Four Parts, No Waiting

AMERICAN MUSICSPHERES

Series Editor
Mark Slobin

Fiddler on the Move
Exploring the Klezmer World
Mark Slobin

The Lord's Song in a Strange Land
Music and Identity in Contemporary Jewish Worship
Jeffrey A. Summit

Lydia Mendoza's Life in Music
Yolanda Broyles-González

FOUR PARTS, NO WAITING

A Social History of American Barbershop Harmony

Gage Averill

UNIVERSITY PRESS

2003

OXFORD
UNIVERSITY PRESS

Oxford   New York
Auckland   Bangkok   Buenos Aires   Cape Town   Chennai
Dar es Salaam   Delhi   Hong Kong   Istanbul   Karachi   Kolkata
Kuala Lumpur   Madrid   Melbourne   Mexico City   Mumbai   Nairobi
São Paolo   Shanghai   Taipei   Tokyo   Toronto

Published by Oxford University Press, Inc.
198 Madison Avenue, New York, New York 10016

www.oup.com

Oxford is a registered trademark of Oxford University Press

Library of Congress Cataloging-in-Publication Data
Averill, Gage.
Four parts, no waiting : a social history of American
barbershop harmony / Gage Averill.
p. cm. — (American musicspheres)
Includes bibliographical references (p.   ) and index.
ISBN 0-19-511672-0
1. Barbershop singing—United States—History and criticism.
I. Title. II. Series.
ML3516 .A94   2002
782.8′0973—dc21   2002000696

3   5   7   9   8   6   4

Printed in the United States of America
on acid-free paper

To the memory of my father,
Gage Averill Sr., a self-described barroom tenor
who used to sing "Buffalo Gal (Won't You Come Out Tonight),"
"I've Been Working on the Railroad," "Oh, You Beautiful Doll,"
and other chestnuts of the close-harmony era while
dancing my sister and me around the room.

Credits

Preface: "I Don't Know Why (I Love You Like I Do)"

No single question has dogged my presentations on barbershop harmony more than "How did you ever get interested in barbershop?" Allow me to get this one out of the way once and for all. In 1987 I was a Ph.D. candidate in ethnomusicology, ready to go to Haiti to research Haitian popular music. I had recently depleted my savings purchasing a small arsenal of ethnographic research equipment from New York's Forty-Second Street Photo, and, as I visited with my mother in southwest Florida, I suffered a late-night panic attack realizing that I hadn't the slightest notion of how to use most of it. Worse still, I was unlikely to find interesting performers on whom to "practice" while stuck in the retirement capital of the nation. Desperate, I scanned the Fort Myers Sun and read that the Caloosahatchie Chorus, the local chapter of the Society for the Preservation and Encouragement of Barber Shop Quartet Singing in America (hereafter SPEBSQSA[1] or the Society), was performing at the Edison Mall in Fort Myers. Admittedly, this was not my idea of ethnomusicology, or of a good time. I expected that neither the music, nor the performers, nor their audience, nor the mall in which they were performing would be of any sustained interest to me, but it occurred to me that that just might be for the better. After all, I could practice some concert videography, snap some photos, maybe even tape a short interview, and leave with no lingering sense of obligation.

I found the group gathered around a small impromptu stage in the center of the mall atrium, waiting for the mall's piped-in music to be turned off. Bob Summers, director of the group, readily agreed to allow me to videotape their performance. Moreover, he insisted that since I was interested in barbershop, I had to drop by the "afterglow," a barbershop party that follows performances; maybe I would even feel inspired to "bust some chords."

Okay, I thought, here was a chance to try out that sine qua non of ethnographic research: participant observation. But of course participant observation is a dangerous method. It creates relationships with real people. It is intended to allow the researcher to get inside a culture and understand it on its own terms; but once having gotten inside, can one then ever fully emerge from the experience to write dispassionately from outside? A little fear crept over me—a fear I would later identify as the "fear of polyester pants." Was I, a white middle-class male researcher, immune to contagion? Moreover, how could I hold on to my impressions of barbershoppers as social reactionaries while partaking readily of their generosity and goodwill? I began to feel somewhat dishonest, like an interloper, a spy perhaps.

This afterglow, held at the home of the chorus director, was dedicated to one of their oldest members and one with the longest history in the barbershop movement (thirty-eight years), whose wife was in the hospital with a life-threatening illness. On the tables and living room walls of the director's house were the mementos of years in barbershop: chorus photos, trophies, plaques, programs, SPEBSQSA souvenirs. I would find this same passion for barbershop memorabilia over the next decade in nearly every barbershopper's home I visited. The women at the party congregated in the living room and kitchen, leaving the screened-in back porch ("Florida room")—with its view of backyard orange bushes and the canal—wholly to the men. Bob Summers sat me down on a lounge chair to explain that the men's barbershop organization was the largest singing group in the world; that it was joined by two organizations for women (Sweet Adelines International and Harmony Incorporated). He spoke about the thrills barbershoppers experience in "ringing chords" and "locking in" a sound, executing chromatic "swipes" and "tags" on series of barbershop sevenths. I recorded our conversation.

After a period of boisterous socializing, the men began to form pick-up quartets. A quartet featuring some of the oldest and most respected singers (including the guest of honor) gathered in the center of the room, and everyone else pulled around. They tentatively struck up the first chords of "Sweet Roses of Morn," and their voices gained strength, transitioning into "I Don't Know Why (I Love You Like I Do)." "I don't know why," they sang as they finished up the final chorus and let loose with a rousing tag, "I just do!" As the final "meat 'n' taters" (dominant seventh) chord dissolved into swipes leading to a sustained tonic triad, the guest of honor—by now in tears—stabbed at the air with his fist and yelled, "Oh boy . . . I love it!"

In the intervening years, I have often mused on the nostalgia, sentimentality, and unabashed enthusiasm that emerged in that moment and that has always seemed to me to be the cornerstone of barbershop style. Readers may recoil at my Capraesque choice of prefatory material, but barbershoppers—both men and women—are undoubtedly some of the most willing exponents of corny, nostalgic sentimentality in American popular culture.

I was struck by the intellectual challenges that this first taste of barbershopping offered. In my fervid graduate-student imagination I saw, lurking behind the striped suits and handlebar moustaches of the barbershop image, deep issues of gender relations, historical idealizations, national imagination, and aesthetics. I considered that I might have inadvertently stumbled on an ideal research topic: statistically important, undertheorized (a so-called lacuna in academic studies), and a fount of important issues and questions in cultural studies.

The more I discovered of this relatively hidden history, the more certain I was of its draw. Here was a story from American musical history that linked such fascinating public figures as Walt Disney, Norman Rockwell, the Marx Brothers, the former New York mayor Fiorello La Guardia, the city planner Robert Moses, Presidents Harry Truman and Dwight Eisenhower, Roy Rogers, the early radio and television host Arthur Godfrey, and the crooner Bing Crosby. I saw in barbershop harmony revealing intersections with institutions (blackface minstrelsy, vaudeville, Masonic temples, world's fairs, Broadway theater, Hollywood cowboy movies) and the great social upheavals of the recent century (racial conflict, urbanization, the Great Depression, world wars). In addition, although the first two decades of the century were quite closely identified with the sound of close harmony quartets, no books or major articles had been devoted to barbershop harmony or quartets.

Back in Seattle, Washington, to finish up my dissertation, I resumed my previous job as program director for the Northwest Folklife Festival and decided to produce a "Barbershop Extravaganza" program at the festival. In addition to using the concert to explore what was "folklife" about barbershopping (and what was not), I also hoped for a colorful spillover effect, with quartets rehearsing on the festival grounds and several workshops featuring Sweet Adelines and SPEBSQSA singers devoted to the barbershop style. I got in touch with the Seattle Seachordsmen, who helped to coordinate the concert and who arranged for seven choruses and many quartets to join the bill. In any case, the barbershoppers were certain to provide an interesting counterpoint to the generally countercultural tone of the festival. However, I remember clearly a little drama that played out as barbershop groups and fans filed into the theater past a small workshop stage set up outside on which a panel concert was taking place. I watched approximately 250 mostly elderly barbershoppers and their fans waiting in line turn around in unison with disbelieving looks as feminist folksinger Peter Alsop sang his children's song about male anatomy called "It's Only A Wee-Wee (So What's the Big Fuss)." (Program director notes for next year: look for potential content conflicts when scheduling two adjacent programs!)

When I first spoke about barbershop harmony at an academic conference three years later, a funny thing happened. Large numbers of audience members came up to talk to me afterward or wrote me in subsequent weeks to say that something about the talk had been moving—that it had reminded them of their father or grandfather, or some place they had once been, or an experience they had once had. My musically academic audience, I discovered, was reacting nostalgically to my academic piece on musical nostalgia.[2]

In 1996 I was asked to give the faculty address to the Wesleyan board of trustees, and, tired of talking about Haiti, I proposed a reflexive piece on my barbershop research. I agonized while preparing the talk, with a mounting sense that the trustees would see my interest in this topic as a symptom of all that was wrong with academia, the tenure system, cultural studies, and their own pointy-headed faculty. I anticipated having to justify my work on the "middlebrow" culture of barbershop harmony, a subject they would have to see as antithetical to the great works of Western civilization, and which also refused to live up to the exotic research they expected from their vaunted ethnomusicology program (I believe I called it "my anti-gamelan topic"). Instead, following the conclusion of my talk, the president of the university and the president of the board of trustees were in the center of the hall leading a quartet, woodshedding "The Sweetheart of Sigma Chi." Wesleyan University, the president of the trustees proudly reminded me, had once upon a time called itself "the Singing University." "Keep this up," he told me. "You could help to bring back the days of the 'Singing University.'" And once again, I found the object of my attention rippling out in little waves of nostalgia.

I am acutely aware that I am writing a book about nostalgia for turn-of-the-(nineteenth)-century America at the turn of a new century and millennium. I am very suspicious of nostalgia, because it so often attributes to people and events in the past a nobler and rosier character and behavior than they exhibited. Nostalgia's lens conveniently frames its romantic revisions of history by leaving out the pain, suffering, oppression, and tragedy. However, is it necessarily a delusion to find value in—and to respect—the past or to recycle aspects of the past as a critique of the present? Even as I grappled with dismantling historical myths (especially racial ones) about the barbershop revival, I discovered within myself a grudging respect for the barbershop revival's emphasis on participatory music making, sociability, service to the community, and concern for leisure—all of which point out many absences in contemporary urban, postmodern life.

Acknowledgments

I have been extremely fortunate in having two hardworking and enormously helpful graduate research assistants at New York University over the past few years, Gloria Lee Pak and Daniel T. Neely, both of whom have contributed in many ways to this study. I also want to acknowledge my students in a graduate methodology class at Wesleyan University who threw themselves wholeheartedly into a class research project on barbershop harmony. They were (in alphabetical order) Chris Bakriges, Mark Braun, Philip Galinsky, Junko Oba, Matthew Reichert, and Kera Washington.

Ruth Blazina-Joyce, the former SPEBSQSA museum curator at the Heritage Hall Museum of Barbershop Harmony, encouraged and supported this project from the beginning and generously contributed her time to helping me in the archives. Her successor, Gina Radandt, was also extremely helpful. Thanks also to other staff members at Harmony Hall, including Brian Lynch, Gary Stamm, Joe Liles, and Dr. Greg Lyne. I also want to express my sincere thanks to Joey Mechelle Stenner, the publications coordinator for Sweet Adelines International, and Nancy K. Foris, the international marketing chairperson of Harmony, Incorporated. A researcher could not pick a topic that would put him or her in contact with a friendlier and more helpful group of people.

Among the barbershop groups that patiently put up with me and my students were the Hill and Dale Songsters, the Lake Washington Skippers, the Big Apple Chorus, the 139th Street Quartet, the Caloosahatchee Chorus, the Bridgeport Coastal Chordsmen, the Sea-Tac Harmony Kings, the Seattle Seachordsmen, and SPEBSQSA chapters in Poughkeepsie, New York; and in New Haven, Hartford, and Danbury, Connecticut. Gary W. Smith kindly sent me the history of the Virginia Harmonizers. If any barbershoppers take umbrage at anything I have said in this book, I ask only that they blame me and not my friends and contacts in the barbershopping movement who have been so gracious and accommodating.

A few ethnomusicologists who are also barbershop singers were especially helpful in their comments and suggestions, and among these I should single out Max Brandt and Robert Provine. In addition, the music sociologist Max Kaplan generously shared with me a number of his early writings and notes on barbershop singing. Lynn Abbott's 1992 article on barbershop music is cited a number of times in this book, and was helpful in clarifying many questions in the present study.

New York University provided a research sabbatical to complete this book, and I received additional research support from both NYU and from Wesleyan University. I want to thank Oxford University Press's former music editor, Maribeth Payne, and the former assistant music editor, Maureen Buja, for their early guidance. This book's subsequent editors, Ellen Welch and Kim Robinson, and its production editor, Christi Stanforth, have served as an unflappable, thoroughly professional, and cheerful support team at Oxford. The editor of the Musicspheres series, Mark Slobin, a close and generous colleague of long standing, helped nurture this book and prod its author when needed. After a few delays on submission dates, I became convinced that Mark, Maureen, and Maribeth must have started calling this book "Four Parts, Lots of Waiting!" My appreciation also goes to Judith McCullough, the music editor at the University of Illinois Press and the first person to suggest turning this research into a book, and to the not-always-entirely anonymous manuscript readers for Oxford University Press, who were exceedingly generous with their praise and their suggestions for improvements.

I will beg the forgiveness of the following people for simply listing their names; all contributed at some stage of this work, if even with suggestions and comments: Ray Allen, Robert Bailey, Max Peter Baumann, Gerard Béhague, Stephen Blum, Katherine Brown, Neely Bruce, David Cannata, Dieter Christensen, Wallace DePew, Mercedes Dujunco, Veit Erlmann, Steven Feld, Aaron A. Fox, Ray Funk, Stuart Goosman, Nancy Groce, Jocelyne Guilbault, David Harnish, Barbara Kirshenblatt-Gimblett, Charles Hamm, Charlie Keil, Ron Kuivila, Robert C. Lancefield, Frederick Lau, Ingrid Monson, Rena C. Mueller, Carol Muller, Dan Neuman, Edward Roesner, John M. Runowicz, David Sanjek, Lorraine Sakata, Margaret Sarkissian, T. M. Scruggs, Tony Seeger, Dan Sheehy, Kay Shelemay, John Shepherd, Jeff Todd Titon, Chris Waterman, Sean Williams, and Su Zheng.

For their help with production of the companion CD I'd like to express my deep appreciation to Val Hicks, Carol Schwartz (Director of Music Services, Sweet Adelines International), Joey Stenner (Sweet Adelines International), Brian Lynch (e-Business Strategist for SPEBSQSA, Inc.), Todd Landor, Einar N. Pedersen, and the ever-helpful Scott Spencer.

And once again, I owe an enormous debt of gratitude to my extraordinary wife, Giovanna Maria Perot-Averill, my chief sounding board, editor, and work schedule coordinator.

Contents

Four Parts, No Waiting

Introduction
Past Perfect

And now we are aged and gray, Maggie
The trials of life nearly done
Let us sing of the days that are gone, Maggie
When you and I were young
          —"When You and I Were Young,
            Maggie" (1866)

A past nostalgically enjoyed does not need to be taken seriously.
          —David Lowenthal, *The Past Is a Foreign Country*

The title of this book is derived from old signs that read "Four chairs, no waiting" and that hung outside countless barbershops across America, encouraging customers to enter, take a chair, and participate in a collective ritual of American male adulthood. Similarly, the four parts of barbershop harmony have come to symbolize a peculiar manifestation of American male musical fellowship or camaraderie, set in a utopian Main Street, U.S.A., of long ago.

A typical definition of barbershop harmony by its contemporary practitioners might run as follows: four-part, a cappella, consonant, close-harmony singing with the voices typically in TTBB (tenor 1, tenor 2 [the lead or melody voice], baritone, and bass), and featuring a flexible tempo, a preponderance of dominant seventh–type chords, ringing harmonics, characteristic arranging devices (swipes, tags, etc.) and a commitment to the popular songs of an earlier period in American history (very loosely, 1890–1930). Where does this peculiar style of quartet singing originate? And what has it meant for participants and audiences in North America, where it has grown up? These are the simple questions that have motivated this study and this book.

Four Parts, No Waiting investigates the role that vernacular barbershop-style close harmony has played in American musical history, in American life, and in the American imaginary. Starting with the first craze for Austrian four-part close harmony in the 1830s, the book traces the popularity of close harmony in minstrel shows, black recreational singing, vaudeville, early recordings, and the barbershop revival that took hold in the 1930s. I argue that barbershop harmony has played a central—and over-looked—role in the panorama of American music; that it has trod a hybrid path between black and white expressive cultural forms; that it has always been a product of a conversation between mediated popular culture and amateur community performance; and that the image and sound of bar-bershop quartets, especially as refined by the barbershop revival move-ment and portrayed in the media, have helped to shape a mythologized vi-sion of turn-of-the-century small-town America, ignoring the formative role of African American quartets in the development of barbershop har-mony. The barbershop revival movement had at its core an implicit theme of innocence, alienation, and redemption (like the literary trope of para-dise lost and found), and it constituted an attempt to recapture a lost structure of feeling. This structure of feeling, imagined in the present and amplified by nostalgia, was held to be a victim of a decline in innocence and sociability in American life following the triumph of industrialization, urbanization, World War I, and the rise of the electronic media. Singing the "old songs"—motivated by a commitment to "old-fashioned values"—was a means of invoking this loss, enshrining a new feeling (nostalgia) as a dominant mode of cultural production, and restoring the fraternity whose loss it mourns. Barbershop has thus been turned into a "heritage" music for a certain proportion of white middle Americans.

As studies of American popular music have proliferated in recent de-cades, various African American close harmony forms such as gospel and rhythm and blues (doo-wop) harmony have received long-overdue atten-tion.[1] Meanwhile, barbershop has remained terra incognita, beyond the horizons of academic scrutiny. For example, Charles Hamm's otherwise pioneering and comprehensive *Yesterdays: Popular Song in America* af-fords barbershop harmony a scant few lines.[2] The two books written spe-cifically about barbershop harmony have treated it within the framework of the sociology of voluntary association, leisure pursuits, and hobbies, but have contributed little to its historical location or its wider cultural rel-evance.[3] This relative neglect of the topic has its roots in the trivialization of barbershop harmony, which began even during its commercial heyday but accelerated as early revivalists adopted stereotypical Gay Nineties out-fits and vaudeville-inspired demeanor. To many scholars, barbershop is all shtick—a corny, nostalgic, pseudohistorical music.

Nevertheless, the threads of barbershop-style close harmony wind their way through the major developments of American popular culture of nearly two centuries, and barbershop has been in the center of the devel-opments in American vernacular harmony.[4] Even its nostalgic evocations in the hands of barbershop revivalists are of substantial sociocultural im-portance; barbershop harmony has exercised an alluring hold over visions of the American past and collective identity—what I am calling the Amer-ican imaginary—that have been recycled in pop cultural representations on the stage, in movies, at theme parks, on television, and in visual art.

This book is an exercise in taking barbershop seriously, in determining its place in the saga of American vernacular harmony, and in understanding its nostalgic appeal to a segment of the American populace.

Rockwell's "Barbershop Quartet" in Black and White

Let us begin our reconsideration of barbershop harmony with a short meditation on a visual icon: Norman Rockwell's "Barbershop Quartet," which appeared on the cover of the *Saturday Evening Post*, September 26, 1936. Rockwell (working in New Rochelle, New York) completed the illustration in the year following the well-publicized first barbershop contest in New York City and two years before the founding of the Society for the Preservation and Encouragement of Barber Shop Quartet Singing in America. According to the Rockwell curator Christopher Finch:

> For Rockwell, nostalgia has always been a valid sentiment and he has never been shy of exploiting its hold on the general public. When he painted this cover he was recalling an era that was already almost half a century in the past. That era may not have been quite as innocent and uncomplicated as he chose to portray it, but he *convinces us of its reality* by making the four singers seem so real. We can almost *hear their voices* as they harmonize some old favorite—"Down By the Old Mill Stream" perhaps—and this in turn *evokes for us the clatter* of horse-drawn buses and wagons on the cobbled streets outside the barbershop.[5]

Finch points to the power of Rockwell's illustration to evoke singing as well as sounds outside of the shop; this illustration demands to be sounded in the imagination. Rockwell's hyperrealism and attention to detail help to sell its message: that there is an ideal America—innocent, hardworking, patriotic, and sentimental—that resembles such representations. Rockwell's illustration was not the first in a barbershop mode to grace the cover of the *Saturday Evening Post*. The October 11, 1924, edition features an illustration by Alan Foster of a quartet in collegiate street clothes singing "Sweet Adeline." The song's title is lettered on a scroll below, and two barber poles flank a shield on which two sixteenth-note stick figures are engaged in a boxing match.[6] The boxing motif may suggest that competition between collegiate barbershop groups was becoming more common in the 1920s.

In the long run, it is not Foster's evocation of barbershop that has endured but Rockwell's. Rockwell was among a handful of the most influential cultural figures of his time. As Warren Susman has observed, "No other paintings ever so caught the American imagination or were so widely distributed in reproduction to eager Americans."[7] This illustration, appearing on the most-read publication of its day and crafted by America's best-

Figure I.1. Barbershop quartet cover art, *Saturday Evening Post*, September 26, 1936. Artist: Norman Rockwell. Courtesy of the Library of Congress. Used by permission.

Figure I.2. Barbershop quartet cover art, *Saturday Evening Post*,
October 11, 1924. Artist: Alan Foster. Courtesy of the Library of Congress.
Used by permission.

loved artist, did as much as anything else to help establish the look and feel of barbershop revival practices for the early revival and for succeeding generations.

Unlike Finch, I suggest that Rockwell was not *"recalling an era"* as much as participating in the construction of a national myth of this innocent time and place in American history, remembered as a utopian "Main Street, U.S.A." saturated in four-part harmony. To call this image of America's past a myth is not to say that it is patently or completely untrue, only to stress that it represents a selective snapshot from a much more complex social and cultural panorama, processed through a nostalgic filter and developed in such a way as to cultivate its warm, romantic glow. I surmise that Rockwell was aware of the campy nostalgia of the New York barbershop contests and captured this tone for national consumption. I also expect that, in another of those odd American reinterpretations of rural and small town life through the eyes of the urban metropolis, Rockwell's iconic representation of barbershop singing helped to shape the character of the midwestern revival a few years later and secure for it an eager national membership base.

Most North Americans know barbershop quartet singing by just such representations in the media (magazines, movies, television, cartoons, and comics). My approach in this study is admittedly iconoclastic: I intend to smash a few of these icons and to demythologize barbershop's evolution. My research departs rather significantly from the "conventional wisdom" histories of barbershop harmony written by those whose primary concern was to promote barbershop singing. In contrast, this book explores the ideological implications of barbershopping and barbershop's role in the production of an American national imaginary formed in the crucible of conflicts over class, race, gender, and ethnicity.

The best-known barbershop myth was popularized for some decades by the Society's many chroniclers of barbershop history. The rough outlines were that barbershop harmonizing is an ancient activity practiced by white Anglo-Saxon amateur male singers in small-town barbershops. The two founding accounts on which this intertextual mythology of Anglo-American "barber" singing is founded were both included in early Society histories: "[Barbershop harmony] was well established in Elizabethan England when Pepys, the diarist, wrote in the early 1600's: 'My Lord called for the Lieutenant's cittern (ghittern or lute, daddy of today's guitar) and with our candlesticks and money for symbols (cymbals) we made barbers' music with which My Lord was well pleased.'"[8]

The second of these accounts comes from Percy A. Sholes in the 1938 edition of the *Oxford Companion to Music*: "One of the regular haunts of music in the 16th, 17th and early 18th centuries was the barber's shop. Here customers waiting their turns found simple instruments (apparently always the cittern) on which they could strum. The barbers themselves, in their waiting time between customers, took up the instruments and thus acquired some skill as performers."[9]

To link these accounts to barber music in the United States, Joe Stern cited a Boston musical instrument dealer named Steinert who spoke of a man he knew in Georgia around 1860: "As once upon a time he had been a barber, he knew how to play a guitar." Stern continued, "The impresario [*sic*] Hammerstein in 1908 cancelled his promise to put on a certain Spanish opera because the score called for a large number of guitar players . . . more than I could get together readily; I should have been obliged to engage all the barbers in New York."[10] The mythology of the origins of the Anglo-Saxon barbershop quartet is thus constructed on a few tenuous references to the playing of music in barbers' establishments. There is no evidence that this music involved vocal harmonizing, nor is there any connection demonstrated or even argued between the songs or repertories involved in these early barber shops and the barbershop harmony of the early twentieth century. On the matter of whether any significant number of white close-harmony quartets sang in barbershops in the nineteenth century, the historical record (of reliable first-hand testimony) is surprisingly weak. Although many revivalists speak of this as received history, I have run across only a couple of clear and unambiguous examples, such as a description of an eighty-six-year-old white Tampa barber who began singing with a quartet in 1879 in his own barbershop and has photographs to back up his story.[11]

A counterhistory of barbershop harmony dating back to the 1920s provides original credit for barbershop-style close harmony (and for a connection to barbershops) to nineteenth-century African Americans. This history was reconstructed first by James Weldon Johnson (author, composer, lawyer, and founder of the National Association for the Advancement of Colored People [NAACP]), a towering intellectual of the Harlem Renaissance. Johnson wrote: "Pick up four coloured boys or young men anywhere and the chances are ninety out of a hundred that you have a quartet. Let one of them sing the melody and others will naturally find the parts. Indeed, it may be said that all male Negro youth of the United States is divided into quartets. . . . In the days when such thing as a white barber was unknown in the South, every barbershop had its quartet and the young men spent their leisure time 'harmonizing.'"[12]

Johnson's slightly hyperbolic rhetoric was motivated by his abiding concern that minstrel music not be confused for the authentic products of the black experience, that black composers be given recognition for their achievements in art music, and that popular genres fashioned by black musicians and composers (which in his view included ragtime, jazz, and barbershop harmony) not be credited to their numerous white imitators. Johnson's thoughts on this latter question anticipated a lively discourse over the course of the twentieth century on the appropriation of cultural alterity by the dominant or mainstream culture.

The African American–origin view occasionally slipped through the cracks of the dominant myth in SPEBSQSA discourse, and it is important to note that certain barbershop revivalists recognized their debt to African

American singing, if only through crude rhetorical figures involving the "naturalization" of black singing (making of it something natural and instinctive). For example, the following appeared in a 1948 Society publication: "Barbershop harmony is a misnomer. There is no basis in fact that close harmony started in barbershops, or was confined to barbershops. There is a greater indication that close harmony originated in the south, with the negro slaves singing—their worksongs on the plantations and levees, and their singing of spirituals, and folksongs during their leisure time. This most certainly was not arranged music. It was original, and spontaneous. . . . It would be a safe bet that a great majority of our members were singing close harmony before they ever heard it called barbershop."[13]

In an offhand tribute to the reputation of African Americans as harmony singers, many of the barbershop revivalists mentioned that nineteenth-century white close-harmony singers often drafted "porters" (a common occupation for African Americans) when white singers were in short supply. Joe Stern reported that "often as not, the Negro porter filled in the baritone or some other part." Deac Martin echoed this passage four years later: "Often as not, the porter filled in some part."[14] Note that in these accounts the African Americans are always "filling in" for an absent white singer and that they consistently are assigned the baritone voice—the least prestigious part.

Following the lead of James Weldon Johnson, the gospel researcher Lynn Abbott in 1992 wrote an article called " 'Play That Barber Shop Chord': A Case for the African American Origin of Barbershop Harmony" in order better to document the African American origins of barbershop.[15] Abbott's careful scholarship, which grew out of his research on black gospel quartets in the New Orleans area, demonstrated that black quartetting extended back decades into the nineteenth century and had a close connection to black barbershops. This work reinforced Johnson's assertions that barbershop harmony had its origins in authentic black experience and that white performers and audiences appropriated it for their own amusement. Barbershop singing, like banjo playing and tap dancing, could be understood, therefore, in a history of crossover cultural influences from black to white: an African American expression alienated from its community of origin and consumed by the dominant group, the powerful trope of appropriation in American cultural historiography. A recent dissertation by James Early Henry attempted to substantiate the claims for historical continuity through detailed comparisons of transcriptions of early recordings by white and black harmony groups.[16] Despite their many important contributions, these scholars ignore the various forms of continuous white close-harmony singing throughout the nineteenth century, they underestimate the importance of minstrelsy in spreading these forms in the first place, and they fail to emphasize the truly syncretic nature of close-harmony singing among African Americans. In general, they ascribe to the term "barbershop singing" too much solidity. In contrast, I note that what became known as barbershop harmony embraced a number of different genres and can scarcely be said to have evolved outside of the realm of popular, mediated, commodified culture.

When I began my research on barbershop history in the late 1980s, I had in mind at first a thorough rewriting of the racial history of barbershop to redress the silences and erasures of the official historiography. However, the complex histories that I uncovered have pushed me to focus on barbershop's hybrid and miscegenated history. An analysis of the interplay of white and black aesthetics, musical forms, repertories, performance styles, motor behavior, and choreographic practice reveals close harmony to be a music of racial encounter, of a profound cultural intimacy, a short circuit in the hardwiring of racial separation and segregation, and the product of the convoluted history of cultural transgressions, borrowings, mimicry, miscegenation, and cross-cultural homage that has characterized black-white relations in North America.

Close harmony, like so much American vernacular and popular music, has provided an expansive terrain for both blacks and whites to experiment with racial identity in sound. Decades of research have substantiated and documented the fascination that blackness has held for whites. This research project has illustrated how some whites have explored alternate cultural locations and have played with the liberating potential of black cultural expressions while maintaining a privileged social position. Black culture in America was shaped both by exclusion and by pressure to think, act, and live according to normative models. Despite the pressures on blacks to acculturate, we cannot dismiss the aesthetic appreciation of Euro-American music that inspired many African Americans to emulate it or adapt it. Blackness and whiteness in America have been mutually interdependent phenomena, and the history of American popular culture is rife with what Jeffrey Melnick has termed "multiple, and often unexpected, racial posturings."[17] The hyper-hybrid identity of barbershop harmony argues against assigning it too precise a racial location. As Russel A. Potter has said, "For even as popular music embodies and evokes a mosaic of racial identities and histories, its relationship with identity has never been as deterministic as those who see race as an essence have tried to construe it."[18]

The metaphor of "masking," cited in some studies of white appropriation of black expression, is drawn chiefly from blackface minstrelsy, the pervasive nineteenth-century theatrical travesty of black culture. In chapter 1 I argue against the subtle visual bias of the "blackface" label and for a deeper appreciation of "blackvoice"—the stereotyped representations of black dialect, vocal mannerisms, and musical style that was a product of the minstrel stage. Blackvoice provided white singers with a vocal mask from behind which to experiment with identity and style. To move from the visual (blackface) to the auditory (blackvoice), it is helpful to recall that in African studies the notion of a masque (masquerade) is often stretched to include sound. For example, although many West African spirit figures appear in ceremonies in full visual masquerade, others may appear only as sounds, with the voices of those making them disguised by mysterious-sounding devices (for example, mirlitons, such as one would find in a kazoo). These vocal disguises, meant to suggest otherworldly spirit voices, are accorded the status of vocal masques. I believe it is productive to examine the vocal masques that both blacks and whites have adopted throughout the history of American music, as part of the play of racial and cultural identity.

There are two essential stylistic devices in barbershop singing that can metaphorically predicate its racial history: echo effects (an immediate restating of melodic material—often transposed—in another voice) and "swipes" (chord changes produced by one or more voices changing their pitch while others remain constant). These terms suggest the myriad imitations, borrowings, and shifts in meaning, association, and value as close harmony has moved back and forth in black and white social fields over two centuries of development. But "swipe" has another meaning—little theft—that I find playfully revealing here, because it is these little thefts of cultural capital that have pushed close-harmony singing forward. Even the African American term for "swipes," "snakes," can suggest the history of vernacular harmony "snaking" its way through white and black cultural locations.

Throughout this book, I will look at how black and white close harmonies grew together and apart, drawing from each other and in the process producing barbershop harmony. This is the first of the two narratives of race that run throughout this book. The second has to do with the construction of barbershopping as an exercise in white nostalgia. Imagine Rockwell's "Barbershop Quartet" once again, and substitute one black face for a white one (perhaps the ubiquitous "porter baritone"). Now, imagine four African American singers in Rockwell's tableau. If you are a white reader, is the illustration still an exercise in nostalgia? Does it feel as safe and folksy? Does the razor in the hand of the gentleman on the left suddenly look more like a switchblade? In this little Rorschach test of race, when one is dealing with nostalgia and the American imaginary black or white matters.

Unreal Estate: Nostalgia and the American Imaginary

In discussing the barbershop revival movement, I faced two problems of terminology: whether to use the term "revival" and whether to use the term "movement." In the Americanist literature, "revival" is often found attached to "folk music" as in "the American folk music revival," employed by folklorists to distinguish "revivalists" (mostly outsiders who hoped to become competent performers of a musical culture) from traditional practitioners and those who had grown up in a musical culture ("culture bearers"). At worst, the term implied an equivalency between the new and old musics, overlooking the myriad reinterpretations and invented traditions involved in the new practices.[19] Distrust of revivals was part of a multidisciplinary "worrying" in the 1980s and 1990s that challenged the ways in which traditions, histories, cultures, and notions of authenticity were known and represented. Scholars came to consider ethnographies, histories, cultural revivals, and representations as ideologically motivated and tied to specific subject positions and interests. In the process, the term "revival" fell on scholarly hard times.

On the contrary, I find it a very handy term (and I use it often in this book) as long as my readers share with me in the understanding that there is no authentic historical experience that is made to be relived in this way. The term "revival," in the sense in which I am using it, refers to the intent on the part of participants to recreate some vision of the past in the present. My focus throughout is on how the past is filtered, imagined, and redeployed in the present to address contemporary desires, fears, and needs, and especially on how nostalgia for an idealized past shapes actions in the present.[20]

One aspect of the mythology of barbershop harmony that has seldom been challenged is the notion that it has always been a music of amateur socializing. Even Lynn Abbott, in his critique of racial ideologies in barbershop, fails to uproot the pervasive view of the history of barbershop (white or black) as having been characterized by informal, noncommercial amateur or recreational singing. Some have argued that barbershop quartet singing has not only stood outside of commerce, but that it has stood somehow in opposition to the commodified and commercial nature of American popular culture—even that it is a last vestige of premediated entertainment. In an article called "Three Eras of Barbershop," the barbershop revivalist Deac Martin stresses this view, conspicuously failing to mention the importance of commercial recording quartets, sheet music, the record companies, Tin Pan Alley, minstrelsy, or vaudeville.[21]

I argue that barbershop harmony can only be understood as a product of—and not an alternative to—commercial music trends of its era. If I am right, how then do the mediated and commercial aspects of barbershop intersect with its amateur, informal, and recreational elements? What has been the relationship between passive and active modes of consumption of vernacular harmony over time in America? How have audiences domesticated and incorporated the commodities produced by culture industries as signets of personal and social identity?

Profitability in culture industries has been linked throughout the twentieth century to turnover and disposability. Culture industries have attempted to match market tastes at any given time with cultural products that capture (and help create) the peculiar zeitgeist of a moment in time. The media and industries have reinforced the notion that in modern times each generation, indeed each graduating class, needs its own cultural pantry stocked with the products of these same industries. They have also ensured that these products have a short popularity shelf life. As a result, popular music hits have come to stand for their eras. The yearning in the hearts of millions for the sounds of their adolescence has created, in turn, a market for recycled sounds—former hits now consumed as cultural memory. Musical nostalgia is part and parcel of the system that enshrines disposable hits and fads as the centerpiece of cultural attention. It is a means to extract resale value when a commodity's initial "legs" have been exhausted. This book suggests that the entertainment industry has colonized cultural memory to create nostalgia (and demand on the secondary market) for the discarded husks of its own planned cultural obsolescence and turnover.

Barbershop is, of course, not the only nostalgic performance practice or heritage art to have been "revived" in contemporary America. On the contrary, hundreds of spectral performances haunt the cultural landscape of America: swing dancing, New England contra dancing, sock hops, the Society for Creative Anachronism's reenactments of medieval fairs, Civil War battle reenactments, the recycling of Renaissance and baroque style in "goth" rock, historical theme parks, and Grateful Dead concerts, for a few examples. Musical nostalgia has a long pedigree in this country (as a quick look at the antiquarian "Old Folks Concerts" of "Father" Robert Kemp during the mid-nineteenth century will confirm—see chapter 1). Even the dominant theatrical form of the nineteenth century, the minstrel show, was steeped in nostalgia for an agrarian and pastoral past, reexperienced through the mask of blackface. Hamm has argued that "nostalgia for youth home, parents, old friends, lost innocence and happiness" is "one of the most persistent themes of the nineteenth century."[22] But what is it about this young country with so little past of its own that drives it to manufacture nostalgia for the past?

Maurice Halbwachs uses the term "collective memories" for those memories that stress the continuity of the past and the present and help construct social identity.[23] Within collective memories, according to Halbwachs, will be certain arrested moments that resist tampering and change. The turn-of-the-century small Victorian town with its Main Street (and barbershop as a site of cultural production) is one such arrested moment enshrined in collective memory. Mieke Bal uses a similar term, classifying nostalgia as an emotionally charged form of cultural memory in which the past is idealized and invested with a present longing. Nostalgia, she argues, is a "structure of relation to the past" rather than a set of explicit meanings.[24]

Coined by a seventeenth-century Swiss physician, "nostalgia" (Greek *nostos*, a return home, and *algos*, a painful condition) came to mean a pathological condition of homesickness.[25] Anthropologist Renato Rosaldo focuses on a "particular kind of nostalgia, often found under imperialism, where people mourn the passing of what they themselves have transformed," as in the "elegiac postures toward small towns and rural communities." He notes that much of nostalgia's power "resides in its association with (indeed, its disguise as) more genuinely innocent tender recollections of what is at once an earlier epoch and a previous phase of life," but he also stresses its "historical and cultural specificity."[26] I would suggest that Rosaldo's nostalgia is less an imperialist than a modernist nostalgia, the progenitor of an aesthetics of disappearance that motivated folklorists and anthropologists in the century. This form of nostalgia reaches back to a period of European history when connections to the past and to tradition were being violently severed—a time when, as Rousseau wrote, "everything is absurd but nothing is shocking, because everyone is accustomed to everything."[27] Suffering from this radical disconnection from tradition and history, humans are, according to Frederic Jameson, "condemned to seek the historical past through our own pop images and stereotypes of the past, which itself remains forever out of reach."[28] Nostalgia triumphs when the continuities with the past (especially collective identity) are disrupted or threatened.

In the narratives generated by the barbershop revival, the golden era of barbershop harmony has an edenic quality. In contrast, the period from World War I through the Great Depression is characterized as a paradise lost, in which Americans are seen as suffering from feelings of alienation and distrust. That the revival is then credited by its participants with helping to restore a utopian male fraternity should not be surprising, for it completes the narrative of paradise lost and found that is at the heart of so many nostalgic literatures.

Barbershop harmony also points out the inability of nostalgia to be divorced from ideas of space and place. The various names for barbershop harmony at the turn of the century—"lamp post harmony," "curbstone harmony," "barroom harmony," "street corner harmony," and "barbershop harmony" (along with the "woodshed" as a locus of vocal improvisation)—all imply a spatial reference for musical activity. At the heart of the nationalist and nostalgic American imaginary are small Victorian towns with wide-open Main Streets—friendly sites of junction, assembly, and encounter.[29] It is apparent that this kind of spatial imagination, while it may help in envisioning an abstraction such as Jeffersonian democracy, also constructs an ethnically and ideologically homogeneous utopia that, far from having disappeared, can barely be said to have ever existed.[30]

Throughout the latter chapters of this book, I examine the complex interpenetration of past and present in barbershop singing and to understand how the past is performed and to what ends and goals. As Barbara Kirshenblatt-Gimblett suggests, heritage "is a mode of cultural production in the present that has recourse to the past."[31] Like Mieke Bal and Renato Rosaldo, Kirshenblatt-Gimblett is concerned that we not map the contemporary cultural practices motivated by an interest in heritage onto our history and our past. Barbershop, with real roots in the nineteenth-century mix of white and black vernacular harmonies, and with instantiations in the pioneer commercial recording era, was adopted as a heritage music for a segment of the American populace. Mark Slobin suggests looking collectively at heritage musics to understand their commonalities, noting that, like barbershop since the 1930s, they are typically "sub-commodified."[32] Unlike many of the heritage musics that were revived in the efflorescence of ethnicity in the 1970s, however, barbershop quartets seldom made use of what Slobin calls the "heritage music infrastructure"(festivals, small folk labels, and so on), having constructed their own infrastructure of organizations, competitions, recordings, and communications since the 1930s.

Barbershoppers themselves call their activity a "movement," and so I am on safe ground from the perspective of ethnotheory in borrowing this term. However, I am more comfortable with the general analytical term formation, which is favored by Raymond Williams in his various sketches for a sociology of culture.[33] While "formation" implies more or less concerted activity in the production of culture, it does not have the political overtones of "movement," nor does it suggest the same zealousness. Many barbershoppers are indeed harmony fanatics or zealots, but I have tried not to use too broad a brush in characterizing the many and diverse members of the barbershop formation. As a rule, I will use the term "movement" but interpret it as a formation. It is important to recognize that affinity formations such as the barbershop movement, brought together by an aesthetic appreciation for an expressive form and by shared interests and even worldviews, cannot be analyzed as bounded social and cultural universes. The members of these groups consume, participate in, and are exposed to a wide range of cultural expressions. Their affinity to a specific form is informed by their much more diverse soundscapes and culturescapes.

The nostalgic spaces of barbershop singing are gender specific, and close-harmony singing has long served as form of recreational gender segregation. The neo-Victorian models of proper male comportment, the construction of a certain model of masculinity, and the space for nostalgic male fellowship are at the heart of the barbershop revival ideal. The barbershop revival thus took place at an intersection of issues of race, class, and gender. Chapter 4 examines the formation of women's barbershop societies and addresses some of the peculiar issues of gender and aesthetics that women barbershoppers have had to confront, but one of the defining issues in the history of the barbershop revival has been its normative maleness. Even women barbershop revival singers adopt the TTBB voice designation (tenor 1, tenor 2, baritone, bass).

Tag: "You're As Welcome as the Flowers in May"

This study is a historical one, informed by ethnography; but what does it mean to be "informed by ethnography?" Throughout the more than ten years during which this project was in progress, I attended numerous barbershop rehearsals, performances, workshops, competitions, conventions, and afterglows. My students and I videotaped and recorded many of these. I interviewed barbershop singers and administered questionnaires. I also visited SPEBSQSA headquarters and offices. Yet through all of this activity focused on the experience of barbershopping and its meaning for contemporary participants, I kept stumbling into issues of a historical nature, and I came to appreciate that these constituted the principal lacunae in the academic understanding of barbershop singing. Therefore, most of this book explores how and why this singing style evolved. Chapter 5, however, returns to the ethnographic present to briefly document contemporary meanings of the sound, texts, performances, and the life of barbershop singing.

In this book I occasionally play agent provocateur to prod readers into worrying through difficult intersections of race, popular culture, nostalgia, and the American imaginary. Although the chapter structure is predominantly chronological, I dislodge the chronological narrative in many places to explore coherently the thematic issues raised. Barbershop harmony is an enormous, sweeping topic, and this book follows its trajectory from the early roots of American close harmony to the 1960s. Subsequent decades were good years for the revival movement, with enormous strides in sound quality and arranging complexity, as well as institutional development, but I am chiefly interested in issues, and I came to conclude that the major issues in barbershop revivalism had been adequately defined (although not necessarily resolved) by the early 1960s.[34]

Chapter 1, "A Little Close Harmony," traces the roots of barbershop harmony in nineteenth-century America and theorizes the contributions of black harmonists to barbershop harmony, especially in "cracking" chords and "snaking" harmonies. This chapter reinterprets blackface minstrelsy, a popular context for close-harmony singing, primarily through its sound, which I paraphrase as *blackvoice*, an imitation (usually for comedic effect) of black southern dialect, diction, timbre, and vocal mannerisms. By analyzing the interplay of white and black musical forms, repertories, performance styles, motor behavior, and choreographic practice, I conclude that close harmony has developed in a complex interplay of black and white aesthetics and performance practice. This chapter, and the one that follows, are built chiefly on an examination and reinterpretation of some primary and many secondary sources, harnessed to buttress an argument.

Chapter 2, "The Golden Era," follows close-harmony singing at the turn of the century, the period of its greatest commercial success, especially through Tin Pan Alley quartet arrangements, the early pioneer recording quartets, and vaudeville "comedy fours." Quartets, which were well suited to the rudimentary recording technology available, recorded many of the most popular songs of the period and were some of the most successful (and now most forgotten) artists of the twentieth century. Quartets recorded both anti- and pro-war songs of the World War I era and featured heavily in the sound of the war era, but they declined in stature and importance after the war owing to factors chronicled in the latter part of this chapter. During the golden era, close-harmony quartets received the "barbershop" designation and achieved the status of sonic icons for the period, a status they shared only with the ubiquitous village brass band. This status was increasingly bestowed on them by posterity, especially from the vantage point of the nostalgic yearning that churned in white America during the Great Depression. I argue that barbershop harmony was never the truly amateur and noncommercial activity imagined by barbershop revivalists, but that it was always a product of—and participated in—culture industries and commercial popular culture.

Chapter 3, "The Lost Chords," examines the emergence of a revival movement and fledgling barbershop society in the context of the Great Depression and of an increasingly urban and modernist America, in a period that represented a tectonic shift in the aesthetics of American popular culture. Nostalgia for small Victorian towns with wide-open Main Streets—conceived of as friendly sites of sociability for white, largely middle-class men—inspired a number of neo-Victorian revival movements, among them one for barbershop quartet singing. Fraternal societies (both business-oriented and secret) were significant models for the organizational identity of the fledgling barbershop movement. This chapter introduces the notion that the revival movement was institutionalized first in the competitions organized in New York City by New York's most famous politicians (Al Smith, Robert Moses, and Fiorello LaGuardia) and soon after in the heartland revival, which gave birth to the Society for the Preservation and Encouragement of Barber Shop Quartet Singing in America (SPEBSQSA). The New York and heartland initiatives joined forces to stage a barbershop extravaganza at the 1939–40 New York World's Fair but soon split over the question of allowing African American quartets to perform in competition.

Chapter 4, "On Main Street, U.S.A.," treats the period of the institutionalization of the men's and women's barbershop societies and culminates with the success of the Broadway musical *The Music Man*. The chapter traces the increasing seriousness with which revivalists treated barbershop singing during the conflict against fascism and the early years of the cold war. It also documents the tension between building an international organization—which required bureaucratization, centralization, and literate transmission—and the homespun, loosely knit, and largely extemporized approach to quartet singing of the early revival. The chapter includes four case studies of barbershop harmony's mediation and circulation in pop culture that demonstrate the cultural impact of Roy Rogers movies, Disneyland, Arthur Godfrey's radio and television shows, *The Lucy Show*, and the Broadway musical *The Music Man*, among others.

Chapter 5, "Romancing the Tone," uses the barbershop revival movement's approach to "selling the song," to look in succession at barbershop lyrics, musical sound, and performance practice and to probe the various meanings that each of these has in contemporary barbershop practice. Arguing that the texts of the old songs, drawn from the golden era, function as repositories of social memory, this chapter explores some of the ideologies of gender, race, and class that have been distilled in these song lyrics and that resonate in the worldview of many barbershoppers. The revival movement, especially its competition system, helped to consolidate certain turn-of-the-century sonic practices and redefined barbershop style, insisting on a cappella singing, a melody harmonized by a tenor above, a predominance of dominant seventh chords, circle-of-fifths progressions, swipes, certain arranging conventions, and a vocal production that emphasizes expanded sound. The production of ringing chords has become a paramount aesthetic goal in barbershop singing. It serves as a metaphor for group unity and camaraderie and takes on a quasi-mystical significance for many barbershoppers. A final section looks ethnographically at the performance of an SPEQSQSA international competition to listen in on the informal discourse on musical aesthetics that surrounds competition and to communicate the passion for barbershop singing that characterizes so many of its devotees.

1

A Little Close Harmony
A Medley of Nineteenth-Century Harmony

Johnson Jones from Tennessee,
Father of sweet harmony
Organized a quartette, goodness me!
And they sang so wonderful,
Kindly let me tell you, when
It comes down to singing men
I've just got to say again, They're wonderful!
Chorus:
Come on and hear that harmony sweet
Come and have a musical treat
From your head down to your feet
You'll be fairly hypnotized, they harmonize
Most any old place
Alto, tenor, baritone, and bass
Every other chord
Is a message from the Lord
When you hear old Johnson's Quartette harmonize
  —"When Johnson's Quartette Harmonize,"
   Irving Berlin (1912)

merica of the early nineteenth century was awash in vocal harmonies. There were exuberant and homespun harmonies of the singing schools, where they taught from books like *The Easy Instructor* using patent or "shape" notes (or, in the vernacular, "cabbage" or "buckwheat" notes), and there were the schooled harmonies of Boston's Haydn and Handel Society. Psalms and hymns were arranged for two, three, or four voices.[1] African Americans employed a range of African multipart techniques, responsorial forms, and rhythmic play to create complex polyphonic textures. Soon there were "singing family" and blackface minstrel harmonies as well, joined in the latter half of the century by harmonized American spirituals from the black colleges. In the face of this profusion of harmonies—black and white, a cappella and accompanied, through-harmonized and verse-and-chorus, professional and amateur, improvised and scored—America was increasingly passionate about its multipart (es-

21

pecially four-part) vernacular harmonies. Although a comprehensive treatment of the emergence of close harmony as an American vernacular style has yet to be written, it is worthwhile to consider here how this style came to prominence.

Roots of Close Harmony

The best-known legacies of the singing school approach to sacred choral music of the early nineteenth century are the Sacred Harp conventions (some of which have endured into the twentieth century in the Deep South, where they constitute a "survival" of a widespread practice originating in New England). Although arranged in four parts, the Sacred Harp style of singing differs dramatically from close harmony. In the words of its chief early chronicler, George Pullen Jackson, Sacred Harp "has been composed in such a manner that each voice-part is equally balanced. The tune is submerged more deeply because each part except bass is sung by both men and women. This gives 'Sacred Harp' music distinctive qualities that differentiate it from all other types of music, and it is known as *dispersed harmony*."[2] Like the other part-singing approaches coming out of the singing school movement, Sacred Harp was considered a vernacular harmony, written by enthusiastic Americans with little regard for the "science" of music as understood by their European counterparts. During Reconstruction, African Americans participated enthusiastically in shape-note singing throughout the South, but there is little or no evidence that the approaches to harmonizing represented by shape-note singing had much tangible influence on the development of African American close harmony.[3]

Members of the "Better Music" movement attacked the populist approach to music education of the regular singing schools, objecting to the dominance of fuguing tunes, to the many violations of European harmonic conventions (parallel fifths and octaves, among many others), and to the patent or shape-note approach to notation. Reformers, some of whom were associated with Boston's Haydn and Handel Society, argued for a more conventional, "scientific," and European approach to harmony and notation.

Germans and Austrians played a significant role in the maturation of American part-singing. Germans often worked as schoolteachers and tutors and frequently included music and harmony among their lessons. Germans formed concert and singing societies in the United States, and as we shall presently see, tours of German and Austrian minstrels precipitated the formation of American quartets. The German Franz Abt wrote many hundreds of part-songs for vocalists, some of which were popular among Germans in America. The German-speaking regions of Europe were also home to a popular choral movement called the *Singverein* movement, which nurtured an interest in four-part arrangements of *volkslieder* (folk song). Among the art-music composers with more than a passing interest in the movement were Carl Maria von Weber and Franz Schubert. Popular on university campuses in midcentury, the movement was transplanted to America by German immigrants such as Gustav Stoeckel, the founder of one of the first American glee clubs at Yale University in 1863 (Harvard's glee club claims to have been founded in 1858). The Yale group accompanied their harmonized school songs and folk songs with banjos and guitars. The term "glee" had been used for over fifty years in England to refer to a species of part-song arranged for three or four voices. During the latter half of the eighteenth century, English glee clubs popularized these arrangements and similar songs. American glee clubs, following a century later and owing more to the German tradition, were simply university choral societies, although there were a few community-based glee clubs as well, such as New York's Mendelssohn Glee Club, organized in 1865. Glee clubs became fixtures on American campuses during the 1860s and 1870s, decades during which recreational close-harmony quartets were also proliferating. Glee clubs demonstrate little direct influence over the development of barbershop harmony, although their repertory, which often came to include popular and commercial songs, overlapped significantly with that of the minstrel, recreational, and concert quartets.[4] Another manifestation of German four-part singing in America was the New York–based Liederkranz Society, an all-German group dating from the 1840s that was devoted to singing TTBB and SATB arrangements.

America's passion for close harmony built up steam in the late 1830s during a series of tours by singing troupes from the Austrian and Swiss border region of the Alps. The Rainer family (Anton, Franz, Maria, Felix, and Joseph) had been touring Europe for a decade when they decided to bring their act, the Tyrolese Minstrels, to America, performing German part-songs and Tyrolese folk songs in arrangements for solo voice, trios, and quartets. After their successful concerts starting in 1834, this first group of Tyrolese Minstrels was followed by the German Minstrels (1837), the Alpine Minstrels (1837), and then by a different set of Rainer family members (Margaretta, Ellena, Lewis, and Semir), again calling themselves the Tyrolese Minstrels,[5] who toured the United States between 1839 and 1843. At a concert at the Alexander Hamilton Monument near Trinity Church in Manhattan, the Rainers premiered "Silent Night [Stille Nacht]" for American audiences. The Rainers and another singing family, the Strassers, were chiefly responsible for spreading this song (which they mistakenly understood to be a Tyrolean folk song) throughout Europe.[6] Also known as the Rainer Family or the "Tribe of Rainer," this last incarnation of the Rainer family was the most influential of the European touring vocal ensembles.

American audiences were thrilled by the Rainers' precise enunciation and timing and by the impression they created of a harmony that was so well blended the audience 'could not determine which singer was singing which part. Soon groups of American singers, such as the Euterpian Quartette, the Hughes Family, Ossian's Bards, the Illsleys, the Boston Minstrels, the Alleghenians, and, most important, the Hutchinson Family Singers had formed quartets in their likeness, singing sentimental ballads, comic songs, martial airs, and patriotic and topical songs.

John Hutchinson first heard the Tyrolese Minstrels when the attended the Rainers' concert in either Lynn or Boston, Massachusetts, around 1840. About the concert, he said, "I was overwhelmed, though of course I could not understand their words. Ditson soon published their songs, with English words, and of course I remembered their Tyrolean style of singing, and taught the rest how to sing them as the Rainers did."[7] The Hutchinson Family Singers gave a singing concert in Milford, Massachusetts, in 1840, and this was followed by a concert at Lynn in 1841 featuring four of the twelve Hutchinson brothers: John, Judson, Asa, and Jesse. Jesse soon removed himself from regular concretizing in order to devote himself to songwriting and to managing the group's affairs (hence their sobriquet "Tribe of Jesse," which they appended to their stage name as an homage to the "Tribe of Rainer"). Without Jesse, the brothers concertized as a trio called the Aeolian Singers, but in 1842 the brothers experimented with a quartet involving their twelve-year-old sister Abby on the high tenor part. This combination proved irresistible to audiences.

The quartet aimed to integrate voices to the standard set by the Rainers. Some years later, John Hutchinson described their approach to blending voices: "Judson had a naturally high voice, a pure tenor. My voice was a baritone, though I sang falsetto easily, and Asa had a deep bass. Abby had an old-fashioned 'counter' or contralto voice. The result was *an effect like that of a male quartet,* Abby's part being first tenor, Judson's second tenor, mine first and Asa's second bass, respectively. But we practised an interchange of parts as we sang, and the blending of the voices was so perfect that it seemed quite impossible for the audience to distinguish the several parts."[8]

Thus, by 1840 the family featured a close harmony blend of voices in classic TTBB arrangements, with the lead harmonized above by a tenor (or contralto) voice. Their subsequent popularity made them the first wildly successful homegrown close-harmony quartet.

Their approach to composing settings and arrangements of poems and texts was to start with the tune, composed measure by measure by Judson, and to add their own harmony parts as they went along. The Hutchinson Family Singers toured New England in 1842. By this time they were grossing as much as $130 per concert. In 1843, Jesse penned their signature song, "The Old Granite State" ("composed, arranged and sung by the Hutchinson Family, words by Jesse Hutchinson, Jr.," 1843; see figures 1.1 and 1.2). This was a song about the Hutchinson Family, describing how they came from the Granite State (New Hampshire), left their parents (with their parents' permission), and toured around the world singing harmony. The lyrics listed the names of the singers and those of their family members. Over the years they added verses in favor of emancipation ("We despise oppression"), temperance ("We are all teetoatlers [*sic*], And have sign'd the Temp'rance pledge") and Yankee virtues such as prudence. The arrangement, with the second tenor or lead voice written on the top staff, is enlivened by a few contrapuntal passages, as on the responsorial line "with a band."[9]

Figure 1.1. Cover art to "The Old Granite State," by the Hutchinson Family (New York: C. Holt Jr., 1843). Courtesy of Daniel T. Neely.

Following Jesse's lead, the Hutchinson siblings threw themselves into the emancipation movement, temperance, and the campaign for woman suffrage. They spent nearly a year in England in 1845, having traveled there with Frederick Douglass, and they wrote reform anthems such as "Right over Wrong," "Get Off the Track!" and "The Slave's Appeal."

Figure 1.2. Excerpt from the sheet music to "The Old Granite State," by the Hutchinson Family (New York: C. Holt Jr., 1843). Courtesy of Daniel T. Neely.

In the late 1840s the group's membership began to vary considerably: a fourth family member often replaced Abby, owing to her fragile health, and John and Asa split with Jesse in 1851. Jesse took over as agent for one of the best known of the Hutchinson's rivals, the Alleghanians, and toured with them through California. Gradually, a second generation of family "tribes" emerged to carry on the performing tradition. The Hutchinsons,

Figure 1.3. Flower City Harmonists, Rochester, N.Y., 1865. This local close-harmony quartet, formed in the mold of the Hutchinson Family, featured three cousins and a friend and performed at the popular Forest Hotel as well as for the ceremonies commemorating the Rochester visit of Abraham Lincoln's casket, which arrived by train as part of a national tour in 1865. *Left to right:* William Cowles, William Corkhill, John Boyd, and J. Franuken. Heritage Hall Museum of Barber Shop Harmony. Used by permission, Society for the Preservation and Encouragement of Barber Shop Quartet Singing in America, Inc.

although only one of many touring close-harmony groups after 1840, helped to establish and to define this tradition and its repertory by virtue of their popularity, which spanned decades.

The success of the Hutchinson Family tribes helped to inspire many family singing groups. One of these was the African American Luca family, led by Alexander C. Luca Sr. (b. 1805). Alexander C. Luca Sr. had sung in a mixed quartet in New Haven, where he worked as a Congregational church choir director. His family quartet consisted of four of his sons: Simeon G. Luca, first tenor; Alexander C. Luca Jr., second tenor; Cleveland O. Luca, soprano; and John W. Luca, bass or baritone. The family sang quartets alternating with solo and duet performances and accompanied themselves on various instruments. A. C. Luca's wife, Lisette, and his sis-

ter Diane also appeared with the group. (Although they sang in close harmony, the Hutchinsons, the Lucas, and the Alleghanians all included
women singers.)

Their first public appearance seems to have been as early as 1848. The
group toured New England and the mid-Atlantic states in the early 1850s.
In 1853 over 5,000 people attended the Luca Family performance at a ben-
efit concert for the Anti-Slavery Society. The Lucas teamed up with the
Hutchinson Family in 1859 for a month of tours just before the outbreak
of the Civil War. The two family troupes ended their collaboration when
Cleveland Luca, who was better known for his remarkable pianistic skills,
was hired by the president of the young African nation of Liberia to teach
music. Researchers point to a Hutchinson influence on the group, and it is
likely that they included close harmony arrangements in their repertory.[10]
In the Hutchinsons and the Lucas, America had examples of a dignified
concert quartet lineage that would serve as a staid foil to the generally
comical quartets of the minstrel—and vaudeville—stage. White and black
quartets similar to these two groups continued to perform throughout the
century. The Lucas always included art music songs and instrumentals in
their shows. They were considered part of the African American concert
tradition in the nineteenth century that also embraced the Hyer Sisters,
the piano prodigy Blind Tom, Harry T. Burleigh, and others.

"Father" Robert Kemp (1820–1879), from Wellfleet, Massachusetts, presented nostalgic shows featuring old-fashioned psalm singing as well as
four-part harmony in the years just before the Civil War. Kemp and his antiquarian variety troupe, the "Old Folks' Show," dressed in "costumes of
one hundred years ago" and performed what passed at that time for old-
fashioned musical repertory. An amusement reviewer from the *Cincinnati
Enquirer* said in a 1859 review: "Their music . . . calls to mind early associations long since buried in the 'dead past,' and revives the pleasantest
recollection of the spring-time of existence, when 'life was full of sunny
years,' and our hearts were free from the 'mountain of care' which weigh
them down in after years."[11] In Kemp's time, as the threat of secession and
war plagued Americans, people longed for the tranquility and simplicity
that they identified with eighteenth-century life.

One of the "Old Folks'" show-stoppers was a close-harmony quartet song
in German about a multi-instrumentalist named Johnny Schmoker (see
figure 1.3) who teaches instrumental technique by singing imitative nonsense syllables such as "Pily, wily, wink, das ist mein fi-fe." In performance,
the quartet members pretended to play the instruments they were imitating. The melody or "air" was sung by the second tenor. Kemp's "Old Folks'
Shows" demonstrate elegantly just how old the siren call of nostalgia really is in American life.[12]

A deep appreciation of four-part close harmony found expression in concert attendance and home and recreational singing using commercial
sheet music arrangements. Dating at least to the 1840s, there were numerous sheet music publications for men's four-part harmony (TTBB), including hymns for Masonic lodges, early college fraternity songs, and mil-

JOHNNY SCHMOKER.

In this song, an old German musician tells his friend, Johnny Schmoker, about the instruments upon which he can play, and describes them by motions while he sings. When performed by a chorus, especially of men, the movements being in exact time, and all together, an effect is produced which has not been equalled by anything of the kind ever produced in this country. Observe, that the motions are made only when the words describing the instruments are sung, as for example, at "Rub a dub a dub," the roll of the drum, is imitated, beginning, (as in the case of all the instruments) with the first, and ending exactly with the last word; at "Pilly willy wink," the hands are placed as if playing the Fife and the fingers only move; at "Tic knock knock," the right hand strikes three times under the left as if playing the Triangle; at "Bom bom bom," the hand is mov-ed forward and back as if playing the Trombone; and so on the last, which is imitated by crooking both arms and striking with them against the sides as if playing the Bagpipe. Observe that the singing at some of the instruments is loud and at others soft, also that the phrase where each instrument is first mentioned is repeated, and that the first movement, which is sung when each instrument is introduced is, to save room printed but once. Sing until you come to D.C. then begin again, and omitting that which is marked 1st time, go to that which is marked 2nd time, and when you come to the next D.C. go back again to the begin-ning and omitting both that which is marked 1st time, and that which is marked 2nd time, and go to that which is marked 3rd time and so on. The effect of this with a company of children is highly amusing and entertaining.

GEO. F ROOT.

Harmonised and Arranged by B. F. RIX.

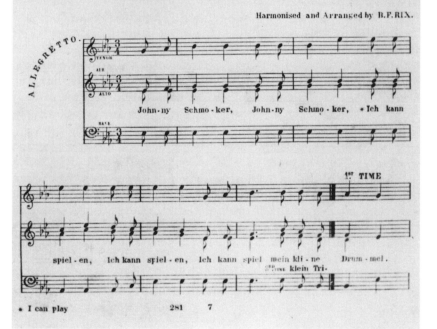

ALLEGRETTO.

TENOR
AIR
ALTO

John-ny Schmo-ker, John-ny Schmo-ker, * Ich kann

BASE

1ST TIME

spiel-en, Ich kann spiel-en, Ich kann spiel mein kli-ne Drum-mel.
klein Tri-

* I can play   281   7

Figure 1.4. Excerpt from the sheet music to "Johnny Schmoker," composed by B. F. Rix (Chicago: Root and Cady, 1863). Courtesy of the Rare Book, Manuscript, and Special Collections Library, Duke University. Used by permission.

itary, patriotic, sentimental, and comic ballads. The majority of sheet music published in four-part harmony between 1840 and 1870 consisted of SATB arrangements (soprano, alto, tenor, bass for two female and two male voices). Certain repertories, though (notably those listed above), were apparently deemed more appropriate for male voices. For example, an arrangement of the song "The Sword and the Stone" (1843) has a chorus in TTBB, with the melody sung by the high tenor.[13] SATB arrangements could, of course, be rearranged for male voices, sometimes by lowering the soprano lead by an octave, resulting in a second tenor lead underneath a high tenor (formerly alto) harmony. This transposition of voices between SATB arrangements, with a soprano lead, and TTBB arrangements, with a second-tenor lead, was sometimes noted in instructions on the sheet music itself, providing a clue that it was commonly done in practice. Many of the SATB arrangements were, in fact, based on the performances of all-male groups to begin with (minstrel quartets and the like) and would have originally been sung in TTBB harmony.

Despite many decades of scholarship to the contrary, it is still common to hear variations of the formula that African American music inherited "rhythm" from Africa and "harmony" and "melody" from Europe. Of course, "rhythm," "melody," and "harmony" are European terms that represent musical abstractions, none of them isolated in musical performance. For example, West African multiple drum and percussion orchestras typically produce complex polyphonic structures to which each drum contributes its own patterns (with its own pitch and timbre). These may combine with vocal melodies as well. It is well documented that many African people sang in polyphony or even (nonfunctional) harmony before contact with Europe. Gerhard Kubik has offered a theory to account for the "abstract structural idea behind some of the most diverse bi-part and multi-part harmonic singing styles in Africa," which he identifies as the selection by singers of nonproximate pitches (i.e., every other pitch) in a scale to produce simultaneous sounding of two or more concordant pitches, which he calls the "scalar skipping process."[14] Different parent scales generate different combinations of allowable tones; this theory accords well with the observable coincidence of tones in contemporary African musical practice. In one example Kubik cites, the parent seven-note (heptatonic) scale used by a group in the Central African Republic generates alternating four-note "chords" that are similar to Western "major sevenths."[15] Kubik provides a catalog of numerous heptatonic harmonies from the Guinea Coast and West Central Africa.

A widely cited account of slave singing from William Francis Allen provided a description of African American polyphonic singing from a decidedly naive perspective:

> There is no singing in *parts, as we understand it,* and yet no two appear to be singing the same thing—the leading singer starts the words of each verse, often improvising, and the others, who "base" him, as it is called, strike in with the refrain, or even join in the solo, when the

words are familiar. . . . And the "basers" themselves seem to follow their own whims, beginning when they please and leaving off when the please, striking an octave above or below . . . *or hitting some other note that chords,* so as to produce the effect of a marvelous complication and variety, and yet with the most perfect time, and rarely with any discord.[16]

This account represented slave singing as primarily heterophonic, responsorial, and characterized by improvised "harmonizing." To "base" in this account means to sing the responsorial part or chorus. The most important word for our purpose, however, is "chords," used as a verb to mean what we would refer today as "accords." I suspect that "hitting some other note that chords" may be an apt description for the variety of harmonizing that flourished in black communities in the nineteenth century outside of the domain of Western functional tonality.

Another extraordinary description of early African American harmony came from Frederika Bremer, who noted while traveling in Virginia in 1851: "I first heard the slaves, about a hundred in number, singing at their work in large rooms; they sang quartettes . . . in such perfect harmony, and with such exquisite feeling, that it was difficult to believe them self-taught."[17] Virginia was a cradle for black harmony (especially in the Hampton Roads region near Norfolk) for generations.

I speculate that African American approaches to part singing in the Americas resulted from the following processes:

1. application of African "scalar skipping" harmonic approaches described above,

2. incidental harmonies resulting from overlapping responsorial parts (overlapping call-and-response),

3. heterophonic singing, in which two or more voices sing the same text using similar melodies but diverge appreciably in interpretation,

4. combinations of dronelike vocal or instrumental parts with a melody,

5. frequent repetition of one or more "riffs" or short ostinati (melodic-rhythmic formulae) coincident with a melody, and

6. cycling different texts and melodies against each other in African polyphonic style.

African slaves in the Americas and their descendants were privy to a repertory of multipart, dialogic, and interactional techniques that were combined with European functional harmony in the construction of American styles of harmonic singing. These well-established African approaches to part-singing are responsible, I believe, for William Francis Allen's observation of "marvelous complication and variety . . . rarely with any discord." I argue that some of these techniques are audible in contemporary barbershop and related close-harmony styles.

Kubik also weighs in on the interaction of African and European harmonies in North America: "While at the end of the nineteenth century one social class of musicians emulated European popular song forms and harmonic patterns in the process of creating ragtime piano *and vocal quartet music*, there was another social class on the plantations and in the urban back streets that was little affected by Western formal music education. Musicians from that mould remained faithful to tonal-harmonic principles inherited from one or another place in Africa, through enculturation processes within families and communities spanning several generations."[18] I think Kubik has overstated the case for a separation between these two "molds." In contexts such as minstrelsy, and even in the African American singing college (jubilee spiritual) groups, there was actually considerable give and take between rural, African American, and oral-tradition harmonizing, on the one hand, and written, functional, and Euro-American harmony on the other.

One example of this convergence may even explain the importance of the circle-of-fifths harmonies in ragtime. European composers developed these progressions in the nineteenth century, constructing longer cadential progressions by first interpolating the V^7 of the V^7 chord before the final cadence, then adding increasingly distant secondary dominant progressions, leading to a resolution on the tonic. Although the logic is an outgrowth of functional harmony, the introduction of the initial secondary dominant—often many modulations away from the tonic key and containing many accidentals—can be, and was, jarring to nineteenth-century ears. In addition, the chromaticism introduced by these progressions (there are at least two chromatic movements possible in each resolution) led to new styles of voice leading. This may explain how Europeans developed these novel harmonic progressions, but it does not explain their popularity among harmony singers or their ubiquity in "rag" progressions.

Many scholars have speculated that the blues scale is a North American retention of common African scalar models, with "neutral" pitches that fall outside of Western diatonicism. When this African model is juxtaposed to Western major diatonic scales, Western observers describe the blues scale as having microtonally lowered thirds, sevenths, and, to a lesser degree, fifths. When blues scales are performed on fixed-pitch chromatic instruments, the inflected thirds, sevenths, and fifths are represented as choices or combinations of two chromatic pitches (i.e., major and minor third). Kubik terms this the "African pitch area concept"; in it, neighboring notes in the Western chromatic "scale" "can be compounded to form a pitch area" to preserve African scalar relationships.[19] He further suggests that barbershop harmony is a product of African American pitch equation relationships (expressed in chromatic voice-leading). Although this ignores the relationship of barbershop harmonies to European dominant seventh resolutions—and as a result probably greatly overdetermines the African contribution—I agree that African American aesthetic preferences for shading a tone or for sliding between neighboring tones has in all likelihood played a role in the evolution of barbershop harmony and in the cultural preference for secondary dominant progressions in ragtime. Portia K. Maultsby has noted that "'Playing' with pitch or 'worrying the line,' as Stephen Henderson calls it—is a technique integral to the solo style of many black performers."[20]

Given the prevalent play with close harmony in African American communities of the mid to late nineteenth century and the practice of "snaking" chords (moving from one chord to another by changing one or more nonmelody notes), it is reasonable to assume that one of the most common techniques for snaking chords was to substitute alternative pitches within these "African pitch areas" to produce new chords. This would have given to black improvised harmonizing of the period a chromatic tint that could be readily evoked within the sequences of secondary dominant chords that eventually became known as "ragtime progressions." The introduction of ragtime progressions (often by white composers of ragtime) and the extemporized chromatic chord sequences of some of their black interpreters created new performative logics and chord vocabularies that flowered in black close harmony and its minstrel evocations.

Ragtime rhythms may have very well developed in a similar process; European songs had their metrical structures "ragged" by African American performers who interjected crossing and contrasting rhythmic accents.[21] "Ragging" can be understood as a pervasive aesthetic principle of African American treatments of Euro-American music. It is an interpretive move that can be understood as a form of signifyin(g), in the vernacular sense used by Henry Louis Gates Jr. and applied insightfully to black musical practices and tropes by Samuel A. Floyd Jr.[22]

In Blackvoice: Minstrelsy and Variety Entertainment

One of the earliest and most popular of contexts for the performance of close harmony was the blackface minstrel theater. For well over a century, white Americans were fascinated, even obsessed, with exploring racial and cultural difference through the medium of theatrical presentations by whites in blackface. Although most works on the subject have explored its theatrical conventions, few have taken its sound seriously. Blackface ("blackvoice") delineators were the medium through which millions of Americans and audience members throughout the world encountered a simulated African American "essence," including speech, vocal mannerisms, music, dance, and movement. Songs, skits, and oration were typically delivered in blackface (in which the performers' faces were made up with "burnt cork"), but they were, perhaps more importantly, performed in blackvoice, an often crude parody of black southern dialect, diction, timbre, and vocal mannerisms. Instrumental performances employed stereotypical plantation instruments: bones, tambourine, fiddle, banjar or banjo, and sometimes a jawbone. Minstrel performers learned an entire code of black simulacra, including stereotyped motions, gestures, steps, and moves that were thought to represent black plantation body language.

Thomas Dartmouth Rice was one of many "burnt cork delineators" who performed in shows and circuses around America in the first few decades of the nineteenth century, a practice that has its roots in the eighteenth century. Rice claimed to have patterned his Jim Crow character on an African American singer and dancer. True or not, by 1828 Rice was performing the song and dance he called "Jump Jim Crow." He elaborated his piece into an entire play and took his act to New York's Bowery Theater in 1832. A small army of blackface delineators followed. George Washington Dixon introduced another long-lasting song and character, his dangerous urban dandy "Zip Coon" in 1834, adding to the stock of black stereotypes available in minstrelsy.[23]

The Virginia Minstrels, a foursome formed in 1843 and led by the fiddle player Dan Emmet (Daniel Decatur Emmet, 1815–1904), appropriated the "minstrel" part of their name from the Rainer Family (which sometimes called itself the Tyrolese Minstrels), which had recently toured the United States.[24] There were a few similarities: the American group would perform something not entirely divorced from folklore, and they would do it in costume like the Tyrolese Minstrels; indeed, they would perform as a quartet and include music. The four Virginia Minstrels popularized the minstrel-style show as a collective theatrical performance and instituted the standard instrumentarium of the minstrel show: bones, tambourine, violin and banjo. One of their lasting hits was "Buffalo Gal (Won't You Come Out Tonight)," originally "Lubly Fan Will You Come Out Tonight" (1844) by "Cool" White, also known as John Hodges (1821–1891). By 1845 C. Bradlee of Boston had already published four-part minstrel arrangements of songs such as "Where Is the Spot That I Was Born On" and "Miss Nancy Paul," from a series of "Carolina Melodies" as sung by the minstrel troupe the Harmoneons. The Harmoneons' version of "Nancy Paul," published in 1843, has the earliest minstrel sheet music with a TTBB chorus that I have found, although the Campbell's Minstrels TTBB chorus of "Bella Rosa" ("Bella Rosa! Tender Flower! Come and cheer this darkey's heart") from 1848 follows by a few years. Minstrel troupes, therefore, were singing four-part TTBB arrangements of their choruses from the earliest years of their existence.

In 1846 E. P. Christy (founder and manager of the Christy Minstrels) created the lasting tripartite structure for the minstrel show: (1) repartee and comic dialogue between the interlocutor and one or two endmen (Bruder/Mister Tambo and Bruder/Mister Bones were the stock endmen characters); (2) the Olio or variety show, the direct predecessor to vaudeville, which was performed typically in front of a scrim or curtain while the set was assembled backstage for the final skit; and (3) a short skit or play, usually on plantation life—sometimes with musical interludes. The size of the troupes expanded through the 1870s and 1880s, when they could be eighty strong. Along with circuses and touring Wild West shows, these were *the* entertainment spectacles of their day.

There is good reason to believe that the singing Hutchinson Family had a strong influence on quartet singing of the early minstrel show. The Congo Minstrels advertised as early as 1844 that "their songs are sung in Harmony in the style of the Hutchinson Family."[25] Many of the early songs for troupes that performed minstrel material, such as Ordway's Aeolians (Boston), the Harmoneons, Campbell's Minstrels, Wood's Minstrels, Kunkel's Nightingale Opera Troupe, Buckley's Serenaders, and Palmo's Burlesque Opera Company, were also written in three- or four-part male harmony.

Stephen Foster was an early master of the minstrel musical interlude, and he wrote or adapted many of his songs for the minstrel stage. Many of Foster's songs were in the "courtly serenade" and chivalric genre of mid-nineteenth-century popular songs ("Jeanie with the Light Brown Hair" and "Beautiful Dreamer," for example). He is better remembered, however, for his interpretation of minstrel songs in mannered black dialect, as in "Old Folks at Home" and "Camptown Races." He began to compose in the "Ethiopian" fashion to supply a small circle of friends, his "Knights of the Square Table," with songs for informal singing. In these, Foster sought a song style with an indelible minstrel feel. In imitation of African American call-and-response songs, Foster settled on short, tuneful choruses, often sung in four parts, followed by solo verses, a form that was commonly called a "refrain song" at the time and that was closely identified with African Americans, although it had been circulated in some English glees and arrangements to Thomas Moore's *Irish Melodies*. Although he did not invent the refrain song, Foster helped to popularize and standardize the verse-and-chorus form of the minstrel song.

Foster wrote a four-part chorus to "Oh! Susanna" (1848), which was made famous by the Christy Minstrels and performed by countless minstrel quartets such as the Continental Vocalists. The latter published a songbook called the *Continental Vocalists Glee Book* in 1855. Foster also set "Gwine to Run All Night" (or "Camptown Races" [1850]) for the Christy Minstrels and published "Old Folks at Home" (1851), with an agreement to allow the Christy Minstrels to perform it prior to publication (he labeled it "Ethiopian Melody as sung by Christy Minstrel's"). Foster's songs were part of a subtle evolution of the minstrel song away from the crude and comical caricatures of "Jump Jim Crow" and toward songs full of sentiment dubbed "plantation ballads."[26] The melodic and harmonic content of Foster's minstrel songs were in the vein of the Irish melodies popular in midcentury, but with light touches of African American syncopation.

After midcentury, the four-part chorus in the style of Foster became a commonplace of song composition, and not only in minstrelsy. Jon Finson notes that "while it may not have invented the multi-voice refrain, ensemble minstrelsy enshrined the four-voice chorus in song for at least three decades, and popularized a narrative structure in which a story unfolds in the verse while the chorus provided a moral, commentary, or sentiment."[27]

In the introduction to this book, I discussed the nostalgic function of blackface minstrelsy. Finson argues that minstrelsy used African Ameri-

Figure 1.5. Chorus from "My Brudder Gum," by Stephen Foster (1849)

cans as "symbols of rural longing," betraying "covert admiration" of rustic common sense and virtue.[28] Similarly, Eric Lott demonstrates in his appropriately titled *Love and Theft* a complex reception of minstrel theater among white audiences, who approached it with "envy as well as repulsion, sympathetic identification as well as fear."[29] This helps to explain why songs from this theatrical tradition became anthems of Southern states and of the Southern rebellion, despite their associations with African American life. "The Yellow Rose of Texas" (1858), for example, was about a "yellow" or mulatto woman ("We'll play the banjo gaily and we'll sing the songs of yore"). Another minstrel tune, "I Wish I Was in Dixie's Land," attributed at the time to the pioneering blackface minstrel Dan Emmet, was performed as a minstrel "Plantation Song and Dance" in 1859, just before the opening of hostilities between the North and South. It swiftly became the most popular song in the country and served as a marching tune for the Confederate troops.[30] "Carry Me Back to Old Virginia," later the official song of its namesake state, was written by an African American composer for minstrel shows, James Bland. These songs and various southern pastoral ballads of subsequent decades became mainstays of white barbershop revival singing. Anecdotal evidence suggests that quartetting was popular among troops in Northern and Southern regiments during the Civil War, setting a precedent for the next several wars. For example, the original version of the antislavery song "John Brown's Body" was popularized by a quartet from the Second Battalion of the Massachusetts Infantry. This too may have accounted for the popularity of TTBB arrangements of a military character.

Although much attention has focused on "blackface delineators" in minstrelsy, by the time of the Civil War African Americans were beginning to move into the blackface theater in search of work in entertainment. The minstrel stage offered opportunities to what were being called "authentic Ethiopian" performers to learn and practice show business arts and to build a reputation and career.

I have found references to three black minstrel troupes performing before the Civil War. The Mocking Bird Minstrels appeared in Philadelphia in the 1855–56 season and may have been the first black group to adopt the "minstrel" label, and there is also mention of a group called the Apollo Minstrels in 1857 in Ohio.[31] Sometimes called the "first successful black-owned minstrel troupe," Hicks' Georgia Minstrels was run by Charles Hicks, a light-skinned black, and it first performed during the denouement of the Civil War in 1865. Hicks' troupe was the successor to an even earlier group, Brookes and Clayton's Georgia Minstrels, which Hicks managed.

As evidence of the importance of black barbershops as centers for entertainment in African American communities, Henry T. Sampson noted that Hicks selected members for his troupe "from ex-slaves who were giving extemporaneous performances in the barber shops and other places of amusement in and around the city."[32] Hicks' Georgia Minstrels toured Panama and Europe, among other places, but after running into economic difficulty, Hicks sold the troupe to a white tavern keeper, Charles Callender, whereupon it became Callender's Georgia Minstrels. Under Callender, the group continued its rise to become the best-known black minstrel group of all time. By 1975 Callender had recruited the Hamtown Students close-harmony quartet—Messers. Little, Morris, Jones, and Devonear—as the troupe's resident quartet. This is one of the earliest examples of a named quartet in African American minstrelsy. Prior to this, quartet numbers seem to have involved assorted performers from the minstrel show.

Charles Hicks later organized troupes under his own name again, and many others organized imitation groups under similar names. Following the second formation of Hick's Georgia Minstrels, a black minstrel named Lew Johnson formed his own group, Lew Johnson's Minstrels. Between 1866 and 1897, Johnson toured with four successive groups. His first group included a quartet featuring the ballad singer F. M. Proctor, a Mr. Hardey (tenor), and George Catlin (bass). His other groups were Lew Johnson's

Plantation Minstrels (1871–96), with Alf Lindsey and O.T. Jackson as singers, and his most successful effort, Lew Johnson's Baby Boy Minstrels, with a resident quartet called the Black Baby Boy Quartet (1887–88).

Although staged shows have been the central concern of all the books written about minstrelsy, the minstrel parade was often the main attraction of a visit by a minstrel troupe. When minstrel groups came to a town, especially in the later part of the century (after some troupes had swelled to gargantuan proportions), some promoted their performance by parading to the theater, led perhaps by a horse-drawn wagon carrying the managers of the minstrel group. Following the managers and stars came the "walking gents," which included singers, acrobats, and comedians, after which came the baton-twirling drum majors and local boys carrying the group's banners. The parades were musical extravaganzas as well, featuring the troupe's brass band, quartet, or chorus, or some other musical attraction. More people saw these parades than bought tickets for the stage shows, and the parades (especially those made up mostly of African Americans) made a lasting impression on American towns.

After the success of the various black college singing groups, Callender's Georgia Minstrels and Haverly's Genuine Colored Minstrels began to include jubilee quartets in minstrel shows. Hicks and Sawyer Colored Minstrels starred an early version of the Magnolia Quartet. The Standard, Unique, Magnolia, Twilight, Diamond, Excelsior, and Knickerbocker Quartets were some of the outstanding black close-harmony groups of the late nineteenth century. Most were involved in minstrelsy at some stage in their professional careers, although many also sought recognition as concert artists and as performers in more legitimate stage productions (see chapter 2). Their performances inspired many of the white quartets of the later decades, including groups that assumed the names of earlier black quartets, such as Peerless, Knickerbocker, Criterion, and others.

Outside of the minstrel show, one heard boisterous close harmonizing in tents shows, patent medicine shows, and concert saloons. The patent medicine shows sold cheap medicines and trinkets in their travels through small-town America during the mid- and late nineteenth century. The one-man shows later became small-group variety acts, with singers, dancers, and banjo players. The Hamlin Company of Chicago, one of the bigger patent medicine firms at the time, sent around large stage shows, as did their main competitor, the Kickapoo Indian Medicine Company of New Haven. Hence the shows were often called kickapoo (or "kick") shows. During the Civil War, Hamlin's Wizard Oil was "sold from wagons drawn from town to town by handsome four- or six- horse teams. Each wagon carried a driver, a lecturer, a vocal and instrumental quartet, and a parlor organ built onto the wagon."[33] The wagons offered free shows to entice customers and used the full range of pre-vaudeville variety, comedy, song, and dance, including close-harmony quartets. Smaller towns, which might not have been able to afford a large minstrel troupe, were still visited by the medicine shows and traveling tent theaters.

Concert saloons (honky-tonks or free-and-easies) were a fixture of the western frontier before making their way into the urban areas. By the 1850s, New York City's concert saloons were concentrated in the Bowery neighborhood, also host to brothels and gambling houses. In a bawdy atmosphere of drink, smoke, and male patronage, concert saloons presented low-concept variety shows featuring off-color comedy, music and dance numbers, novelty acts (juggling, acrobatics, contortionists, and animal acts), skits, and farces. The bill was less organized than that of the minstrel shows, and its polyethnic humor supplanted the "darky" humor of minstrelsy. By the 1880s, there were over three hundred concert saloons in the Bowery area alone.

Tone on Tone: Black and White Recreational and Concert Quartets

Lynn Abbott cites a fascinating review in an African American paper, the *Indianapolis Freeman*, from 1900, discussing the place that "the barbershop quartette with its barbershop harmony" plays among African American singers. "It doesn't take much of an effort of memory to *recall* the time when all quartettes sang their own self-made harmonies. With their oft-recurring 'minors,' diminished sevenths and other embellishments, this barber shop harmony, although pleasing to the average ear, and not altogether displeasing to the cultivated ear, is nothing more or less than a musical slang" (italics mine).[34] I emphasize the word "recall" in the account because it provides a timeframe, situating African American recreational barbershop harmony in the 1880s and perhaps the 1870s as well. This is, as far as I know, the first written example of the use of the phrase "barbershop quartet," and it strongly suggests that the association of close-harmony quartet singing with barbershops was a product of the African American musical experience. By contrast, the term does not seem to have become popular among whites until after the song "(Mr. Jefferson Lord) Play That Barber Shop Chord" became a vaudeville hit in 1910–11 (see chapter 3).

The composer James Weldon Johnson reflected back on the "crack quartets made up of waiters in the Jacksonville hotels" in the 1870s. He and his brother Rosamond formed their own quartet in 1886, when Rosamond was just thirteen. Johnson noted, "when a white barber was unknown in the South, every barber shop had its quartet, and the men spent their leisure time playing on the guitar . . . and 'harmonizing.'" Similarly, the minstrel Billy McClain discussed working in Kansas City in the late 1880s when "about every four dark faces you met was a quartet."[35] Johnson also remembered hearing a locally renowned quartet of black barbers in Jacksonville of the 1880s. To conclude, as some have, that Johnson's experience of quartets constituted "the first documented observation of one-on-a-part, four-part singing by blacks" is to ignore many other manifestations of minstrel and concert quartets dating back to the 1860s.[36] For example, the Luca Family quartet performed well before this time, and James M. Trotter noted the presence of many elite concert quartets active in the early 1870s [see below]), but there are numerous references to minstrel quartets in the years before the Jacksonville report.

Too great a reliance on Johnson's observations may exaggerate the uniqueness of Jacksonville. According to Abbott, "Taken on its own merit, the 'Jacksonville connection' theory of an African-American origin of barbershop harmony is more plausible than any published speculation from the white perspective."[37] For Abbott, acceptance of the "Jacksonville connection" helps to separate racist from nonracist accounts of barbershop's origins: "After Sigmund Spaeth's initial enthusiasm for the 'Jacksonville connection,' 'white origins' theorists vacillated between reckless, second-hand interpretation and faceless unawareness of it. Spaeth eventually played the 'Jacksonville connection' theory down, and he never did grace it with a footnote. It is totally invisible to Deac Martin; *emasculated* by James McClelland; and most recently circumvented or rejected, or perhaps suppressed, by Val Hicks. It has yet to be publicly recognized by the SPEBSQSA."[38] It is likely, however, that such scenes were being played out in black barbershops, on street corners, in saloons, and in black men's fraternal organizations all across the South. The pervasive nature of barbershop harmonizing in black neighborhoods of the late nineteenth century argues against attaching too much significance to the Jacksonville story in and of itself, except as an instance of a wider pattern.

Reflecting on the ubiquitous black harmony quartets of the 1870s through the 1890s, the composer Scott Joplin decided to compose a close-harmony quartet song, "We Will Rest a While," for his "ragtime opera" *Treemonisha*, published in 1911. The quartet was sung by characters portraying field workers. Edward Berlin states that this provides Treemonisha with "additional value as a record of black, rural musical practices of the1870s–90s. The sections with folk types of music are, in effect, re-creations by a skilled and sensitive participant. . . . In Joplin's day it had not yet been forgotten that close-harmony quartet singing was characteristic of black culture, both as a religious expression and as a secular entertainment. . . . Here, Joplin confirms that the quartet was integral to black rural practice of the 1880s."[39] While Joplin does not include swipes per se, he does include various echo effects associated with the barbershop quartet style ("ve-ry good"), some of the characteristic chromatic voice leading (note the parallel chromatic motion in the bass and second tenor voices in m. 3 on the syllables "a-while 'Cause it makes"), and conventional barbershop chord progressions. The latter include the circle-of-fifths resolutions ("us feel very good," VI^6–II^7 V^7 and so forth (with a short "tiddly" to a half-diminished chord on the echo); note the fully diminished chord at "'Cause it," resolving back to the tonic.

African American audiences saw the jubilee quartet or chorus, personified by the Fisk Jubilee Singers, as a more refined and dignified alternative to the traditional minstrel quartet, and even black minstrels adopted some

Figure 1.6. Vocal harmony excerpt, "We Will Rest Awhile," from Scott Joplin's opera *Treemonisha* (1911)

of the conventions of the jubilee quartets. Featuring spirituals arranged in European four-part harmony, Fisk and the other school groups strove to achieve respectability through a dignified concert demeanor and a largely sacred repertory, and by emulating European harmony.

The world tour by the Fisk Jubilee Singers was a watershed event in the history of African American music, especially in its reception by North American whites, and the validation provided by European concert audiences helped to raise the status of African American music at home. The early group was not a quartet, but it did sing four-part arrangements in SATB voicings. In the 1890s the school launched a men's quartet, the Fisk Jubilee Quartet, which became the seminal jubilee quartet, widely imitated by other black schools and by community- and church-based quartets.

Hampton Institute developed its own group of singers (sixteen singers on four parts) in 1873, and some version of the Hampton Singers (and later the Hampton Institute Quartet) persisted for over sixty years. In the same year, the Central Tennessee College formed the Original Tennesseeans, and thus by 1873 there were three or more school harmony groups active. A host of schools organized touring quartets during the next few decades: the Dinwiddie Colored Quartet of Dinwiddie, Virginia (of the John A. Dix Industrial School); the Florida Normal and Industrial Quartette; the quartets of Tuskegee Institute, Southern University (in Baton Rouge, Louisiana), and Atlanta University; the Bennett College Quartet; the Biddle University Quartet; the Invincible Quartet of Rust College; the Livingston College Male Quartet; the Moorehouse College Quartet; and many others. Although the harmonized spiritual formed a fairly distinct repertory and style, it cannot be considered completely apart from the minstrel show or its community-based, recreational, secular cousin (barbershop). This is because (1) the minstrel and recreational groups (both black and white) incorporated many spirituals into their repertories, (2) some of the jubilee spiritual quartets maintained a repertory of secular material indistinguishable from minstrel songs, and (3) musical styles and techniques flowed freely between the sacred and secular repertories.

Black secular concert quartets were also numerous in the early 1870s. In 1875 James M. Trotter surveyed literate black concert-music making around the country for his book *Music and Some Highly Musical People*. He mentioned that "Boston contains . . . several [African American] vocal quartets. *The Auber Quartet* have attracted much attention by their very pleasing rendering of *some of the best popular music of the day*."[40] In a playbill reproduced by Trotter (1875), the Auber Quartet was described as Messrs. Smith, Hill, Ruffin, and Henry, and their songs included "Sighing for Thee"; "The Image of the Rose," by Reichardt (with female lead); "Soldier's Farewell," by Kinkel; an untitled march; and "Man the Life-Boat." Trotter also identified a Cincinnati quartet called the Arion Quartet featuring Messrs. Andrew D. Hart and John Lewis.

Trotter's remarks are significant because they demonstrate an active African American quartet life in the urban North in the 1870s featuring a vernacular and secular repertory performed in elite concert style with little connection (at least in this account) to minstrelsy. Trotter's casual recitation of the names of mid-1870s quartets in a number of localities, with no hint that these represented novelties, suggests that these may have formed as early as the 1860s. With the influence of the Luca family still fresh in the minds of concertgoers, it is likely that the arrangements of popular tunes for these concert groups were in close harmony, but I have no proof of that. The publication date of Trotter's manuscript—1875—at least demonstrates that there were African American concert quartets throughout the North playing by the time of the earliest mention of a named quartet in an African American minstrel show, the Hamtown Students Quartet, around 1875.

Many accounts by prominent African American musicians who were later involved in jazz, classical music, ragtime, and blues mention quartet activity early in their lives, especially during the latter quarter of the nineteenth century. Some of these remembrances point to the formative role quartet harmonizing had in the development of black instrumental music. Here I will mention accounts by Scott Joplin, W. C. Handy, Willie "The Lion" Smith, and Louis Armstrong.

The composer Scott Joplin had a long association with quartet singing. Around 1894 he formed the Texas Medley Quartette, which he took on tour. The quartet was really a double quartet with eight singers (including two of Scott's brothers, Will and Robert). Two other members of the double quartet later sang in Joplin's Sedelia Quartette.[41] While living in Sedelia, Missouri, in the late 1890s, Scott Joplin was a regular contributor to two black fraternal associations, the Maple Leaf Club and the Black 400 Club, both of which featured entertainment. Many of the regular performers at the Maple Leaf Club were associated with vocal quartets. For example, the drummer Emmet Cook (of the Queen City Cornet Band) was a member of Joplin's Texas Medley Quartette, and Jake Powell was with the Cuba Quartette.[42]

Handy, the "Father of the Blues" and composer of one of the most popular songs of the twentieth century, "St. Louis Blues," sang in numerous quartets in his youth. His early music instruction took place in the chorus of the Florence (Alabama) District School for Negroes, directed by a music instructor who had been in the first graduating class of Fisk University. Handy also studied cornet by watching through the window of a local barbershop when a stranded circus music director gave lessons to a local band. At the age of fourteen, he arranged the song "Come and Kiss Me Annie Darling" for a female close-harmony quartet as a present for a girl on whom he had a crush. He wrote that around 1888, he "sang with a quartet that often serenaded the moon until the wee hours. Shortly afterwards, when Bill Felton, a minstrel man and a singing banjo player, came to Florence and organized a home town minstrel show, I joined up as first tenor for his quartet. I was fifteen at the time and my colleagues told me I looked pretty funny stepping along with the 'walking gents' in my father's Prince Albert."[43] The Felton minstrel group toured Tennessee and northern Alabama but became stranded in Jasper when their manager abandoned them. Afterwards, the minstrels toured for a while on their own without a manager, "playing for buttermilk and biscuits."

Handy later joined a quartet in Birmingham, Alabama, called the Lauzetta Quartet. Their repertory included a spoof of a spiritual that they adventurously renamed "Gwine Chop 'Em In the Head with a Golden Axe." In 1892 the group bummed railroad passage and sang along the way for handouts in order to make their way to the World Columbian Exposition but to their dismay, the fair was postponed until 1893, and the quartet soon disbanded. Handy received his big break when he was invited to join a well-known touring minstrel show in 1896 called Mahara's Minstrels. There is also a photograph from a San Francisco Minstrel show of 1897 with Handy singing tenor in the Ponce de Leon Quartet.

The early jazz and ragtime pianist Willie "The Lion" Smith recalled that that his uncle was an ardent quartet singer. Although he does not specify a year, he does seem to be referring to the period around the turn of the century when he describes his uncle in the following terms: "When he wasn't busy on his perfume wagon he devoted his time to a quartet around town that he managed. Many times I would go out and hear them sing on street corners and hear their audience holler at them to 'pep it up' or 'rag it' while they were harmonizing away."[44]

Jazz musicians recalled quartet experiences in New Orleans of the 1890s. Jelly Roll Morton was singing in a quartet for wakes, and Louis Armstrong, a tenor, assembled a quartet of neighborhood boys before he was eleven years old. His group paraded through the Storyville district, singing in the street for donations from pimps and prostitutes. The quartet also sang at funerals, at tent shows, in theaters for variety shows, and in bars. Armstrong said of the latter, "I used to hear some of the finest music in the world listening to the barroom quartets, who hung around in the saloons with a cold can of beer in their hands, singing up a breeze while they passed the can around. . . . When I was a teenager, those old-timers let me sing with them and carry the lead, bless their hearts." In describing a friend of his with whom he occasionally sang, he said, "You should have heard his good old barroom tenor sing 'Sweet Adeline' or 'Mr. Jefferson Lord—Play That Barbershop Chord.'" Few have questioned to what extent Armstrong's quartet experience informed his trumpet playing and improvising. According to Armstrong, "I had been singing for a number of years, and my instinct told me that an alto takes a part in a band same as a baritone or tenor in a quartet," by which he meant that the alto fills in the chords.[45]

It is striking how many African American figures considered foundational to their genres (Joplin to ragtime; Smith to stride piano; Armstrong and Morton to jazz; Handy to blues; and James Weldon Johnson and Roland Hayes to African American art music) had roots in or experiences with barbershop quartet singing. Such potential influences from close harmony on these other genres have never been sufficiently analyzed.

Abbott cites the early experiences of the concert tenor Roland Hayes, who had a "curbstone quartet" at the turn of the century and whose "harmonies were personal discoveries, although a good deal of our musical improvisation perhaps was illegitimate. Sometimes we imitated the minstrel singers with whose harmonizations my ear had become familiar before I 'came out from amongst them' going from the tonic chord into the minor mode, thence into a deep minor and back into the major. Barbershop harmony, if you will, but good practice for the ear. When we got into bad habits we stood a good chance of having them corrected in the choir of the Monumental Baptist Church."[46] Hayes's reminiscences support a number of my arguments about early quartet singing. First, he makes clear the impact that minstrel quartets had on recreational quartet singing: it was most often the minstrel theater that helped to spread four-part close-harmony singing in black neighborhoods and communities. Secondly, he speaks to the importance of improvisation, with all of its unintentional violations of "correct" harmony. And thirdly, he alludes to the conventional chords employed by extemporizing singers, which he calls minors and deep minors and by which I believe he means seventh chords and diminished seventh chords. And, as I have mentioned, the "curbstone" was one of those cultural locations associated with young black men.

The range and diversity of black close harmony of the second half of the nineteenth century is staggering. There were amateur and professional groups, spiritual/jubilee and secular quartets, concert and minstrel groups. Black quartets staked a claim for close-harmony singing as an African American form by putting an indelible stamp on quartet singing, transforming European close-harmony performance practice and style. Lynn Abbott observes that "at the heart of this all-absorbing quartet activity was a spontaneous and highly infectious approach to harmonizing, or 'cracking a chord.' Ballads and sentimental tunes were most susceptible to it, but no song, religious or secular, traditional or Tin Pan Alley, was immune. The basic idea was to improvise, linger on, and bask in the immediate warmth of hair-raisingly unusual close-harmony chords."[47]

This observation gets to the meat of African American transformations of harmony singing. Many contemporaneous accounts speak of the improvised search for new harmonies obtainable by "cracking a chord," with its image of either breaking open a harmony and exposing it (as in cracking corn or a nut) or of startling the listener with sharply executed chords, as in the crack of a whip. Those who are accustomed to thinking about black contributions to music of the Americas in terms of the rhythm section and "groove" may wonder at my emphasis on African American contributions to disrupting the flow of rhythm, to establishing rhythmically free vocal interpretations, to "cracking" chords, and to snaking from one interesting chord to another. These techniques bear more than a superficial relationship to the changes in psalm singing among African slaves, which involved, in Christopher Small's words, "vocal improvisation around each single note in turn of a melody, over a beat slowed down almost to immobility, in what has been described as a volume of florid sound which ebbs and flows slowly, powerfully and at times majestically in successive surges."[48] We have journeyed far from the crude old saw about African rhythm and European harmony, and yet we have only begun to theorize about the contributions of African Americans to American vernacular harmony and vocal performance practice.

Even in the 1870s and 1880s, when close harmony was so popular in black communities, there was still a thriving and continuous white quartet tradition of recreational singing and concert performances that was distinct from the blackface minstrel show; if one includes the glee clubs, then one might argue for a number of parallel singing traditions. Offshoots of the Hutchinson Family (and its Tyrolean antecedents), glee clubs (many of which performed folk and popular songs), and parlor quartets (specializing in sentimental or "hearth and home" songs as well as comic songs, minstrel songs, and even spirituals) sang (and in some cases toured) throughout the second half of the nineteenth century. Chautauqua playbills, sheet music cover lithographs, and concert programs all support this. There may have even been considerable overlap between this white tradition and the "whiter" African American groups, such as the Luca Family or the Aurion Quartette. Sheet music for quartets was released throughout this period with a white target market. In 1878–1879, Dr. J. B. Herbert's *Male Quartet and Chorus Books* and W. T. Giffe's *Male Quartet and Chorus Books* were published for white quartet singers. The books included arrangements for male quartets of songs such as the black spiritual "Swing Low, Sweet Chariot"; the sentimental ballads "In Silent Mead," "A Little Farm Well Tilled," and "My Old Ox Team"; the comic songs "Ladies Tobacco Song," and "How Goes the Money"; and the "Singers March," which consisted entirely of nonsense vocables such as "la, la" and "boom chin boom."[49] The songbook featured a picture of the Aldine Quartet (a double quartet, eight men).

An 1887 edition of Stephen Foster's "Old Folks at Home" for male quartet (TTBB) contains some possible hints of the crossover influences that were shaping the contours of close harmony at the time. In figure 1.6, we can see that a number of gestures that I believe were meant to be evocative of African American vocal style have crept into Foster's "plantation song."[50] The figure comprises a prototype of a "swipe" at m. 12 and an early "tag" at m. 24. Various clues in the arrangement reinforce the importance of these gestures. For one thing, these measures are the only ones in the arrangement that feature contrasting dynamic markings. In the tag, two voices hold their notes (and syllables) for the entire measure while the other voices swipe in contrary motion using short text fragments and execute a crescendo. The crescendo emphasizes this contrary motion, and it ends with slurs, also in contrary motion. The slurs in this measure and the previous one are imitative of African American vocal style. In addition, the chord sequence of the swipe in the tag at m. 24 is a very common cadential progression in barbershop.

Tag: The Gray Areas of Black and White Harmony

The nineteenth-century history of barbershop harmony that I sketched in this chapter begins in earnest with the popularization of the German *Singverein* tradition of close harmony through tours of European singing families and through songbooks and sheet music. Close-harmony choruses were adopted by blackface (blackvoice) minstrel singing in verse-chorus structures, and African American minstrels subsequently embraced them as their own. Black and blackface minstrels carried this form of close harmony chorus to white and black singers all over the country, and I have

Figure 1.7. Swipe and tag, "Old Folks at Home," by Stephen Foster; arranged by Wilson G. Smith (Boston: Oliver Ditson, 1887)

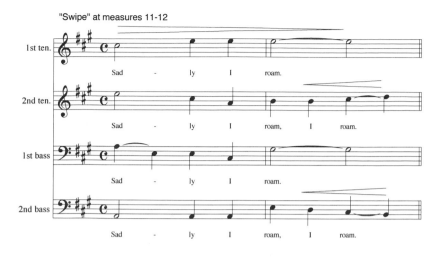

noted that black recreational singers effected a transformation of close-harmony singing in informal contexts throughout the South.

Most important, no form of harmony, close or otherwise, was hermetically sealed off from the others. Harmonized spirituals, plantation ballads, sentimental parlor songs ("hearth-and-home" songs), comic ditties, work songs, glees, and novelty songs such as the impersonations of animal and industrial sounds were all available to—and popular with—the range of quartet formations. Even the Fisk Jubilee Singers were not entirely immune to the attractions of the popular minstrel repertory.[51] Throughout the nineteenth century, therefore, close harmony was already a seasoned traveler between popular culture contexts and home and recreational settings, and what would become known as barbershop harmony incorporated repertory from minstrelsy, parlor songs, spirituals, and early Tin Pan Alley and ragtime songs.

Determining with precision the cultural origins of elements of barbershop singing has proven vexing for musicologists. For example, the popularity of echo effects in barbershop arranging may derive either from their similarity to African call-and-response techniques or from the popularity of echo effects in eighteenth-century British popular song. The elastic rhythm of barbershop singing, its secondary-dominant progressions, the verse-chorus structure, the exaggerated portamento, and the tags all have European prototypes but also seem to respond to deeply traditional aspects of African American performance practice. Even snaking and swiping chords, so closely identified in the nineteenth century with African American singers—an identification I am inclined to ascribe to black sources—is a form of voice-leading in four-part harmony singing and is not entirely unrelated to non-chord-tone embellishments in functional harmony.

The ambiguity inherent in these efforts is not entirely a product of the scarcity of sound and written sources, but also a product of the seamless syncretism evident in nineteenth-century forms of close harmony. Thus I view the development of barbershop-style close harmony as a complex interaction of black and white forms, performers, aesthetics, styles, and sounds. Nonetheless, when culture industries (chiefly vaudeville and the recording industry) popularized close-harmony singing at the turn of the century, the hybrid form was associated with an African American cultural "address" on black street corners, in black bars, in minstrel evocations of plantation life, and in black barbershops.

2

The Golden Era
Quartets in Show Business and the Music Industry

There's a time each year that we always hold dear
Good old summertime
With the birds in the trees-es and sweet scented breezes
Good old summertime
When your day's work is over then you are in clover
And life is one beautiful rhyme
No trouble annoying, each one is enjoying
The good old summertime
> — "In the Good Old Summer Time"; words by
> Ren Shields, music by George Evans (1902)

For barbershop enthusiasts, 1890 marks the beginning of the golden age of American barbershop song. That year was, of course, also the start of the decade dubbed the "Gay Nineties," a decade at the climax of the country's industrialization—capped by the Spanish-American War—in which the United States established itself as a global superpower. Although it began with America firmly mired in a deep depression, the economic climate improved after 1895, and optimism among middle-class whites, and many northern middle-class blacks, rebounded. Americans perceived that a new technological era was in the offing. The incandescent light bulb was displacing the flickering glow of gaslit street lamps, and the railroad and telephone connected Americans coast to coast. The 1893–94 World Columbian Exposition in Chicago summed up these marvels in a display of America's coming global dominance.

The end of the century was also a period of insecurity. Disparities in wealth nurtured resentments that could, and sometimes did, spill over into class warfare. Organized violence and Jim Crow laws threatened southern blacks. Rising immigration from southern Europe and Asia led to anti-immigration organizing, legislation, and riots. The so-called Gay Nineties thus capture an America of terrible contrasts, flexing its economic and military power while worrying through the consequences of its increasing pluralism and modernity. Pop culture emerged as a democratic forum for working through the nation's cultural contradictions.

The Gay Nineties: Black Quartets,
Tin Pan Alley, and Ragtime

African American quartets were well established by 1890 and regularly headlined performances; their names were almost always included on posters and playbills for the shows in which they appeared. Although not well known today, even among barbershop enthusiasts, these black harmony groups advanced close-harmony aesthetics in the late nineteenth century and were models for white recording quartets. However, the 1890s was a dangerous decade for touring African American minstrel groups; there was always the threat of attack from white racists, especially if a performer happened to be out of costume. A few black minstrel performers were killed and some minstrel trains delayed or stoned by mobs.

Among the hundreds of black quartets in show business were the Golden Gate, Knickerbocker, Calliope, Meadowbrook, Criterion, Standard, Unique, Twilight, Eclipse, Diamond, Acme, Peerless, Orpheus, Oak Leaf, and Trocadero Quartets. Some broke through into concert careers, others performed in progressive African American revues, but the great majority toiled in minstrel shows (both black and integrated), night after night in towns serviced by the railroads.

The Golden Gate Quartet (Henry Winfred, Sherman Coats, Frank Suttor, and James Grundy) worked continuously throughout the decade in minstrel shows, concert appearances, revues, and variety shows. Over the decade they performed in Sheridan and Flynn's Big Sensation Company, Slavery Days Company, a white burlesque troupe called Metropolitan Burlesque Company, and a musical farce called "A Hot Time in Dixie" (1899). They toured with the Williams and Walker Company in 1901, went out on the Park vaudeville circuit in the same year, joined Al and Mammie Anderson's Lady Africa Company, and toured with a white company during the fall of 1901.

The Twilight Quartet (Isaac Hines, Joseph Hodges, Robert Martin, and Billy Moore, bass) performed with Cleveland's Colored Minstrels in 1890–91. The San Francisco playbill for the minstrel group's performance in 1893 included both the Twilight and the Sans Souci Quartet. Twilight joined McCabe's Minstrels in 1894, performing in a spectacular olio that included Hindu jugglers, a bullfight scene, and a circus parade. In 1896 Twilight's Isaac Hines founded the Theatrical Professionals Club of Greater New York (also called the Colored Professional Club). This was, I believe, the first black professional entertainment organization in New York, preceding the Frogs and other clubs, and many of its members sang in black close-harmony groups such as the Golden Gate, Knickerbocker, Calliope, Meadowbrook, and Unique Quartets. Before it closed, sometime after 1905, the club came to include a reading room, rehearsal rooms, and a picture exhibit of famous African Americans in entertainment.[1]

These leading black quartets, many of them associated with the Colored Professionals Club, helped advance the "dignity agenda" later championed by James Reese Europe, James Weldon Johnson, the comedians Bert

Williams and George Walker, and other performers during the Harlem Renaissance. The quartets advocated more-refined performance venues, better treatment and pay for black performers, and control over the representation of African American culture. Early efforts to revise the portrayal of plantation-era slave life took shape in the African American revues of the 1890s. Lew Johnson's Refined Minstrels staged *Out of Bondage* in 1890 with the Lime Kiln Quartette. The Slavery Days Company opened at Brockton, Massachusetts, in the fall of 1893 with two quartets, the Eclipse and the Golden Gate. Soon afterwards, the South before the War Company went on stage with the Buckingham Quartet. For the opening of *The South before the War* in New York, the Colored Professional Club threw a reception for the performers.

Perhaps one of the greatest extravaganza performances of any kind to be staged in New York during the 1890s was a production by the minstrel entrepreneur Billy McClain called *Black America*. Far too large for a theater, *Black America* was staged in Brooklyn's Ambrose Park in the summer of 1895. Along with the U.S. Army Ninth Cavalry, exhibition boxing, cakewalking, and a reconstructed plantation (with livestock and cotton plants for realism), were over sixty-three African American quartets![2] I assume that McClain had to recruit locally as well as draw on his extensive contacts on the minstrel circuit to assemble such a large number of quartets. In January 1898 a smaller but similarly named production, *Darkest America,* came to New York, and the singer Gussie L. Davis organized an evening's entertainment at the Douglass Club, another black social organization, in honor of the cast. The roster of acts at the Douglass Club event included the Golden Gate Quartette and the Silver Leaf Quartette, along with the comedy team of Williams and Walker and Professor Henderson Smith's Concert Band. These pioneering Negro revues represented earnest efforts to elevate the minstrel show, to do away with despised stereotypes, and to depict antebellum life more realistically while preserving the entertainment value (and thus box-office draw) of minstrelsy, and they attracted considerable numbers of white patrons, especially after the success of *In Dahomey,* which opened on Broadway in 1903. Most pertinent to the current topic is the prominent place that black quartets played in these productions.[3]

Among the groups performing in concerts mostly outside of minstrelsy in this period were the Cyclone Quartette, which played concerts for three weeks straight in a Spokane, Washington, opera house, and the Black Arts Harmony Quartette of Nashville, Tennessee. However, minstrelsy remained the most secure form of employment for black quartets throughout the 1890s. Among the most active concert groups that also performed on the minstrel touring circuits was the Knickerbocker Quartet, which played in the Billy Jackson's Minstrels in 1894 (this troupe performed at Worth's Museum in New York and the People's Theater in Paterson, New Jersey). The Magnolia Quartet (Will Wade, Fred Jones, Ollie Hall, and L. Lucas) toured with Fields's Negro Minstrels and with the Canadian Jubilee Company. McAdoo's Original Jubilee Singers and Virginia Concert Company (known for their international tours) sported two quartets, one male (the Orpheus Quartet, which included O. M. McAdoo, bass) and one unnamed female quartet. The men's group sang the comic number "B.I.N.G.O." and the female group the maudlin "Lost Chord." The Excelsior Quartet went on tour with the Old Swanee River Company after performing in Hicks and Sawyer's Minstrels. Of this quartet it was said that they "had more steady engagements than any other colored quartette in the country" and that they were "filling engagements in Colorado, Nevada, and California."[4] Excelsior's routine included a vocal imitation of Barnum's steam organ. There were a number of integrated minstrel shows, such as Washburn's Double Minstrels (c. 1898), which included the Queen City Quartet, a "colored" band and orchestra, and a drill corps of "thirteen Negro boys." All of the quartets, minstrel shows, revues, and concert groups that I have cited in this section constitute but a tiny sample of the African American performance activity in the 1890s.

Abbott notes that the black press tended to disparage barbershop harmony and its conventions in favor of more "legitimate" approaches to harmony. The critic who wrote under the nom de plume of Tom the Tattler in the *Indianapolis Freeman* complained, "Their chief aim is to so twist and distort a melody that it can be expressed in so-called 'minors' and diminished chords. The melody is literally made to fit their small stock of slang-chords, instead of the chords being built around the melody." The same author praises William Coleman of the Excelsior Quartette who, in his words, "has done more to advance quartette singing from *the slough of barber shop harmony* than any man living." Abbott also cites a review of the black Military Quartette of San Francisco, in which the author noted, "They do not sing coon songs or about 'Way down Yonder in the Corn Field,' with accompanying barber shop chords."[5]

Whether a black group sang "Way down Yonder in the Corn Field" or not, nearly every black quartet included at least a few songs written by white Tin Pan Alley composers in their repertory. In the 1890s songwriting and publishing achieved a remarkable geographic center, spread out over only a few blocks of New York City. As hit songs tumbled out of the early New York–based firms such as Charles K. Harris, T. B. Harms, Willis Woodward, Joseph Stern, and Leo Feist Music, publishing houses from around the country gravitated to New York's Lower East Side to emulate their success. Clustering at first in the vaudeville theater district around Union Square and Fourteenth Street, publishing firms soon followed M. Witmark and Sons up to Twenty-eighth Street near Fifth Avenue. Pianos graced the lobbies and offices in this district in which songwriters plied their trade and sold their material to publishers. The journalist Monroe H. Rosenfeld is credited with coining the name "Tin Pan Alley" after remarking that these pianos (often muffled with paper) sounded like the rattling of tin pans.[6]

Sheet music was advertised by performances of songs on stage and in vaudeville. Musicians, especially singers, functioned as agents for the songwriters and publishers by plugging the latest hits. Publishers paid artists to sing a particular song in concert, on the street, in a bar, or outside a music shop. They also paid audience "plants" to request a particular song or to sing or whistle along with the performer to create the impression that a song was well known. A given tune could be plugged by being performed by a popular tenor, a close-harmony quartet, a male-female duet, or a brass band; on the heels of any popular rendition, the publisher could supply the relevant arrangement as sheet music.[7]

If Tin Pan Alley was a Mecca for producers of popular culture, Coney Island enshrined pop culture consumption. With rides, a carnival midway in the style of the Chicago World Columbian Exposition, a variety of eating establishments, and any number of entertainment houses, Coney Island was an outdoor vaudeville fantasy land, and vaudeville stars made it a regular stop on their summer itinerary. As a result, a lay historian of early popular music, Ulysses "Jim" Walsh, titled his articles for *Hobbies* magazine "The Coney Island Crowd." To advocates of elite or highbrow culture, Coney Island symbolized the siren call of cheap, popular culture and novelty—in essence, all that was wrong with mass taste. Quartets were active in the debate over the relative merits of popular music and the recording industry, especially in the choices they (and their labels) made regarding the choice of repertory (rags and comic songs versus parlor songs and light classics, for example).

Tin Pan Alley songsmiths were typically immigrants or children of immigrants working in New York City with little or no contact with the "heartland," yet they wrote many songs that ingratiated themselves deeply in the nostalgic culture of turn-of-the-century America, becoming a new American musical vernacular. Nineteenth-century parlor music's fascination with medieval chivalry and pastoralism was already dimming by the 1890s, supplanted by a new realism and brashness concerning technology, romance, and ethnicity.[8] By late century, lovers "spooned," "sparked," and "courted" (unchaperoned!). Novel consumer goods and machine technology, including tandem bicycles, merry Oldsmobiles, flying machines, world's fair attractions, and telephones, supplied themes for many songs.

The early Tin Pan Alley songs depended on economically reiterated motives attached to memorable text phrases, the precursors of the ubiquitous "hooks" in popular song. Songs were often in waltz time, considered the most suitable rhythmic accompaniment to songs of young love and attraction. After two decades of popularity, however, the waltz became increasingly associated with old love and nostalgia. Ragtime and the related coon songs, on the other hand, emerged as the vehicle for all that was brash and modern. In a voice that imitated black Americans, white (and a few black) songwriters could explore more explicit and frank treatments of relationships.

In vocal as well as instrumental performance, "ragging" was an African American term that implied spirited improvisation on a song's rhythm, a treatment or version of an existing song, and a form of musical transformation and play. When Euro-American songs were ragged by African American performers, the resulting rhythms syncopated the melodic rhythm but within a clear European metrical framework. Consistent with this framework, the basic style of ragtime piano and accompaniment that developed later in the 1890s consisted of a left-hand alternating bass in march time, against which the right hand provided a syncopated melody. Contrary to the Joplincentric theories of a few years back, ragtime was probably very much a vocal as well as an instrumental form, developing in the "sporting" districts of Mississippi River cities such as St. Louis, Memphis, and Louisville.

Although antecedents of rags and ragtime percolated for some time under the surface of American popular entertainment, the popular coming out of ragtime is linked to Chicago's World Columbian Exposition in 1893. The exposition was a temple to American technological progress housed in a series of enormous Greek revival buildings on the Chicago waterfront. For two years, news of its planning, construction, opening, and operations made front-page news across America. With all the talk of progress and internationalism, however, it was the midway (officially the "Midway Plaisance") that made the most indelible impression on visitors. With the motto "Make Culture Hum," it dished out 1890s novelty entertainment to over twenty-seven million patrons. Pavilions devoted to exotica hosted performances from Dahomey, China, Cairo, Java, Lapland, and the South Seas. America's own exotica, especially African American music and dance, made the biggest impact. Ragtime was introduced to Americans and the world through the first performance of Jesse Pickett's "Dream Rag" in the entertainment district around the exposition. A parade of cakewalks, coon songs, and piano rags soon followed.[9]

The first published use of the term "rag" in song arrangements was on a vocal score in 1896—"All Coons Look Alike to Me," by the African American composer Ernest Hogan. Similarly, the first ragtime piano compilation (in 1897) consisted of songs in piano reduction. By 1897, however, instrumental rags were appearing in sheet music form. A variety of song types thrived under the label of ragtime, which was applied indiscriminately; any song with a real or asserted connection to African American culture could be dubbed "ragtime." By the late 1890s, many white composers (and some African American ones, such as Hogan) were using the term for songs that recycled minstrel stereotypes, such as the violent urban dandy ("Zip Coon"). Although these themes had been explored in countless minstrel songs, ragtime provided them with a new melodic, rhythmic, and harmonic foundation. The objectionable portrayals in these turn-of-the-century coon songs have resulted in their gradual excision from later compilations of period sheet music and recordings, but in their time, they exercised a powerful hold over the tastes and imagination of white Americans.

The more inflammatory racist lyrics of coon songs were tempered a bit after the New York City race riots of 1900 (some critics argued that the stereotypes fostered by coon songs were one of the causes of the riots). But even with tamer topics, ragtime provided a spicier update of the mildly erotic or salacious waltz. In its syncopated rhythms was encoded the continuing fascination with racial and cultural difference and the allure of a black urban demimonde. In ragtime, coon songs, and fads generated by the World Columbian Exposition lay the roots of the common association in America of black culture with modernity and novelty. Paradoxically, in "plantation songs" and in the songs of southern nostalgia, African Americans remained objects of nostalgic attraction for songwriters. Both images of African Americans were reproduced in close-harmony arrangements of ragtime and plantation songs.

Ragtime's syncopated melodic figures and secondary-dominant chord progressions provided the final elements associated with barbershop harmony. These songs, with their many seventh chords, were ripe for four-part harmony, and they authorized new chromatic voice-leading. Ragtime chestnuts from the turn of the century include "Hello, My Baby" (Joseph E. Howard and Ida Emerson [1899]), a celebration of the telephone in ragtime syncopation; "Goodbye, My Coney Island Baby" (Les Applegate [n.d.]); "Bill Bailey, Won't You Please Come Home" (Hughie Cannon [1902]); "Mandy Lee" (Thurland Chattaway [1899]); "The Levee Song" (also known as "I've Been Workin' on the Railroad" [n.d.]); and "Down Mobile" (also known as "Way down Yonder in the Cornfield" [n.d.]). The last three songs probably served as the most popular close-harmony tunes before the twentieth century and before the appearance of "Sweet Adeline" and "By the Light of the Silvery Moon."

E Pluribus Vaudeville

The New York entertainment district that entertained an increasingly rootless urban population after the Civil War was renowned for its vices and its ruffian clientele.[10] Responding to public clamor for prohibitions on indecency, proprietors of some concert saloons in New York's Bowery district renamed their establishments "music halls," "concert gardens," or "opera houses," taking a cue from reputable English music halls. One such proprietor, the former minstrel and songwriter Tony Pastor, opened an opera house in the same Bowery neighborhood, hoping to attract a more diverse clientele to his variety shows. Pastor segregated the entertainment from the drinking and cleaned up the obscenity, attracting women and even children to his shows. To further separate his theater from its Bowery roots, Pastor moved his theater to the Rialto District on Fourteenth Street near Union Square in 1881. According to the publisher Edward Marks, Pastor advertised his theater as "the first specialty and vaudeville theater of America, catering to polite tastes, aiming to amuse, and fully up to the current times and topics." Marks claimed that "this was the first professional use of the word 'vaudeville' that I have seen."[11] The term "vaudeville" is a French word for an urban ballad or light entertainment, said by Robert W. Snyder to derive from *voix de ville* ("voice of the city").[12]

By the 1890s theater owners in the United States were using the French term to designate variety theaters. As early as the beginning of the decade, variety theaters had opened up in cities across America, even before the national vaudeville circuits were organized. Benjamin Franklin Keith introduced "continuous" vaudeville (an ongoing staged variety show) in 1883 at his Boston museum, advertising a "colored" singing group, the Olympian Quintette, as a main attraction. Some claim that the first use of the term "vaudeville" in America was by Keith to describe this museum show.[13] In 1886 Keith and Edward F. Albee moved the variety show from the museum into a Boston theater, expanding in 1888 to Providence and then to Philadelphia and New York. Their Union Square House opened in 1893.

These theaters were the germ of a far-flung network under the Keith and Albee name, the first of many circuits or "wheels" for touring vaudevillians. In addition to Keith and Albee's Union Square Theater, New York's vaudeville theaters included the Alhambra Music Hall, Miner's Bowery, Koster and Bial's, the Atlantic Gardens, the National Theater, the Haymarket, Tony Pastor's Opera House, the Winter Garden, and the Abbey. By the turn of the century, the center of the vaudeville district had moved from Union Square up to Twenty-third Street; from there it moved to Times Square, where, by 1915, the Palace Theater was serving as vaudeville's flagship venue. Drawing much of its big-name talent from immigrant performers living in the New York tenements, vaudeville created a novel kind of entertainment for Americans, full of crass ethnic stereotypes of Germans, Dutch, Jews, Irish, and Italians revealed in dialect songs and slapstick skits.

Many of the best-known songs of the period were commissioned for, premiered in, or popularized by vaudeville. Tin Pan Alley and vaudeville were eagerly symbiotic: vaudevillians consumed new tunes from Tin Pan Alley songsmiths, and Tin Pan Alley used vaudeville to boost sheet music sales. Some of the sentiments in these tunes would have been at home in the Victorian-era parlors of the previous century, but much of vaudeville and Tin Pan Alley represented a clear break with Victorian respectability and a source of transgressive thrills. According to Snyder, "In vaudeville, Victorianism was only one element of a complex and volatile cultural equation that simultaneously recognized Victorianism's lingering power and asserted alternatives to it."[14] These contrasts are apparent if one looks at the differences between Victorian sentimental songs ("My Mother's Rosary" or "Mother Machree") and ragtime expressions ("If You Knew Susie"); between songs of rural longing ("Down by the Old Mill Stream") and urban ethnic slice-of-life songs ("The Bowery"); between the nostalgia of "When You and I Were Young, Maggie" and the technological optimism of "Come, Josephine, in My Flying Machine"; between the sentimentality of "A Bird in a Gilded Cage" and the lighthearted wordplay of "Ida, Sweet as Apple Cider"; and between normative Anglo-American ballad subjects ("Grandfather's Clock") and the subjects of coon songs ("All Coons Look Alike To Me") or European ethnic novelties ("Down Where the Wurzberger Flows").

In the words of the barbershop enthusiast Joe Stern, "At the height of its popularity, no minstrel or burleyque [burlesque] was complete without a barbershop quartet. The dozens of Musical Tabloid shows which toured the country all had them." Close-harmony arranger George Botsford claimed, "No vaudeville program was complete without a barbershop quartet."[15] There were serious musical quartets on the vaudeville stage, but most were comedy groups that interspersed songs with ethnic comedy routines and dialect songs. A 1912 magazine listed among various types of vaudeville performers "young boys who have procured most of their training on the streets, learned a song and dance from some source or other and graduated on the stage as Musical Comedy Fours."[16] Nicholas Tawa draws a distinction between the two types of groups: "The traditional quartet, dressed similarly in dignified clothing, sang sentimental ballads in close harmony—the tenor taking the lead in Irish, and the baritone in mother songs. The comic quartet included a straight man, a sissy boy, a dialect man, and a tramp bass, all dressed for their parts. Rough comedy was interspersed among their songs."[17]

A column by Damon Runyon called "Brighter Side," which ran in the Hearst papers in 1943, reminisced about That Quartet (Frank Morel, Harry Aylvester, Aubrey Pringle, and leader Poodles Jones, renowned for his rendition of the novelty number "Down Where the Wurzburger Flows"). According to Runyon, the quartet earned $1,000 per week at their peak, playing engagements at Hammerstein's in New York. One former vaudeville singer recounted his experiences with the Troy Comedy Four in 1912: "The characters were 'Messenger Boy,' 'Tough Kid,' 'Brokendown Actor,' and I did 'Dutch.' We played the Sullivan-Constantine Time on the West Coast, also the Bert Levy Time. About 19 weeks all told. We followed the Primrose Four, who called themselves a Thousand Pounds of Harmony. So we billed ourselves the Little Men with Big Voices. The songs we sang in the group were 'College Man,' 'Red Rose Rag,' 'Roll Dem Bones,' and 'When I First Met Kate Down by the Golden Gate.'"[18]

In vaudeville, the four acts, comedy fours, and variety quartets mixed with an extraordinary assemblage of comedians, musicians, jugglers, dancers, and novelty acts, as in the following recollection:

But there is no denying that when the page boy stepped rapidly across the stage to the easel, took down the card reading, "Carl Emmy's Pets" or "Mme. LaRue's Cockatoos," or "Landon Bros. in Feats of Strength," and put up "Maple City Four" (not that a swell quartet was wont to follow an opener), and that four came on, singing something like "I don't want a hammock built for two . . . ," the effect was something, but right along about there, that four was apt to do something that seems to make an exception to our rule of get on with the tune. They have entered singing as above noted, it sounds swell, the customers are promptly lulled into a state of bliss, and the four have proceeded to where they sing ". . . just a little rocking chair and. . . ." Masters that they are, they've led up to and prepared the paid customer for that last word, but without supplying it, they go into a bit of comedy business, after which they sing again. Their whole routine is founded on hard experience, based on the old idea of always leave 'em wanting more.[19]

Many stars of the American stage and cinema got their starts in four acts. The Marx Brothers started out as a quartet called the Nightingales, with each brother taking on the persona of one of the standard ethnic stereotypes (Groucho in the role of the Dutch or German professor, Harpo as the Irishman with a shock of red curly hair and a harp, and Chico as an Italian casanova; the fourth brother played the straight-man role). Al Jolson first performed with the Casion Four and George Burns with the Empire City Quartette.[20] (Empire City was discovered, according to Willie "The Lion" Smith, singing on the street corners of Newark. They were booked into a club called Johnson's that was a haunt for traveling vaudeville acts of the time.)

The best-known quartets were considered "big-time" acts: these included the Avon Comedy Four, the Casion Four, the Monarch Comedy Four, the Empire City Four, the Primrose Four, the Quaker City Quartet Four, That Quartette, and the Monarch Comedy Four. The spread of vaudeville into even small American cities led to a drain on big-time acts and openings for imitators and no-name quartets. When in New York City, most of the famous quartetters hung out at Dowling's, an uptown vaudeville district watering hole at the corner of Forty-third Street and Seventh Avenue on Times Square. Quartets that frequented Dowling's included Empire City, the Primrose Four, the Bison City Four, the Quaker City Quartet, That Quartet, the Avon Comedy Four, and Three White Kuhns [sic].

Although vaudeville was typically segregated and therefore a forbidding environment for black performers, a number of successful black vaudeville variety and burlesque troupes toured America to great acclaim, including the Lady Africa Company (with the famous Golden Gate Quartet), Rockwell's Sunny South Company (a minstrel-oriented variety show with two quartets), and Robert Edmond's Sunny South Ladies' Quartet and Sunny South Men's Quartet. Other African American quartets in vaudeville included the Four Chocolate Dandies and the Dixie Comedy Four or Dixie Four. Black vaudeville achieved its greatest exposure in 1911, when the celebrated black singer, actor, and comedian S. H. Dudley organized a "colored" touring circuit called the Dudley Circuit or Dudley's Theatrical Circuit; it was in operation for five years.

Quartetting was still predominantly a male occupation, but some female harmony trios appeared in vaudeville (the Boswell Sisters, the Pickens Sisters, and the Three X Sisters, among others). It is most probably on this model that the revival of female trio harmonizing in New York City around 1938 was based ("Gibson Girl Trios"; see chapter 3).

The consortium uniting the Keith and Albee circuit and the western Orpheum Circuit dominated the national scene, but at least twenty other vaudeville companies operated circuits or wheels by the 1920s, including Loew's, Shubert, F. F. Proctor, and William Morris. By this time, the United States could boast of an estimated one thousand theaters booking big-time acts and four thousand featuring small-time acts. Perhaps ten thousand to twenty thousand acts were competing at any time for tours of the wheels and circuits.[21] This circuit's infrastructure allowed vaudeville to dominate the popular culture of its era and to launch countless careers.

The best-loved vaudeville quartet was perhaps Avon Comedy Four. In 1900 a blackface song and dance team of Joe Smith (b. Joe Sultzer, 1884) and Charles Dale (b. Charles Marks, 1881) that had been formed in 1898 was invited to join the Imperial Vaudeville and Comedy Company for an engagement in the Catskill Mountains. The rest of the troupe consisted of the straight man and ballad singer Jack Coleman, the dialect comedian Will Lester, a piano player, and a group of four singers who provided a comedy quartet. After finding themselves in debt to the hotel for their stay, the group broke up. Smith and Dale later discovered Coleman and Lester playing in a Harlem venue called the Avon Cafe. They reunited and created an act that balanced close-harmony arrangements of songs such as "My Gal from Dixie" with slapstick and buck dancing, a form of percussive dance that preceded tap dance. They played for their first week at the same cafe and renamed the group the Avon Comedy Four.

Their "New Schoolteacher" routine was their most memorable comedy act, and it featured a "Hebrew type," a German, a tough guy, and a sissy. A *Billboard* review of their performance in January 1914 at Keith's Theater in Philadelphia reported: "The Avon Comedy Four, in the singing farce, which has provoked more laughter in this theater than any act since its erection, cleaned up again today. Their New Teacher was new here in 1902 and has been a regular riot about every three months since."[22]

"New School Teacher" was recorded for Victor, as were many of their comedy sketches and songs. They recorded for the first time in August of 1916 and had a modest hit the following year with "Way out Yonder in the Golden West." They continued with a series of hits in subsequent years, including the war-oriented "I'm Crazy over Every Girl in France" and "Come On, Papa," both of which were recorded for Columbia. The catalog of recordings for Victor listed many of their (largely ethnic) comedy routines, including "Gila, Galah, Galoo," "New School Teacher," "Cohen's Wedding," "Hungarian Restaurant Scene," "I'm Going Way Back Home (and Have a Wonderful Time)," "Yaaka Hula Hickey Dula," and "Ginsberg's Stump Speech." In 1914 the quartet headlined the first All-American bill at London's Finsbury Park Empire, and in the spring of 1929 they starred in a show at London's Palladium. Sometime before the entry of the United States into World War I, Irving Kaufman and Harry Goodwin replaced Lester and Coleman, and over time many other singers filled in the other parts around Smith and Dale. The popularity of the Avon Comedy Four peaked in the war years when Kaufman was a member, during which time they recorded with Victor, Columbia, and Edison.

Three entertainment offshoots of vaudeville gained momentum in the first two decades of the century: chautauqua, burlesque, and musical revues. Chautauquas had their origins in a summer school for religion launched in 1874 by the minister John H. Vincent. On the shores of Lake Chautauqua, New York, the minister hosted the first Sunday School Teachers Assembly under brown tents. The chautauquas initiated a speaker's bureau and circuit and eventually recruited show business acts that performed "clean." They evolved into a nondenominational "inspirational" movement that provided performances under tents around the country featuring variety acts, dramatic sketches, song, dance, and even minstrel acts and comic operas.

The first traveling chautauqua premiered in Marshalltown, Iowa, in July 1904 with a Boston male quartet called the Temple Quartet. The Temple Quartet had been formed to open a Masonic temple in Boston and sang professionally for years thereafter. Other quartets that specialized in chautauquas were the Four Embers, the Weatherwax Brothers (Charles City, Iowa), the Mendelssohns, the Panama Singers, and the Whitney Brothers (singers of the "Rio Grande Rag"). As one scholar noted, "Bands pulled the crowds into the tents, but chautauqua was born to the accompaniment of the male quartet."[23] By 1912 there were over a thousand chautauquas visiting over twelve thousand North American towns and cities. Playing to rural and marginal markets not covered by vaudeville and emphasizing a more wholesome entertainment, the chautauqua traveling tents carved out an important niche market and brought men's close-harmony quartets to the farthermost corners of the continent.

Like vaudeville, burlesque drew on the range of pre-1900 entertainments (medicine shows, concert saloons, etc.), but it specialized in the display of female anatomy and in bawdy humor, making it vaudeville's raunchier cousin. In 1905 Samuel Scribner organized the Columbia Circle for burlesques. The level of risqué activity increased in the 1920s with the organization of the Mutual Burlesque Association. Burlesque may have reached the height of its popularity around 1915, but it lasted through the 1950s, with an increasingly sexualized entertainment, often including stripteases; eventually the striptease became the centerpiece of the entertainment. The aforementioned Empire City Quartet performed for years in burlesque shows.

"Pioneer-Era" Close-Harmony Recordings

Although Thomas A. Edison recognized in 1878 that his invention of a wax cylinder recorder the year before would be "liberally devoted to music," he expected that it would prove most lucrative as a dictation machine.[24] Edison marketed his talking machines through thirty-three regional subsidiaries of the North American Phonograph Company; but with revenues stagnating, salesmen experimented with alternative uses for the contraption.

A West Coast distributor placed two coin-operated music playback machines in a saloon in San Francisco and scored an instant success. Rustic predecessors of the jukebox, the nickel-activated phonographs allowed customers to select songs and listen to the selection through a tube. The regional phonograph subsidiaries, foremost among them Columbia Phono-graph Company, introduced the nickel phonographs (nickelodeons) into saloons, hotel lobbies, train and trolley stations, stores, carnivals, arcades, and phonograph parlors. Well into the first decade of the twentieth century, the "coin-ops" were the primary means for consumption of recorded sound. Phonograph parlors competed with vaudeville theaters and music halls for patrons. Edison, who had at first opposed the idea, opened his own parlor in New York's Union Square. Many early recordings were considered to be content for the phonograph parlors (and thus as a new means of plugging a song for sheet music sales).

Edison's Standard Phonograph, which cost $20 when it debuted in 1896, was the first recorded sound playback machine priced for widespread home use. Home phonographs reconfigured the relationship of audiences to sound; sounds could now be captured and reexperienced at will, making hearing a repeatable experience. A Decca advertisement announced: "HERE THEY ARE, your favorite stars of radio, screen, and stage—in their greatest performances of instrument and voice! . . . Hear them *when* you want—as *often* as you want—right in your own home."[25] Nineteenth-century parlor-style pieces—what Edison marketed as "hearth and home songs"—became a means of interacting with memories of mother, childhood, and small-town or country life. Women, especially, took control of the emotional climate in the house by selecting humorous, romantic, or inspiring music. It was to vocalists that the industry turned to interpret the lyrical inventions of Tin Pan Alley. The range of content was a response to this market-driven demand for emotional and repeatable experiences.

The three big labels that had emerged by the early years of the twentieth century—Edison Studios, Columbia Graphophone (later Phonograph) Company, and the Victor Talking Machine Company—competed to establish their divergent playback formats. The main contenders in the early format wars were Edison's cylinders, Victor Records' twelve-inch flat disc (with three and a half minutes of recording time, versus two minutes for cylinders) with vertical-cut ("hill-and-dale") grooves, and Columbia's side-cut grooves and double-sided recordings. A host of other formats followed on the way to the triumph of double-sided discs. Recordings promoted these competing technologies.

Early recording technology favored men's quartets. Sound was recorded through an acoustic horn that transferred waves onto a cylinder (or a zinc disc, in the case of Emile Berliner's gramophone); as a result, sound sources had to be strong, directional, and not overly complex. Early recording engineers developed a rule of thumb that good recordings should contain fewer than fifteen instruments, or if vocal, four or fewer voices. Another limitation on early recordings was in range: narrow ranges close to the male tenor and baritone range worked best, while soprano and basso profundo ranges were more difficult to capture. Male vocal quartets singing in close harmony, either a cappella or with a small ensemble, were thus ideal recording units. Close-harmony quartets came to play a significant role in the expansion of the new medium, a medium that revolutionized music listening tastes and habits, home and family life, and recreation.

The first quartet to record seems to have been an African American close-harmony quartet called the Unique Quartette of New York. In December 1890 the Unique Quartette, consisting of Joseph M. Moore (lead), William Tucker (tenor), J. E. Carlson (baritone), and Samuel G. Baker (bass), recorded for the New York Phonograph Company (a later version of the group featured Ben Hunn as baritone and Walter Dixon as bass). Dixon and colleagues note that "according to surviving ledgers of the New York Phonograph Company, the Unique Quartette was paid for three further sessions in December of 1890, thirteen sessions in 1891, three sessions in April and June, 1892, and a final session on Tuesday, March 14, 1893."[26] Their first session for which documentation is available (fall 1893 for the Edison label) lists, among twenty tunes, "Mama's Black Baby Boy," "Ise Gwine Back to Dixie," "Ham Bone Medley," "Parthenia Took a Fancy to a Coon," and spirituals such as "Who Built the Ark." The group recorded many other sides before 1897 for the New Jersey and New York subsidiaries of Columbia and for the Phonograph Record and Supply Company. The Standard Quartette, described as "Men of Color" in the Columbia catalog, began to record cylinders for Columbia (New York) in August 1891, although the bookkeeping records from those first sessions have been lost along with the cylinders. Their sessions from 1894–97 produced recordings of songs from the coon repertory ("Way down Yonder in the Cornfield" and "Little Alabama Coon)," southern pastoral numbers such as "My Old Kentucky Home," and spirituals such as "Steal Away to Jesus." The personnel appear to have been H. C. Williams, Ed DeMoss, R. L. Scott, and William Cottrell.[27]

The first white quartet to record was probably the Manhansett Quartette (often called *the* first quartet to record). The original group included Gilbert Girard (first tenor), George J. Gaskin (second tenor), Joe Riley (baritone), and someone known only as Evans (bass). The Belfast-born Gaskin sang almost twenty of the most popular songs of the decade and was known as the "Silver-Voiced Irish Tenor." Evans was replaced by the bass Jim Cherry, and about 1892 the tenor John H. Bieling (1869–1948; sometimes spelled Bierling) joined the group. Bieling grew up "down in the old Fourteenth Ward—born and raised there; around Spring Street and the Bowery. Four of us fellows used to 'barber shop' on Saturday night and Sunday—good old fashioned melodies and sentimental ballads."[28] Bieling later joined the Haydn Quartet and then the American Quartet, singing with either the most or the second-most popular quartets of each decade. Bieling pursued a short solo career (his "Sweet Bye and Bye" was a number one hit in 1903), but he was always known best as a quartet singer.

Gaskin had heard about a record company executive, Victor Hugo Emerson of the U. S. Phonograph Company in Newark, New Jersey, who wanted to record a quartet, and Gaskin and Bieling contracted to have Emerson record Manhansett. They gathered in "a loft over some meat packing houses about 50 by 100 and 20 feet, littered with machine boxes and barrels . . . piled up everywhere."[29] In an interview with the record collector Ulysses "Jim" Walsh, Bieling spoke of the conditions encountered in the early recording studio: "The recording was done with Edison machines, run by storage batteries placed on shelves. They were grouped so that the horns into which we sang would focus as nearly as possible to a center on the opposite side of the rack. There were usually seven horns into which we sang. The cylinders, of course, were wax ones, made by the Edison Company."[30]

A single song, generally sung into five to seven horns, was what was known as a "round." Performers would be paid by the round, at about seventy-five cents to a dollar per round. Harry MacDonough of the Edison Quartet recalled that "at that time they made five masters at each performance of a song and from each master they could make from twenty five to seventy five duplicates before the master wore out."[31] Thus a round could result in 125 to 525 individual cylinders or discs. If a performer recorded thirty rounds of a single song in a morning's work, the record company could produce anywhere from about 4,000 to 16,000 units. If a recording sold well, the artists were often invited back for successive recording sessions devoted to the same song until market demand was satiated. The "piecework" sessions (which lasted until the invention by Edison of the "gold-molded" process for making a durable master) were considered lucrative work for artists in demand. As Samuel Holland Rous said, "I was making $12,000 a year, which was real money in 1900! But boy, it was hard work! We singers of that period would come home at night with our voices all but gone; not daring to speak above a whisper to our families for fear of wasting those precious vocal cords. I have made as many as 85 records in one day. A bad cold usually cost a singer about $500."[32]

Recording for the North American and New Jersey labels, Manhansett produced the best-selling recordings of 1892: "The Picture Turned toward the Wall" and "Sally in Our Alley." Likewise, their 1894 recording of "The Old Oaken Bucket" was among the most popular recordings of its year. None of these songs were newly composed; their novelty derived from having been recorded. Over the course of four years, Manhansett recorded with a number of labels, including Columbia, Berliner, Xonophone, Reed and Miller, Isaac Norcross ("Jumbo" six-inch cylinders for Howley and Haviland), and Leeds and Catlin (first cylinders and later discs). The Norcross "Jumbo" six-inch cylinders contained perhaps the earliest recorded advertisements. The tenor Albert Campbell's songs were distributed as advertising gimmicks by Quaker Oats, each one concluding with the sign-off, "Thank you, madam. Remember, Quaker Oats are good for children."[33] Manhansett also did a demonstration recording for an early foray by Edison's company into commercial recording. The group broke up in 1896 when Gaskin signed an exclusive solo contract with Columbia, before Edison was ready to start production.

The Manhansett Quartet set many precedents for subsequent white recording groups. Although individuals within the group may have participated in popular theater, the group as a whole was not closely associated with vaudeville or minstrelsy. They tended to dress in suits rather than in thematic or comedic costumes, and although their repertory borrowed heavily from vaudeville and topical songs, they were always closely identified with the hearth-and-home material. In all, they cut a more dignified image than the comedy fours of vaudeville and minstrelsy.

A lovely example of turn-of-the-century restrained close harmony in a hearth-and-home-style song is "Beautiful Isle of Somewhere"[34] (see fig. 2.1), made nationally famous by the women's close-harmony Euterpian Quartette when they performed it at the 1901 funeral of President William H. McKinley. In the four measures from the beginning of the refrain (fig. 2.2), we see both a subtle swipe in m. 4 and the use of a more active bass line in the first two measures (the bass part has its own text for this contrapuntal passage). This arrangement places the lead part in the highest voice rather than in the second voice, the latter being more typical of what would soon be known as "barbershop" or "lamppost" harmony.

One of the tenors from the Manhansett Quartet, Jim Reynard, joined with three other singers, Steve Porter (baritone), Will C. "Billy" Jones (bass), and Albert Campbell (tenor), to form a vaudeville-style troupe called the Diamond Comedy Four, and they plugged songs for the publishing firm run by Joe Stern and Edward B. Marks. Stern and Marks viewed the phonograph as an ideal plug, and they built a small studio in a loft near their Tin Pan Alley publishing house to record songs composed by their own songwriters. The Diamond Comedy Four recorded hundreds of sides at seventy-five cents to a dollar per round, and their "Imitation Medley" and "Cornfield Medley" were two of the first offerings from the Stern and Marks publishing house.[35]

In one of the few examples of artist-controlled recording companies, the quartet singers Steve Porter, S. H. Dudley (a white singer, not the black comedian and music entrepreneur), and William F. Hooley formed a short-lived enterprise called the American Recording Company to cut out the middlemen and produce their own recordings. This kind of direct involvement of artists and music publishers in the recording business was soon crowded out by the independent recording companies, but at this early stage of the recording industry, it was unclear whether the production of discs and cylinders would eventually be controlled by independent companies, by makers of playback devices, by song-publishing companies, or by artists themselves (eventually all would lose out to the radio companies, which bought up almost all the major recording establishments).

Close-harmony recording in the early twentieth century was led by three quartets: the Haydn, Peerless, and American Quartets. Joel Whitburn estimates that the Haydn Quartet was the thirteenth most popular group between 1900 and 1950, followed by the Peerless Quartet at fourteen and the American Quartet at sixteen.[36] During a number of years between 1900 and 1920, quartets—principally these three groups—produced more than 20 percent of all hit recordings. If one adds to their hit recordings the number of hits by soloists closely associated with quartets, the combined figure would be over half of the forty or so most successful recordings each year.

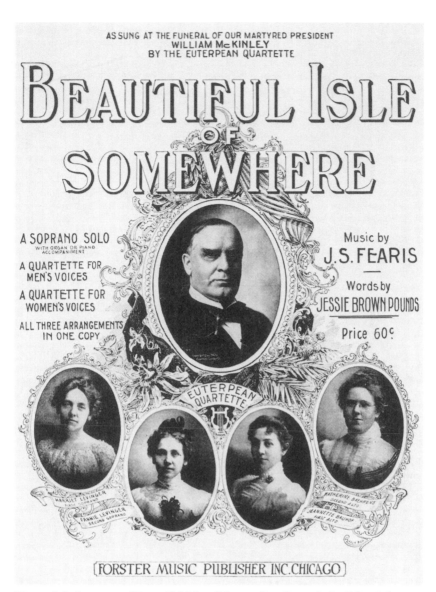

Figure 2.1. Cover art, "Beautiful Isle of Somewhere"; music by John Sylvester Fearis, lyrics by Jessie Brown Pounds (Chicago: Forster Music Publisher, 1901). Courtesy of the Rare Book, Manuscript, and Special Collections Library, Duke University. Used by permission.

The early recording sessions of the Unique and Standard Quartets notwithstanding, recording opportunities for African American groups were quite restricted up until the advent of "race record" labels. Among the exceptions at the turn of the century was the Dinwiddie Colored Quartet, which recorded six discs in 1902 for the Monarch label, including

Figure 2.2. Women's quartet harmonies to "Beautiful Isle of Somewhere"; music by John Sylvester Fearis, lyrics by Jessie Brown Pounds (Chicago: Forster Music Publisher, 1901). Courtesy of the Rare Book, Manuscript, and Special Collections Library, Duke University. Used by permission.

"Down the Old Camp Ground."[37] Another was the Fisk University Jubilee Quartet, which recorded songs such as "They Kissed," "The Soldier's Farewell," and "B.I.N.G.O" starting in 1909 for Victor Records and later for labels such as Silvertone (under the name Booker Male Quartet). This group was not the original group of Fisk Jubilee singers, of course, but a later all-male quartet led by John Wesley Work II (tenor). Their Victor session featured a number of jubilee spirituals in the great tradition of Fisk, but it also included an unreleased recording of "My Old Kentucky Home." The next day they also recorded the minstrel tunes "Old Black Joe" and the "Banjo Song" along with their sacred repertory.[38] The Tuskegee Institute Singers recorded as a double quartet in 1914 for Victor.

Polk Miller's Old South Quartette was one of the few integrated vocal recording ensembles. Miller, who was white, was raised on a Virginia plantation, where he learned to pick and strum the banjo. He later cultivated a repertory of songs and stories in black dialect (he called himself a "darky dialectician") that he used for the amusement of friends and family. A Confederate partisan, by the 1890s he was touring the country as a solo minstrel artist billed as "the Old Virginia Plantation Negro."[39] Miller's act was praised by, among others, Mark Twain and Joel Chandler Harris, author of the *Uncle Remus* books. Around 1900 Polk Miller joined up with ("hired" is perhaps more appropriate) a black group called the Old South Quartette. He claimed to have found the quartet singing "on street corners and in the barrooms of this city at night to motley crowds of hoodlums and barroom loafers and handing around the hat. . . . I could get a dozen quartettes from the good singing material among the Negroes in the tobacco factories here."[40] By the time the quintet recorded, it featured James L. Stamper on bass and Randall Graves as first tenor, although the composition of the group varied over the years. In minstrel fashion, Miller sang most of the song verses and was joined by the quartet for the four-part choruses.

A 1910 brochure for the Old South act emphasized the authenticity of the quartet in contrast to such groups as the Fisk University Jubilee Quartet:

> Their singing is not the kind that has been heard by the students from "colored universities," who dress in pigeon-tailed coats, patent leather shoes, white shirt fronts, and who are advertised to sing plantation melodies but do not. They do not try to let you see how nearly a Negro can act the white man while parading in a dark skin, but they dress, act, and sing like the real Southern darkey in his "workin'" clothes. As to their voices, they are a sweet, though uncultivated, *result of nature,* producing a harmony unequalled by the professionals, and because it is natural, goes straight to the hearts of the people. To the old Southerner, it will be "Sounds from the old home of long ago." . . . To hear them is to live again your boyhood days down on the farm.[41]

This rather extraordinary text speaks directly to an important but little recognized fact about southern white nostalgia: that the good old days

Figure 2.3. Polk Miller's Old South Quartette, from the January 1910 *Edison Amberola Monthly*. Rodgers and Hammerstein Archives of Recorded Sound, The New York Public Library for the Performing Arts. Astor, Lenox, and Tilden Foundation. Used with permission.

for many whites were the days *with* African Americans, not without them. They were the days when whites were dependent on African slaves and when they developed a discourse around blacks that constructed them as subservient, nurturing, or amusing or comical (as opposed to the parallel discourse that found blacks dangerous and threatening). This is the romantic side of slavery, and it was a part of the cultural orientation of many southern whites. This is why minstrel songs often contain a deep vein of affection and pathos; it is why so many popular southern songs about place and history are in blackvoice; and it is why the white southern "pastoral" is often posited in the subjectivity of blacks. Also note that the narrator typically "naturalizes" the gifts of black performers ("the result of nature").

Polk Miller's Old South Quartette went into the Victor studios in November 1909 to record seven sides, four of which came out on Edison Amberol cylinders and three on standard cylinders. All of the standard cylinder recordings and one of the Amberols were spirituals: "Rise and Shine,"

"That Old Time Religion," "Jerusalem Mornin'," and "What a Time." Polk's delivery on these possesses the charismatic fire of a tent revival preacher. Their respectful, even rapt treatment of spirituals lends some weight to the claims by Polk that his group occasionally performed in black churches, although this may have been another strategy to authenticate the music of the quintet.[42] The other Amberol cylinder recordings consisted of an extremely popular Confederate anthem called the "Bonnie Blue Flag" and two comic novelty songs: "The Laughing Song" and a parody of black eating preferences called "The Watermelon Party."

The collaboration between Miller and the quartet lasted only a year or so after the recording sessions due to the difficulties that an integrated group had in touring in 1910. Miller, interestingly enough, attributed the group's problems to the lower-class white southern "hoodlum" element whose ancestors had "never owned Negroes." Ownership of slaves was associated in Miller's thinking with nostalgic, paternal affection for blacks.

Haydn, American, and Peerless: The Big Three Quartets

After the Manhansett Quartet broke up, Samuel Holland Rous, who used the stage name S. H. Dudley, started a quartet in 1896 to reproduce the Manhansett repertory for Edison's studios. Dudley entered the field of popular music after leaving a career in opera and took the stage name of the popular black comedian and theatrical entrepreneur. The new quartet featured Dudley as baritone, William F. Hooley as bass, and the tenors Jim Reynard and Roger Harding. Walter Miller, the recording engineer for Edison, convinced Dudley to replace the tenors with Jere Mahoney and John Bieling, and the new group took the name Edison Quartet. However, this name would clearly not permit the group to record for Edison's competitors, so when the quartet was booked to record for the Berliner Gramophone Company, it adopted the pseudonym Haydn Quartet in honor of the composer Franz Josef Haydn (they later changed the spelling to "Hayden" so Americans could pronounce it). In 1898 Jere Mahoney contracted inflammatory rheumatism and was replaced by Harry MacDonough (born John S. MacDonald in Ontario, Canada, in 1871); this was the group that performed under the Haydn/Edison name for around twenty years. The group's new tenor, Harry MacDonough, was also one of the most popular solo recording artists of the twentieth century.

Thomas A. Edison exercised great control over the selection of artists for his recordings, and he built a reputation on his conservative tastes. His recordings "exerted a dominant power linked to ongoing memories of the paternal family, respect for the past, and veneration of Victorian values."[43] To perform less-respectable material, artists often sang on other labels under different names. For example, around 1900 MacDonough, Dudley, and Hooley teamed up with Frank Banta to release a series of minstrel show songs and stage patter for Victor under the name "Georgia Minstrel

Aside: "Sweet Adeline"

"(You're the Flower of My Heart) Sweet Adeline," a great hit for the Haydn Quartet, was originally an instrumental tune written at a boxing camp in Boston in 1896 by Harry Armstrong (b. 1879 in Somerville, Massachusetts), a prizefighter with an interest in songwriting. Armstrong called his tune "Down Home in New England" or "My Old New England Home."[45] As Sigmund Spaeth was fond of noting, its initial chorus melody was based on the four-note "Westminster chimes," as was that of "How Dry I Am."

Armstrong and friends harmonized the song after training sessions in the boxing ring, and he developed "great faith in the chorus melody" as a result.[46] Among the many lyricists Armstrong approached to flesh out words for his song was Charles Lawler, who had written "The Sidewalks of New York," but Lawler was unable to fit words to the tune. "Gentleman" Jimmy Walker, the future mayor of New York, also tried to write lyrics to the chorus. Walker then introduced Armstrong to Richard G. Hursch (real name: Richard H. Gerard), who coined the line "For you I pine, Sweet Rosalie," and so Armstrong retitled the song "Sweet Rosalie." A year later in 1903, after the duo had once again failed to find a publisher for the song, Gerard saw a sign for a "farewell performance of Adelina Patti," the famed Italian opera singer. He noticed a possible rhyme with "pine" and changed "Rosalie" to "Adeline." His lyrics begin in an elegiac tone:

> In the evening when I sit alone a dreaming
> Of days gone bye, love
> To me so dear . . .

and lead a little later into its famous chorus, with its persistent echo effects:

> Sweet Adeline (Sweet Adeline)
> My Adeline (My Adeline)
> At night dear heart (At night dear heart)
> For you I pine (For you I pine)
> In all my dreams (In all my dreams)
> Your fair face beams (Your fair face beams)
> You're the flower of my heart, Sweet Adeline (Sweet Adeline)

Witmark published the song in 1903 after, in Anderson's words, "eight years of being kicked around." However, the song languished on the shelves until it was selected by a Philadelphia-based vaudeville quartet, the Quaker City Four, for performance at the Hammerstein Theater, whereupon the song became a sensation. The echoed lines in the chorus were perfect for close harmony treatment, as was the chromatic melody, and the interactional chorus provided comedic material for vaudevillian comedy fours to stage as inebriated street corner harmony. According to Armstrong, "Smith and Dale [and] the old Comedy Four sang it. [S]o did Harry Cooper [and] the Empire Comedy four. John Figg [and] the Orpheum Comedy four. Cunningham of the Clipper four. Willie Howard of the old Messenger Boys trio."[47] Even in its originary performances, "Sweet Adeline" was already serving as a comedic spoof of street-corner or barbershop harmony, and its subsequent renditions array themselves along the continuum between its straightforwardly nostalgic lyrics and its satiric potential.

In 1904 "Sweet Adeline" was recorded by the Haydn Quartet, the Columbia Male Quartet, and the duo of Albert Campbell and James F. Harrison (from the Columbia Male and Knickerbocker Quartets, respectively). All three versions were

Dear Librarian:

_____ This title is available in cloth only.

_____ This title is available in paper only.

_____ Cloth edition of this title is out of print.

_____ Paper edition of this title is out of print.

_____ Publisher advises subtitle of this book was
changed from subtitle stated on your order.

__XX__ If diskette/CD packet is opened or removed
from book, both are non-returnable.

_____ Other:

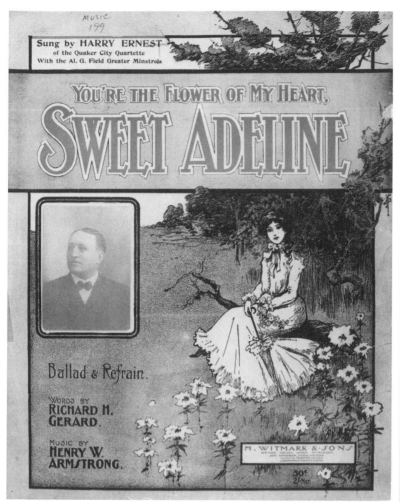

Figure 2.4. The cover art for "Sweet Adeline"; music by Henry W. Armstrong, lyrics by Richard H. Gerard (New York: M. Witmark and Sons, 1896).

hits. Shortly thereafter, Boston's mayor, John F. "Honey" Fitzgerald, adopted "Sweet Adeline" as his reelection campaign song.

"Sweet Adeline" became what one barbershop singer later called "the national anthem of barbershoppers," supplanting the turn-of-the-century favorites "Mandy Lee" (1896) and "Down Mobile (Way down Yonder in the Cornfield)" among amateur close-harmony singers. A book of quartet songs published in 1932 by Deac Martin memorably labeled barbershop singers as "Adeline Addicts." No other barbershop song became as closely associated with drinking and alcohol-induced, off-key harmony, an image reinforced in vaudeville skits. Because of this association the barbershop society, SPEBSQSA, banned the song from competition in the 1940s. In the same decade, however, women barbershoppers adopted "Sweet Adelines" as the name of their society.

Company." This was an especially confusing name because, as mentioned, the stage name of Samuel Holland Rous, S. H. Dudley, was identical to that of a famous black singer and comedian, because the "Georgia" franchise in minstrelsy was associated with black performers, and because it is not clear whether the quartet ever performed on a minstrel stage or whether it was simply a put-together group for recording purposes. Edison's contracts would not allow them to perform this kind of material either under their own name or the Edison imprimatur.

By 1900 the Haydn Quartet had emerged as the country's leading quartet, and in 1901 they signed a contract with the Victor Talking Machine Company that allowed them to continue to record with Edison. In the spring of 1902 the quartet visited England to record for British recording companies such as Gramophone. In 1903 and 1904 the Haydn Quartet scored the best-selling recordings of each year with "In the Good Old Summer Time" and "(You're the Flower of My Heart) Sweet Adeline" (discussed later), respectively. In subsequent years the Haydn Quartet popularized "My Wild Irish Rose" (1905), "Will You Love Me in December as You Do in May?" (1906) and "Put On Your Old Grey Bonnet" (number one in 1909).

The lead tenor Billy Murray joined the Haydn Quartet in 1908 and recorded the group's (and his) biggest hit, "Take Me Out to the Ball Game." The collaboration between Murray and the Haydn Quartet was so successful that Bieling and Hooley decided to form an ongoing group with Murray as lead. Two members of the group were decreasing their commitment to performing: MacDonough had begun work as editor of the Victor catalog, and Dudley had been appointed director of Victor's New York laboratory, so neither had much time to record. Nevertheless, the Haydn group continued to perform in its exclusive contract with Victor, although on a more occasional basis. Bieling and Hooley recruited Steve Porter (who replaced S. H. Dudley as baritone), and Murray (who replaced MacDonough as lead),[44] and the group called itself the American Quartet. Still, Billy Murray collaborated occasionally with the Haydn Quartet—for instance, on the 1910 release "By the Light of the Silvery Moon."

Billy Murray, lead singer of the American Quartet, was born William Thomas Murray in 1877 in Philadelphia, Pennsylvania, of Irish immigrant parents. He grew up in Denver and as a young teenager ran away to join a traveling entertainment troupe called Leavitt's High Rollers. After the Rollers were cheated out of a payment and found themselves broke, they began to hitchhike their way throughout the west. At their stops, Murray was billed as "the Denver Nightingale" (a take-off on the nickname of the Swedish singing sensation Jenny Lind). Impressed by audience reaction to the singing acts, Murray and three other members of the troupe formed a quartet, leaving the High Rollers for engagements in honky-tonks, saloons, medicine shows, and small-time vaudeville circuits throughout the west. In San Francisco, Murray and Keefe wandered into the recording studios of Edison's West Coast distributors, Bocigalupi Brothers, and recorded "The Lass from County Mayo" as a duet. Following this, Murray recorded solos, singing coon songs, Irish ballads, and comedy songs for Bocigalupi. Regrettably for Murray, the company's records were distributed only west of the Rocky Mountains, where they satisfied a market demand that Edison's main studios in New Jersey could not.[48]

Murray had been seriously weakened by a combination of Bright's disease and tuberculosis, and he was able to keep up with the demands of recording and saloon performances only through a strict regimen of cold baths and mountain climbing. Soon after 1900 Murray joined the famous A. G. Fields's Minstrels, to which he contributed his specialty blackface songs. It was A. G. Fields who shortened Murray's stage name to "Billy." Among the songs associated with his act in the early years were "Under the Bamboo Tree" and "Bill Bailey, Won't You Please Come Home?"

In 1903 Murray headed east and tried out for Victor, Columbia, and Edison; his piercing tenor and humorous stage patter earned him recording sessions for all three labels. Murray was thought to have "a 'ping' to his voice that cut sharp into the wax."[49] In 1904 he recorded "Absinthe Frappe" (the drug was popular during this period) and "Meet Me in St. Louis, Louis." Victor records claimed that Murray's recording of George M. Cohan's "The Yankee Doodle Boy" was the biggest seller in the company's history. Murray soon became the best-known interpreter of Cohan's songs, recording "the definitive hit version of nearly every Cohan song from 1905 on."[50] Murray covered other commemorative songs such as "Come Take a Trip in My Air-Ship" (1905), about the Wright Brother's flight, and "In My Merry Oldsmobile" (1905), after an Oldsmobile won the first transcontinental automobile race. Apart from his solo and quartet work, he formed half of one of the most popular male-female singing teams in American history, Ada Jones and Billy Murray.

Murray's involvement in the American Quartet resulted from the 1908 phasing out of the Haydn Quartet. In the summer of 1910, the American Quartet with Billy Murray as lead released "Casey Jones," perhaps the first recording to sell over a million copies in American music history. It was based on a true story about the wreck in 1900 of a train called the "Cannon Ball Express" and the self-sacrificing heroism of its engineer. That year also marked the debut of a tune called "(Mr. Jefferson, Lord) Play That Barber-Shop Chord"(lyrics by William Tracey and Ballard MacDonald, music by Lewis Muir) a vaudeville song from the Ziegfeld Follies of 1910. The African American vaudeville star Bert Williams launched the song in 1910, but the American Quartet (with Billy Murray) covered the song in an influential close-harmony arrangement in 1911. The subject of the song was not a barbershop quartet, but an African American pianist who played ragtime piano with barbershop-style chords.

> Down in a great big rathskeller
> Where a swell colored feller
> By the name of Bill Jefferson Lord
> Played a piano while he'd sing a song

He just sung and played the whole night long
Till one night a kinky haired lady
They called Chocolate Sadie
Heard him playing that Barber shop chord
When he finished Sadie drew a sigh
Every time that she would catch his eye, she'd cry
Chorus:
Mr. Jefferson Lord, play that barbershop chord
That smooth sounding harmony
It makes an awful awful hit with me
Play that strain just to please me again
Cause Mister when you start that minor part
I feel your fingers slipping and a grasping at my heart,
Oh Lord play that Barber shop chord![51]

The "minor part" does not refer to minor chords but to dominant seventh chords.[52] The first four measures of the choral melody (accompanying the first two lines of choral text) exploit chromatic neighbor tones of G (G–F-sharp–G–A-flat) on the words "Mr. Jefferson, Lord" and a chromatic alternation of C and B on "play that barber shop chord." In addition, "Lord" and "chord" are each held for more than a full measure, allowing ample space for the echo effects with swipes beloved of close harmony singers in the period. The relationship between A♯[7] and C chords is also classic, with the A♯[7] resolution providing the contrary-motion, chromatic voice-leading indexical of the barbershop style. As I mentioned previously, this song helped popularize for mass consumption the term "barbershop" as a label for a certain style of close harmony. A response song called "When Tony LaBoard Played the Barber Shop Chord" followed in 1911.

Sales of all sheet music peaked in 1910 with over thirty million copies sold. Two of the decade's biggest sellers, "Let Me Call You Sweetheart" and "Down by the Old Mill Stream," both of which sold six million copies apiece (and were popularized by quartets), provided ample evidence of the power of quartets to sell sheet music.

American Quartet hits included "Call Me Up Some Rainy Afternoon" (with Ada Jones [1910]), "Come Josephine, in My Flying Machine" (with Ada Jones [1911]), "Oh, You Beautiful Doll" (1911–12), "Everybody Two Step" (1912), "Rebecca of Sunnybrook Farm" (1914), "It's a Long Way to Tipperary" (1914), "Chinatown, My Chinatown" (1915). Under the name Premier Quartet, their top hit was "Moonlight Bay" (1912).

In 1914 John Young of the Criterion Quartet replaced Bieling as first tenor of the Haydn and American Quartets, owing to Bieling's worsening throat condition. Bieling's vocal problems developed in a studio recording session where he was required to "yip" repetitively for rounds of "A Cowboy's Romance" on which the American Quartet backed up Len Spencer and Ada Jones.[53] The same year, S. H. Dudley finally left the Haydn Quartet because of his duties at Victor Records. Harry MacDonough reorgan-

Figure 2.5. Chorus to "(Mr. Jefferson, Lord) Play That Barbershop Chord"; words by William Tracey and Ballard MacDonald, music by Lewis Muir (1910)

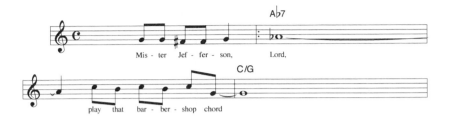

ized the Haydn group, adding the first tenor Lambert Murphy and the baritone Reinald Werrenrath (MacDonough continued on lead and William F. Hooley remained as bass). Werrenrath also sang with the Metropolitan Opera Company and had a distinguished classical stage and recording career, which brought a degree of classical legitimacy to the quartets with whom he recorded.

By 1903 Columbia Records was sponsoring a quartet called the Columbia Male Quartet or Columbia Quartet to compete with the Edison/Haydn Quartet. Its earliest roster seems to have been Albert Campbell, first tenor; James K. Reynard, second tenor; Joe Belmont, baritone; and Joe Majors, bass. Joe Belmont (real name Joseph Walter Fulton) was famous for his whistling and was nicknamed "the Human Bird." By late 1903 the quartet featured Campbell, Henry Burr (lead), Steve Porter (baritone), and "Big" Tom Daniels (bass; sometimes Frank C. Stanley subbed). The group's first success came in 1904 when, following the Haydn Quartet, they recorded "Sweet Adeline." The following year, the Columbia Quartet again covered a Haydn hit, "Tell Me with Your Eyes."

In 1905–6 the bass Frank C. Stanley (real name William Stanley Grinstead) organized a group out of the Columbia Quartet to record for companies other than Columbia; he called it the Peerless Quartet, after the African American close-harmony quartet from the 1890s. Peerless also recorded as the Invincible Four (with the minstrel comedian Byron Harlon as second tenor) and as the Sterling Trio (without a baritone). Many aficionados claim that the Peerless Quartet was the greatest of the era. All four of its original members (Albert Campbell, Henry Burr, Steve Porter, and Frank Stanley) were leading soloists. Stanley started out as a banjo player accompanying some of the biggest stars of the 1890s; as a solo vocalist, he released some forty-four songs that sold among the top twenty between 1899 and his death from pneumonia in 1910. Indeed, Stanley sang many of the lead parts in Peerless Quartet arrangements. The other members, Albert Campbell (tenor) and Steve Porter (baritone), sang together in the Diamond Comedy Four in the late 1890s. Porter started as a vaudeville comedian specializing in Irish dialect sketches and recorded many popular sentimental ballads.

Like Harry MacDonough and Billy Murray, Peerless's Henry Burr was a leading solo tenor. Born Harry H. McClaskey, Burr grew up in New Brunswick, Canada, until he was encouraged by a touring singer to go to New York for coaching and a career in vocal recordings. Burr took his stage name in tribute to his vocal coach, Ellen Burr. Whereas Murray was known for his comedic songs, Burr's reputation was built on his treatment of sentimental ballads. When Peerless was organized, Burr was only twenty years old, but by the end of his recording career he had become the most recorded singer in music history, with an estimated twelve thousand recordings under a variety of stage names.

The Peerless Quartet produced a number of hits under Frank Stanley's leadership, including "Honey Boy" (1907), "My Pony Boy" (1909), and, in 1910, three barbershop favorites: "By the Light of the Silvery Moon," "I Want a Girl (Just Like the Girl That Married Dear Old Dad)," and "Let Me Call You Sweetheart." Although the Haydn bass singer, William F. Hooley, had a much longer tenure in quartets and sang in more groups, some have argued that Stanley was the dominant bass voice of the period. This may be in part a reflection of Stanley's lead vocal role for most of his years with the quartet.

The Peerless Quartet underwent various personnel changes starting in 1909, when a minstrel-style dialect singer, Arthur Collins, replaced Porter.[54] Collins began his recording career in 1898 when he was invited to record for Edison, but he also recorded for Emile Berliner, Zon-o-phone, Victor, Columbia, and others, singing distinctive treatments of coon and ragtime songs. Collins's partnership with the tenor Byron Harlan after 1900 resulted in the best-known comedy singing team of the era. Their recordings evoked a vivid vaudeville stage ambience and featured songs interspersed with comic dialogue. They made hits out of ethnic novelty songs such as "Down Where the Wurzburger Flows" (1902), "The Right Church, the Wrong Pew" (1909), "Under the Yum Yum Tree" (1911), "Alexander's Ragtime Band" (1911), and "When the Midnight Choo Choo Leaves for Alabam'" (1912). The Victor catalog called the duo the "Klassical Koon Komedy Kouple" and the "Black-Face Brothers." Collins and Harlan also joined with Steve Porter and Billy Murray to moonlight at supper clubs as the Rambler Minstrel Company. Rambler made black dialect recordings, with Porter providing the interlocutor material and Murray and Collins singing solos.

Another change in Peerless personnel occurred in 1910 with the death of Frank Stanley. John H. Meyer, a well-known church bass from New York, joined the group as its bass in 1911, staying with them until 1918. With Stanley's passing, the tenor Henry Burr emerged as the group's undisputed lead singer and assumed the role of manager. The revamped Peerless produced many of the epoch's favorite Dixie ballads, such as "Kentucky Days," (1912), "All Aboard for Dixie Land" (1914), and "Virginia Lee" (1915).

Some of the stars of the big three quartets toured in concerts and in vaudeville as the Record Maker Troupe, later known as the Eight Famous Victor Artists. Henry Burr managed the troupe, which included his fellow tenors Billy Murray and Albert Campbell as well as the baritone John Meyer. The solo artists Byron G. Hanlan, Vess Ossman (banjo), and Teddy Morse (piano) rounded out the group.

Although the Edison, American, and Peerless Quartets were the dominant close-harmony groups between 1900 and 1925, many other quartets had hit recordings before 1920, including the Columbia Mixed Doubles Quartet, the Columbia Stellar Quartet, the Criterion Quartet, the Knickerbocker Quartet, and Imperial Quartet of Chicago. Many recordings made by pioneer recording quartets failed to conform to the model of a barbershop arrangement enshrined later on by the barbershop revival movement (see chapter 3). For example, many of the arrangements were not a cappella but included accompanying instruments such as guitar, piano, small orchestras, or brass bands, and it was still common for the lead vocalist to sing the verses solo, interspersed with quartet choruses. Finally, the lead part was sometimes but not always carried by the second tenor.

"Goodbye, My Coney Island Baby": War and the Waning of an Era

The war years were by all accounts still banner years for quartets, which turned out hit recordings that helped to define a war-era zeitgeist for millions of North Americans. In the early years of World War I, a majority of the American public was opposed to intervention, weary of "foreign entanglements" such as the Spanish-American War (1898–99) and of many operations that followed in the Philippines, Panama, and China (the Boxer Rebellion), the occupation of Haiti, and others. The major recording quartets reflected the anti-interventionist sentiment in a string of hits full of maudlin sentiment, but which incorporated brisk martial march tempi. Peerless released the anti-interventionist anthem "Don't Take My Darling Boy Away" (1915), which featured the following chorus:

> Don't take my darling boy away from me
> Don't send him off to war
> You took his father and his brothers three
> Now you come back for more
> Who are the heroes who fight your wars
> Mothers who have no say
> But my duty's done, so for God's sake leave one
> And don't take my darling boy away.[55]

The Peerless Quartet also released a quartet version of "I Didn't Raise My Son to Be a Soldier" (1915), with this plaintive chorus:

> I didn't raise my boy to be a soldier
> I brought him up to be my pride and joy
> Who dares to place a musket on his shoulder
> To shoot some other mother's darling boy
> Let nations arbitrate their future troubles
> It's time to lay the sword and gun away
> There'd be no war today, if mothers all would say
> "I didn't raise my boy to be a soldier."[56]

Once the United States committed to the war, the quartet began turning out pro-war, patriotic march songs such as "America, Here's My Boy" and George M. Cohan's "Over There." In almost all of these songs, the composers interpolated and quoted famous martial and patriotic melodies ("Taps," "Yankee Doodle," "When Johnny Comes Marching Home," and others). The chorus of the spirited march "America, Here's My Boy" functions as an answer to "Don't Take My Darling Boy Away" and offers up multiple maternal sacrifices to the war effort:

> America, I raised a boy for you
> America, you'll find him staunch and true
> Put a gun on his shoulder
> He is ready to die or do
> America, he is my only one
> My hope, my pride, my joy
> But if I had another, he would march beside his brother
> America, here's my boy.[57]

The Peerless Quartet continued their string of soldier-centered traveling songs through to the war's end: "We're Going Over," "I Don't Know Where I'm Going but I'm On My Way," and then the wordiest title of all World War I rallying songs, "Just Like Washington Crossed the Delaware, General Pershing Will Cross the Rhine" (1918). The theme of travel echoed loudly in these songs. This was the war that introduced common Americans (male Americans, at least) to the continent; and as a result, the sophistication of France became a popular leitmotif in Tin Pan Alley songs. The American Quartet took "Goodbye Broadway, Hello France" to a number one position for a short time in 1917. Their other war-era hits included "Oh Johnny, Oh Johnny, Oh!" (1917). The Knickerbocker Quartet's most popular recording in 1917 was "Pack Up Your Troubles in Your Old Kit Bag (And Smile, Smile, Smile)," advertised by T. B. Harms as "a PHILOSOPHY SONG . . . now being sung and whistled by the troops as they march along."

A 1917 song, "After the War Is Over, Will There Be Any Home Sweet Home?" anticipated the many domestic changes that would follow war in which "maps will change entirely." The American Quartet's version of

"How Ya Gonna Keep 'Em down on the Farm (after They've Seen Paree)" was popular in 1919, hinting at the problems of reintegrating the worldly soldiers and convincing them to resume rural, civilian lives. Although many of these songs were also covered by soloists and duets, the all-male quartets seem to have captured for audiences the camaraderie and esprit de corps of the male fighting forces, and they shouldered a large proportion of pro-war songs between 1917 and 1918.

The war ushered in sweeping changes in American society and in the structure of feeling that characterized many American lives. During America's Roaring Twenties, Jazz Age, and Great Depression, close-harmony quartets lost their position at the pinnacle of popular entertainment. In the postwar decades, the major quartets by and large disbanded or consolidated their personnel and never again achieved sales figures comparable to their prewar years.[58] One of the last bona fide hits for the pioneer-era quartets was "My Sunny Tennessee" (1922) by the Peerless Quartet. Billy Murray's last number one solo hit was—fittingly for a singer who spent so many years in various quartets—his 1923 recording of "That Old Gang of Mine," although he continued charting songs as late as 1927.

The war and migration from rural areas had swelled the cities with rural migrants hungry for modern urban distractions, including African Americans escaping rural poverty and racial intolerance. Around 1916, important patents that had protected the Big Three's oligopoly on recording processes began to lapse, and opportunities for black quartets to record improved markedly with the appearance of new labels competing with the Big Three, especially the race record labels and subsidiaries. W. C. Handy and Harry Pace brought their publishing house, Pace & Handy, from Memphis to New York in 1918. Pace soon organized his own company, Black Swan Records, with the Harlem audience in mind and began to record the leading black groups of the era. Three new companies in New York introduced new race record labels: Paramount, Vocalion, and Okeh. The increased competition pushed the industry to seek out new groups, including African American jubilee and blues artists, but also southern white "hillbilly" musicians and musicians of various ethnicities in the urban North. Most of the recordings were made in sessions held in New York City, requiring quartets to travel to New York from all over the South, Midwest and East, but some of the race record labels sponsored field recordings as well. As a result of all this activity, black quartets that had toiled in relative obscurity and with only regional visibility were newly marketed to national audiences on recordings and radio.

In 1920 Congress passed the Volstead Act prohibiting the sale and consumption of alcohol. Many illegal speakeasies were in black entertainment districts that attracted an increasing number of whites to sample jazz, dance band music, and dance variety shows featuring syncopated rhythms, blues-based chord progressions, swing, and improvisation. A series of dance crazes of African American origin swept the country, reminiscent of the cakewalk craze of the late 1890s. James Reese Europe's band accompanied the dance exhibitions of Irene and Vernon Castle, introducing dances such as the turkey trot and tango to new audiences. Within a few years of the introduction by black sailors in New York of an African American dance from Charleston, South Carolina, the charleston became a national fad, complete with exhibitions, competitions, and marathons. This urban modernist culture, heavily indebted to black cultural forms, inspired the epochal labels "the Jazz Age" and "the Roaring Twenties."

Genres of group harmony proliferated in this period: gospel and secular jazz quartets were the newest, but they coexisted for some decades with barbershop and jubilee groups, and even many of the gospel and jubilee groups continued to perform the minstrel and barbershop style repertory. One example of this kind of repertory crossover was the Four Harmony Kings, who first appeared as Lieutenant Jim Europe's Four Harmony Kings. In 1921 the group cut four sides for Black Swan and Emerson in which their sacred repertory was interspersed with such secular songs as "The Queen Street Rag" and "Sweet Adelyne" [sic].[59] Another popular black quartet of the period, the Norfolk Jazz Quartet, also called the Norfolk Jubilee Quartet, recorded nearly 150 sides of its sacred and secular songs over nineteen years, starting with a series of recordings for Okeh in 1921.[60] The Southern Negro Quartette also began to record (for Columbia) in 1921. In 1927 the Harmony Four (also known as the Bessemer Quartet, the Southern Harmony Quartette, and the Southern Serenaders) recorded, among other songs, the minstrel song "You Can Hear Those Darkies Singing." Also recording in 1927 was the Missouri-Pacific Diamond Jubilee Quartette; their releases on Okeh included "I've Been Working on the Railroad," a song they performed countless times. The Silver Leaf Quartet, the Mobile Four, and the Southernaires all embarked on recording, concert, and radio careers and succeeded despite making only an occasional nod to the minstrel conventions. Even with the many advances made by black gospel, spiritual, and jubilee quartets in the early race-records era, many of the recordings featured reverse sides by white quartets, a strategy designed to maximize distribution.

The recording industry fell apart during the Great Depression, and there were few recording sessions in the race record industry between 1929 and 1937. Radio broadcasts, however, carried many of the products of the race record industry, in part because so many of the recordings required little or no royalty payments for airplay, even after ASCAP reached agreements with the major radio networks.

The decline in the fortunes of white close-harmony quartets in this period was rooted in changes in demography and structures of feeling in the wake of World War I. The new worldview embraced rapid cultural obsolescence, turnover, and generational identity differences. Audiences sought new expressions to capture the feeling of dislocation, change, optimism and anxiety that characterized their lives. The reassuring strains of barbershop ballads, whether sentimental or sassy, came to serve as a residue of the era before the jazz era. Moreover, growing numbers of Americans wanted to dance, and barbershop harmony, with its elastic time sense, was a long distance from the dance floor.

Electric recording technology, using a condenser microphone, vacuum tube amplifier, and electromagnetic cutting stylus, made its debut in 1924. The new technology greatly expanded the frequency and dynamic response that could be captured on recordings. Whereas the great quartet singers had specialized in an energetic live sound appropriate for recording horns and for nonamplified performance in large concert halls, with the advent of electronic recording, younger singers experimented with softer and more subtle vocal styles ("crooning"). The new microphones also efficiently captured entire orchestras, and so quartets and small bands no longer had the distinct recording advantages over larger ensembles they once had.

The Shannon Four was one of the few white quartets to record hit songs in the late 1920s. Formed in 1917, the Shannon Four specialized in Irish ballads; its 1926 signature tune, recorded for Columbia, was "Where the River Shannon Flows." After 1925 the quartet experimented with jazz vocals, and in 1926 it changed its name to the modern-sounding Revelers. It charted six hits in 1926, including "Dinah" and "The Blue Room." Owing to contract restrictions, the group appeared under various names such as the Merrymakers for performances in 1927 on NBC's Brunswick Hour of Music.[61] The quartet also recorded with Columbia under the name the Singing Sophomores, producing their last top-twenty hit with Columbia in 1930. Vestiges of the pioneer-era white barbershop quartets could be found on American radio, in commercial advertisements, and on the remaining vaudeville circuits up until World War II, but the Shannon Four/Revelers were the last prerevival group to break through into commercial stardom.

Tin Pan Alley compositional styles were changing rapidly. George M. Cohan and Irving Berlin built songwriting careers on the syncopations of ragtime, and their songs were eagerly harmonized by close-harmony quartets. Nonetheless, quartets largely turned away from the work of other Tin Pan Alley songwriters of the late 1920s to the 1940s (George and Ira Gershwin, Richard Rodgers and Lorenz Hart, Harold Arlen, Cole Porter, Oscar Hammerstein II, and Yip Harburg, among others). The sophisticated lyricism and jazzy harmonies of the show tunes published by these songwriters constituted one of the auditory dividing lines separating golden-era songs from later trends. Whereas the former were full of seventh chords that supported barbershop four-part treatments, the jazzier show and pop tunes featured extended chords (major sevenths, ninths, and elevenths), altered chords (flat fifths, augmentations, etc.), and melodies that often featured large intervallic leaps for emotional or thematic impact.

During the 1910s and 1920s, moving pictures evolved from novelties consumed in pay-for-view parlors (or as vaudeville interludes) into feature theatrical presentations. Because films were cheaper to book than vaudeville acts, vaudeville theaters converted to the big screen. The Vitaphone sound-on-disc system provided a means of synchronizing a film projector with an audio disc turntable to create the first commercially viable soundtrack. The system, marketed by Western Electric, made possible the

Warner Brothers' pioneering 1926 sound film *The Jazz Singer*, which was *about* a vaudeville singer and was shown *in* vaudeville theaters. Between 1926 and 1930 many vaudevillians recorded their routines on Vitaphone films, but these short film recordings of vaudeville performances had the paradoxical effect of hastening the demise of vaudeville: when the Vitaphone shorts were shown as interludes in vaudeville theaters, the live vaudeville routines lost their edge of authenticity and spontaneity and appeared to be redundant versions of the artists' own Vitaphone performances. The Keith-Albee vaudeville circuit attempted to ban name acts from recording for Vitaphone. In response, the Vitaphone Company offered a harmony quartet, the Four Aristocrats, a $52,000 contract for a year (1927), during which Vitaphone would film four or five short subjects featuring the act *and* book the group in vaudeville houses.[62] For most theatrical quartets, however, the dwindling vaudeville circuits meant an end to steady work.

In the late 1920s radio began to out-muscle the recording industry for entertainment dominance. The Radio Corporation of America bought the Victor Talking Machine Company, beginning a string of takeovers. During the depression, radio's profit base in advertising proved more reliable than musical commodities, which faced declining markets. Between 1926 and 1934 radio corporations organized three national broadcast networks: the National Broadcasting Corporation, the Columbia Broadcasting System, and the Mutual Broadcasting System.

Although radio cut into vaudeville (variety hours were now available in the home), they also provided a home for out-of-work vaudevillians, harmony quartets included. In the late 1920s, as radio began to explore the power of performers to pitch products, a barbershop quartet from Minneapolis sang a Wheaties jingle in what some regard as the first jingle ever heard on a radio broadcast.[63] The group thereafter became known as the Wheaties Quartet. They gave their final performance at a General Mills Regional Meeting in 1949, and in the intervening years they sang often at company events and in public.

The Maple City Four, a vaudeville comedy four of the radio era, branched out into live radio shows, movies, and radio advertisements. They came together in 1924 for a talent show at an Elks lodge in LaPorte, Indiana, and were hired to sing radio spots for political candidates in 1926. In the same year they joined the powerful Chicago radio station WLS (Sears' "World's Largest Store"), where they worked for over two decades. The Maple City Four brought to radio their vaudevillian "mixed bag of skits, comedy songs, ballads, barbershop, weird instrumentals, and light patter."[64] Like most radio talent in the early decades, they shamelessly plugged their sponsors' products on live commercial variety shows, taking aliases such as the Caterpillar Crew (for Caterpillar Tractors) and the Checkerboard Singers (for Purina). The Maple City Four performed in their first Hollywood film in 1937, the hit western *Git Along Little Dogies*, starring Gene Autry. In 1938 they made *Under Western Skies* with Roy Rogers. The persistent role for barbershop quartets in westerns of the following decades added another wrinkle to the many associations of barbershop quartets. By the 1940s they seemed to have always been a part of the urban immigrant ghetto scene, with four young toughs singing in the gaslit streets; and they appeared equally at home in midwestern barbershops, in vaudeville shticks, and on the western plains. Maple City released their first and only recording, *Gaslight Ballads,* on Mercury Records in 1946.

Another early radio quartet, the Capital City Four from Springfield, Illinois (formed in 1927) performed on the Schultz Baking Company radio program for eighteen months. In 1939 the group had its debut on the WLS Alka-Seltzer program, and two years later it toured Illinois for the reelection campaign of Governor Henry Horner. The Capitol City Four made six recordings for Victor RCA in 1941.[65] In 1932 the Westinghouse Electric and Manufacturing Corporation's industrial relations department, based in East Pittsburgh, formed an employee quartet they called the Westinghouse Quartet. The quartet sang for over a decade at company events, at charitable events, and in public concerts. The Westinghouse Quartet enjoyed some success in recordings and radio as well. They later joined SPEBSQSA and took third place in the national competition in 1944.

Many of the groups attracted to the barbershop revival after 1938 had long pedigrees as professional, semiprofessional, or amateur quartets. For example, the Flat Foot Four, an Oklahoma City quartet that took third place in the first SPEBSQSA contest in 1939 and placed first the following year in New York City, was started by the mayor of Oklahoma City in 1923 as a police department performing group, touring widely as the official (amateur) quartet of the American Legion. Another group later active in SPEBSQSA events, the Harmony Kings (not the same as the black jubilee group the Four Harmony Kings), was organized in 1917 at an army barracks at Camp Taylor, Kentucky, and performed in an amateur capacity into the 1940s, when they placed in the top five in SPEBSQSA contests for two years in a row. Similarly, Frank Thorne, later of the SPEBSQSA group Elastic Four, recounted singing with the Plow City Four in Canton, Illinois, in 1913, a group that included three later SPEBSQSA leaders, Doc Nelson, Maurice Reagan, and Pete Buckley (bass of the SPEBSQSA group the Misfits). Members of the Four Harmonizers, who won the 1943 SPEBSQSA championship, had loads of previous amateur and professional barbershop experience. The tenor had sung for seven years with the Music Box Four; the lead and baritone both sang with their family quartets; and the bass had played vaudeville with the Troy Comedy Four, the Empress Comedy Four, and the Variety Four.[66]

These examples of barbershop quartets in the 1930s and 1940s illustrate that though the commercial success of barbershop quartets waned dramatically (especially in recordings and in vaudeville), a smaller number of quartets found secure niches in the radio, movies, and advertisements, and as corporate and political pitchmen. It became increasingly clear that barbershop harmony's nostalgic ambience and newly wholesome reputation (its earlier links to the saloon and vaudeville conveniently forgotten) could sell products on radio and advance the political fortunes of candidates in electoral contests.

Tag: Letting Bygones Be Icons

A member of the Globe Quartet (Baltimore, 1905) wrote nostalgically about the amateur quartet scene at the turn of the century: "There were quartets aplenty in the old days and quartet contests were held in dance halls, parks, and everywhere. Quartets sprang up on street corners through the different neighborhoods and there was lots of friendly rivalry."[67] According to another participant, "It flowered also in pool halls, yes, in saloons too. When the fraternal lodge gave a dance, the anteroom or men's room of the dance hall was a formation point for a quartet, later winding up on a street corner or in a restaurant over cups of coffee."[68]

For over half a century, the sheet music industry had supplied material for home-based and recreational quartet performances of popular tunes. The introduction of recorded cylinders and discs did not at first undermine this relationship but rather intensified it by providing audio advertisements for sheet music and audio models for its live reproduction, an aspect of the political economy of popular music that remained stable until it was disrupted by the popularity of radio and by the increasing taste for recorded commodities in their own right rather than as simulacra of live performances or as advertisements for the sheet music that inspired amateur performance. One of the unintended consequences of the thousands of recordings of quartets was that they served as a semipermanent distillation of fin-de-siècle performance practice that could be appropriated and reinterpreted by barbershop revivalists in subsequent decades. The popular music industry at first fueled and later largely displaced amateur and recreational performance. In the end, barbershop harmony quartets fell victim to the passage of time and the demand for novelty. This is not to deny that the decline of vaudeville, the advent of electric microphones, or, a few years later, the deprecations of the Great Depression were also responsible, but only to argue for an underlying tectonic shift in the aesthetics of American popular culture.

During the golden era, close-harmony quartets received the "barbershop" designation and achieved the status of sonic icons for the period, a status they shared only with the ubiquitous village brass band. This status was increasingly bestowed on them by posterity, especially from the vantage point of the nostalgic yearning that churned in white America during the Great Depression.

Many of the hit Tin Pan Alley compositions from the turn of the century filtered into public consciousness and came to be perceived not as commercial ephemera but as a timeless heritage of American songs. These songs served as a canon for a barbershop revival, which also relied on the paradigmatic performances in barbershop style by the pioneer recording quartets. The 1930s-era quartets that sported matching Gay Nineties outfits, handlebar moustaches, and straw hats bear only a glancing resemblance to the popular quartets performing at the turn of the century, and then primarily to the comedy fours rather than the major concert and recording quartets. And the kinship of these quartets to African American close harmony groups was—by the 1930s—whitewashed thoroughly.

3

The Lost Chords
The Early Barbershop Revival

Let's take a trip on memory's ship
Back to the days gone by
Sail to the old village schoolhouse
Anchor outside the school door
Look in and see, there's you and me
A couple of kids once more
　　—"School Days";
　　　　words by Will D. Cobb,
　　　　music by Gus Edwards (1907)

hree important books of sheet music for barbershop quartets appeared between 1925 and 1935 that helped to enshrine the image of
the white amateur barbershop quartet and disseminate paradigmatic examples of barbershop arrangements for later generations. The popular-
music chronicler Sigmund Spaeth published his book *Barber Shop Ballads*
in 1925 with two double-faced phonograph records enclosed. The same
year, the arranger George Shackley published *Close Harmony: Male Quartets, Ballads, and Funnies with Barber Shop Chord*. Five years later, the amateur barbershop singer Deac Martin mimeographed a quartet handbook
as a Christmas present and called it *A Handbook for Adeline Addicts*. He followed with a printed version at Christmas a year later and published it in
1932.[1] All three books were coveted by close-harmony aficionados and
served as linchpins in the consolidation of revival barbershop style and
practice. In general, the arranger-authors glossed over black contributions
to close harmony, studiously avoided references to the famous recording
and vaudeville quartets of the golden era, and treated Tin Pan Alley songs
as a collective cultural commonwealth of white American men. In Spaeth's
words, "We believe the songs . . . are folk-music, and they are sung as folk-
music would be."[2] Note the self-conscious emphasis on amateurism in
Spaeth's remarks a few years later: "While other artists undergo years of
rigorous training with the sole objective of pleasing an audience, the true
barber-shopper performs primarily for himself and the delectation of his

select close-harmony companions. . . . I am addressing the simon-pure amateurs. . . . What we need more than relief for dry farmers is more, and closer harmony that is personalized."[3]

American Neo-Victorianism

The emphasis on amateur pursuits and hobbies that we find in Spaeth's writings was linked to the residue of a broad social change that had been in process since before the turn of the century. The passion for hobbies that swept the country during the golden era was a response to the rise in the standard of living, a shorter work week (resulting in more leisure time), and an increased focus on consumption. A belief in the character-building rewards of hobbies swept up late-Victorian men in a passion for collecting and outdoor activity. The Canadian physician Sir William Osler captured this sentiment elegantly in a speech delivered at his retirement dinner in 1905: "No man is really happy or safe without a hobby, and it makes precious little difference what the outside interest may be—botany, beetles, or butterflies; roses, tulips, or irises; fishing, mountaineering or antiquities— anything will do so *long as he straddles a hobby and rides it hard.*"[4]

The turn of the century also afforded American men multiple forms of association. American participation in fraternal lodges, clubs, hobby networks, and political parties helped them to cope with the decline of traditional institutions and to clarify personal identity in a pluralist and rapidly shifting society. Historians have pointed to the fin de siècle as the period in which this trend accelerated; Neil Harris has therefore proposed that Twain's "Gilded Age" might more properly be called the "Guilded Age."[5] As the prevalent forms of male sociability declined in the 1920s, nostalgia for male camaraderie took hold, reflected in self-referential barbershop songs about gangs, quartets, fellows, and the like. The 1922 song "(Wedding Bells Are Breaking Up) That Old Gang of Mine" exemplifies this trend:

> As they go strolling side by side
> They'll harmonize "Here Comes the Bride"
> What's become of "Sweet Adeline"?
> What's become of "That Old Gang of Mine"?
> *Chorus:*
> Not a soul down on the corner
> That's a pretty certain sign
> Those wedding bells are breaking up "That Old Gang of Mine"
> All the boys are singing love songs
> They forgot "Sweet Adeline"
> Those wedding bells are breaking up "That Old Gang of Mine"[6]

One line of a later verse, "I hear their voices ringing yet / I miss that old quartet"—although ostensibly about the loss of fellowship to marriage— also hints at the passing of a musical era.

Spaeth and Martin certainly did not invent the revivalistic approach to barbershop harmony; there were many groups singing in this style throughout the 1930s. Still, they helped to settle on a number of formal diagnostic criteria for barbershop quartet songs that helped to consolidate, define, and refine the style of group harmonizing. Spaeth insisted that the lead voice should be harmonized above by a tenor, a common but not exclusive practice of earlier close-harmony quartets. He licensed piano accompaniment for part-learning only and otherwise disavowed accompaniment. Spaeth set out to collect the favorite harmonizing songs from the previous era and encouraged his readers to submit their own lists for future volumes, in what was probably the first serious effort to develop a canon of barbershop-friendly songs. What is more, the barber-pole illustrations on every page and the quaint cartoons of quartets helped to set the tone for revival iconography. Spaeth urged his readers on in the last line of his book: "You have joined the vast army of quartettists, harmonizers, barbershoppers—the world is yours."[7]

I locate the institutional origins of the barbershop revival in the period around 1935–36. At this time the United States was still in the grip of the Great Depression, despite Keynesian efforts on the part of President Franklin D. Roosevelt's administration to spark economic growth. With savings lost and businesses bankrupt, families were broken up, and vast armies of out-of-work citizens were moving around the country in search of jobs. Mobile and uprooted on an unprecedented scale, middle-class Americans were experiencing a new level of anxiety. As Warren Susman noted, "It is precisely the middle-class American for whom the experience of the Depression provided a special kind of shock and as a result a special kind of response."[8]

The global economic and political crisis exacerbated general anxieties about modernity that had plagued the developed nations in the nineteenth and early twentieth centuries and that were intensified by the horrors of World War I. Henri Lefebvre described the first decades of the new century as a moment of historical disjuncture:

> A certain space was shattered. It was the space of common sense, of knowledge, of social practice, of political power, a space hitherto enshrined in everyday discourse, just as in abstract thought, as the environment of and channel for communication. . . . Euclidean and perspectivist space have disappeared as systems of reference, along with other former "common places" such as town, history, paternity, the tonal system in music, traditional morality, and so forth. This was a truly crucial moment.[9]

This period seemed to represent for many the decisive break with traditional systems of power, knowledge, and cultural transmission; the end of all that was sure and given. Woman suffrage, labor agitation, and black civil rights were all supported by an increasingly self-conscious, modernist intellectual vanguard, often socialist or communist in orientation. The reaction to all of this among many whites was something of a moral panic, inculcating a desire among large segments of the population, especially the middle classes, "for intimacy, for recognition, [and] for connection to the past."[10] Middle-class Americans not attracted to the dizzying pleasures of modernity found themselves in search of a new sense of commitment to durable traditions, cultural forms, and a secure collective identity.

Many middle-class whites held fast to or resuscitated Victorian ideals in the face of these social changes. American neo-Victorianism was an ideological expression of the predominantly Anglo-American middle class, and its central concept was that of "character," a term that encompassed moral fiber, a work ethic, and self-control. Its most vital institution was the home: it was viewed as a male-dominated refuge from capitalist competition in which modest and moral women were responsible for developing values and character among children. The ideal structure of feeling in Victorian America combined sentimentality with gentility and a perpetually incomplete striving. Victorians were obliged to improve themselves and to aspire to an ideal Stanley Coben characterized as "self-controlled, punctual, orderly, hardworking, conscientious, sober, respectful of . . . property rights, ready to postpone immediate gratification for long-term goals, pious toward a usually friendly God, a believer in the truth of the Bible, oriented strongly toward home and family, honorable in relations toward other Victorians, anxious for self-improvement in a fashion which might appear compulsive to modern observers, and patriotic."[11]

Neo-Victorianism linked up explicitly or implicitly with a range of responses to the crises of the postwar years. Organizations and movements as diverse as the Boy Scouts of America, anti-Catholic campaigns, the Immigration Restriction League, and Prohibitionism all had the stated goal of preserving morals and character. The Boy Scouts, especially, demonstrated the Victorian passion for manly hobbies, combined with a rigorous ladder for self-advancement through the mastery of skills. Protestantism and Anglo-Saxon identity movements increasingly adopted a form of social Darwinism that held that "if a race did not continue progressing upward toward a perfect civilization, it would inevitably backslide and fall into racial decay."[12] Ostensibly to forestall just such a "racial decay," the Ku Klux Klan was reborn in 1915 in Georgia and quickly spread throughout the North and the Midwest, developing particular strength in the so-called heartland states. Its membership topped four million during the 1920s.

Nativism, which spread vigorously during the presidency of Warren G. Harding (1921–23), remained as a stubborn ideological tendency throughout the presidencies of Calvin Coolidge and Herbert Hoover, and even through the progressive reforms of the Roosevelt administration; its adherents argued for "100 percent Americanism."[13] In his 1935 argument for a nativist American culture, the historian Herbert Agar used as his foil a midwestern town he called Sheridan: "It still has the character of a Middle Western small town. But it will not have this character for long, if recent tendencies continue unchecked into the future. For Sheridan is living on its spiritual capital. It is using the virtues that are left over from the past rather than tending the soil from which these virtues grew. *Native America will not win its fight* unless it grows more conscious of the danger, more vigilant in defense." Sheridan's face-to-face social democracy was threatened, in Agar's view, by "the city, the antithesis to Sheridan . . . with its skyscrapers, millionaires, gangsters, *and polyglot proletariat.*"[14] Agar believed, as did many, that the American small town was the repository for the best in American values and character. Henry Seidel Canby, a Yale professor and editor of the *Saturday Review of Literature,* wrote in a 1930s memoir about the late nineteenth century and the strong attraction of small-town life: "You belonged. There has been no such certainty in American life since. . . . Our confidence was an illusion, but like most illusions it had many of the benefits of a fact."[15] This, then, is the genesis of a mythology of the American small town—what I previously called "unreal estate"—that finds expression in the work of Walt Disney, Meredith Willson, and other nostalgic culture brokers of the mid-twentieth century. One of the most succinct statements of the conservative social vision comes from Ellis W. Hawley: "At the core of middle-class rightism, as it appeared in the America of the 1920's, was an idealized community in which sturdy farmers, enterprising but community-spirited businesspeople, and industrious and cheerful workers lived side by side in peaceful and prosperous harmony. The members of this community recognized the mutuality of their interests, and in well-filled churches, character-building homes, and community service organizations they learned the fundamental truths that allowed them to live rewarding and moral lives. . . . That America ever contained such communities was dubious."[16]

The barbershop revival was born from this confluence of conservative reactions to changes in the physical, social, and cultural landscape of America. It was a quest to reconstruct a space of privilege for white American middle-class males based on nostalgia for unchallenged and exclusive sociability and camaraderie located in the adolescent memories of middle-aged men. The rapid spread of this movement and its success in enlisting tens of thousands of Americans in singing harmony arrangements of a popular-song heritage challenges the rather narrow preoccupation among cultural analysts with swing music (and, to a lesser degree, populist folk music) as the sound of the decade, the decade of the New Deal and the Popular Front.[17] The barbershop movement illuminates the large, alienated middle class longing not for the brash, avant-garde exuberance of swing, but for the reassuring four-part chorus of "Sweet Adeline." Neo-Victorian movements and their allied cultural formations can be understood best, perhaps, as "rear guard" cultural activity.

"The Sidewalks of New York"

The nostalgia for turn-of-the-century harmonies was cultivated by two regional initiatives, the first being the almost-forgotten but spectacular stagings of barbershop quartet contests in New York City from 1935 onward, and the second being the better-known barbershop organization that spread from Tulsa, Oklahoma, to national prominence starting in 1938. It is quite possible that with extensive research into local contests a more detailed portrait of local barbershop song competitions or festivals in the 1930s could be sketched. The New York City and midwestern revivals, however, appear to have been the largest and most significant manifestations of barbershop quartet singing. Although they were quite separate at first, they joined forces for a short time in 1939–40 to produce a barbershop contest at the New York World's Fair. Their interactions, mutual influences, and strident break-up provides a window into some of the class, gender, racial, political, and regional differences roiling under the surface of this seemingly cheerful movement.

The idea to first stage nostalgic competitions of barbershop quartets seems to have belonged to the New York City director of recreation, James V. Mulholland, who, in 1935, at the nadir of the depression, "reached far back into the album [of] yesterday for a new idea in public entertainment and came up with a contest for barber-shop quartets."[18] The event quickly became associated with Mulholland's boss, the powerful New York City (and New York State) parks commissioner, Robert Moses, and soon it was embraced by two other titans of the New York political scene: the new mayor, Fiorello H. La Guardia, and the former governor and Democratic Party presidential candidate, Alfred E. Smith.[19] Although barbershop harmony is often linked closely with the United States heartland, the barbershop revival movement's first real institutional presence developed in the most modernist of the world's cities, where it was championed by Mulholland and by the ethnic power elite of the city and state: the city's Italian mayor, its powerful Jewish parks commissioner, and the Irish Catholic former governor.[20] At first blush, this may appear to be an unlikely quartet to launch a barbershop revival movement.

The close association between the city planner Robert (Bob) Moses, a Republican, and the Democratic machine politician Al Smith goes back to Smith's first term as governor (1918–20), when he created a committee to reorganize state government in the wake of World War I and appointed Moses—a Yale graduate with a Ph.D. in public planning from Columbia University—to be its chief of staff. Moses's report laid out a program for centralization and reform that served as the blueprint for governmental reorganization during Smith's terms as governor (1918–20, 1922–28). During Smith's second term, Moses served as his secretary of state, and he drafted many of his most important bills during a period when Smith was distracted by his own presidential election campaign. More important, in 1924 Moses became the chairman of the New York State Parks Commission, demanding successfully that all of the state's parks be placed under a single agency; he also took personal control of the Long Island State Park Commission. In 1933, with a string of large public-works projects on his resume, Moses took over as chairman of the State Emergency Public Works Commission and then (adding to his state parks purview) as Chairman of the New York City Parks Commission under the new mayor, Fiorello H. La Guardia. By 1942 Moses had spent over $300 million on park development in New York City alone, two-thirds of which came from federal work relief money. He was the most ardent spender of Works Progress Administration (WPA) money in the country.

Under La Guardia, Moses transformed almost all of New York City, building bridges, parkways, roadways, parks, and recreational facilities. A year before the first barbershop contest, Moses ran for governor and lost, settling down afterwards to run the city's parks and infrastructure once again. In *The Powerbroker*, Robert A. Caro makes clear (as does Marshall Berman in *All That Is Solid Melts into Air* some years later) that the prewar Moses built and conceived on a more human scale; his parkways, for instance, have an attention to detail and a connection to the surrounding environment that his postwar projects, especially his expressways, lacked. For Moses, a barbershop contest was a means of making his parks come alive with recreational, cultural, and civic activities, an extension of his WPA-funded empire building. But it was also an extension of what, to paraphrase Marshall Berman, might be called Moses's technopastoralism. In his beaches and parks, Moses sought to define a pastoral garden world for leisure activities of the technologically encumbered urbanites, and barbershop singing was its perfect musical correlate.

The connection to barbershop was a more natural one for the genial Al Smith. Smith's gubernatorial and presidential campaigns were accompanied by his theme song, the Tin Pan Alley (and barbershop) chestnut "Sidewalks of New York":

> Down in front of Casey's old brown wooden stoop
> On a summer's evening we formed a merry group
> Boys and girls together, we would sing and waltz
> There we learned the waltz step on the sidewalks of New York
> *Chorus:*
> East Side, West Side, all around the town
> The tots sang "Ring a rosy, London Bridge is falling down"
> Boys and girls together, me and Mamie O'Rourke
> We tripped the light fantastic on the sidewalks of New York.[21]

Smith often reminisced about the urban streetscapes of his childhood in the Bowery, a time of gas lamps, horse-drawn buggies, street vendors, paperboys, and tenement neighborhoods teeming with recent immigrants—the same neighborhoods depicted in "The Sidewalks of New York." Robert Moses called the Bowery, where Smith grew up, an "urban village." "It was the 'old neighborhood' where souls and bodies were saved by the parish priest, the family doctor and the local political saloon keeper and boss who knew everyone and was the link between the exploited immigrant and the incomprehensible distant law."[22] Ironically, these were the same neighborhoods that Moses later intended to uproot with his Lower Manhattan Expressway.

The New York barbershop revival would be built, therefore, on the productive partnership forged between Moses and Smith (his old boss), on the

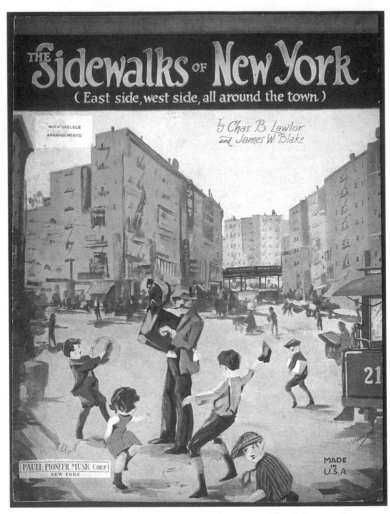

Figure 3.1. This cover art for "Sidewalks of New York" celebrates the tenement culture of immigrant New York City at the turn of the century. Courtesy of Nancy Groce.

one hand, and the often-cantankerous relationship between Moses and La Guardia, on the other. Called the "American Ballad Contest for Amateur Barber-Shop Quartets," the contest was promoted as an exercise in turn-of-the-century nostalgia. The city's power brokers saw an opportunity to capitalize on the burgeoning nostalgia for an optimistic era as a diversion during the hard times of the Great Depression.

Moses and Mulholland scheduled the finals of the Ballad Contest for the Mall in Central Park on September 10, 1935, but borough elimination con-

Respectfully dedicated to Hon. Gov. "AL" SMITH of the State of New York

THE SIDEWALKS OF NEW YORK

EAST SIDE, WEST SIDE, ALL AROUND THE TOWN

With Ukulele Arrangement

Words and Music By
CHAS. B. LAWLOR & JAMES W. BLAKE

MADE IN U.S.A

Hon. Gov. "AL" SMITH
of the "Empire" State

Pioneer · Music · Publishing · Company
119 · FIFTH · AVENUE · NEW · YORK · CITY

Figure 3.2. A competing cover for "Sidewalks of New York" exploits the use of the song as a campaign theme for Governor Alfred E. Smith. Courtesy of Nancy Groce.

tests were held in advance at settings such as Washington Square Park in Manhattan and Prospect Park in Brooklyn. Publicity sparked so much interest that parks outside the city, including Playland in Rye and Jones Beach on Long Island (the latter a Moses creation), demanded their own elimination contests. All told, over eighty quartets signed up to participate in the contest, a number that surprised organizers. This number also suggests that perhaps thousands of amateur quartets were still singing close harmony in various locales across the country.

The first contest featured only amateur men's quartets in barbershop voicing (tenor, lead, baritone, and bass). Matching period outfits were required, but it was left to the quartets to pick their theme. Although organizers at first announced that single-instrument accompaniment (banjo, mandolin, guitar, zither, or lute—not pianos) would be permitted, they later allowed them only to provide a starting pitch. Entrants were solicited with an old-fashioned brochure mailed to clubs and fraternal organizations.

An account of the elimination contests that appeared in the *New York Times* captures this early New York–style revival:

> In a way the Bronx scored a double victory, for when the Metro Male Quartet had finished the last "swipe" of "Down By the Old Mill Stream," with Frank Miller, the second bass, dropping like a ton of coal on the bass phrasing of the line that ends "my village qu-e-e-n," to win by a close decision over the Borden Early Birds in Washington Square, it was discovered that the Metros were Bronxites. . . . In the Bronx, the Bronx Union Y.M.C.A. presented the Little Shavers . . . in costumes of the Nineties, who beat out the Tremont Four. They selected "Drink to Me Only with Thine Eyes" and "I've Been Working on the Railroad." Clad as bartenders, with white aprons and slicked down hair, the Rubsam and Horrman Quartet of Stapleton won out over the Village Four of Tottenville in Staten Island. . . . Seven quartets competed in Manhattan, with the Old Timers, registered from the Mills Hotel, undoubtedly the most barber shoppy. They were awful. Of ten registered for the Bronx, four failed to show and one outfit got stage fright. Barber chairs set up in Washington Square and in McDonald Playground, with white coated barbers shaving and cutting hair of some of the braver in attendance, doing the singing, lent color to the eliminations. Five thousand listened in at Washington Square, and 4,000 in Staten Island, and 3,000 in the Bronx.[23]

Singers and judges arrived for the final competition in antique vehicles, including horse-drawn buggies, early horseless carriages, and tandem bikes, in a parade before the fifteen thousand attendees. The parks design department constructed a Gay Nineties barber shop (named Park's Tonsorial Parlor) in the band shell of the park mall and adorned it with two poles, antique barber chairs, spittoons, a fly-specked clock (broken), a shelf of shaving mugs, a coal-burning pot-bellied stove, and antique photos of prizefighters. Giant shaving mugs flanked the entrance to the audience, and the stage was set up so as to give the audience the feel of being in the back room of the barber's salon. Competition prizes included straight razors, shaving mugs (festooned with the parks department logo), and shaving brushes. Each prize was accompanied by a penny, a nod to a superstition that "money takes the curse off a sharp-edged gift like a razor or a knife."[24] Because organizers thought that period-style shaving mugs would be scarce, one hundred employees of the parks department were assigned to hunt down and buy the mugs, but within hours they had turned up over eight thousand.[25]

The contest was emceed by Moses as parks commissioner. The singer George M. Cohan was proposed as a judge but was unable to participate. Judging for the finals was handled by Sigmund Spaeth, Governor Smith, and Luther C. Steward, president of the Federal Employees Association. The parks department assembled a list of tunes that were allowed for initial songs, but participants were allowed to select a second song providing that it was composed before 1905. Fourteen finalist quartets competed, with the first prize going to Brooklyn's Bay City Four, who sang "Drink to Me Only with Thine Eyes" and "There's a Tavern in the Town." The quartet wore white caps and orange-and-black striped blazers. Second prize went to the Rubsam and Horrman Brewery Quartet of Staten Island (dressed as bartenders), and third place to the Borden's Early Birds of Manhattan (in milkmen's attire). The finale of the concert was a rendition of "Sweet Adeline" by Mayor La Guardia, Commissioner Moses, Sigmund Spaeth, and Luther Steward, a performance that was charitably judged "sour."

The obvious success of his experiment in nostalgic spectacle convinced Moses to make the American Ballad Contest an annual event. Moving the finals to the new Randall's Island Municipal Stadium for the 1936 contest permitted the parks department to expand on the original conception of a barber shop and to create a small-town street with a saloon, a pawnbroker's, a tobacconist's, and a Chinese laundry named Me Sing Loo's.[26] The fire department band held forth with Sousa marches and Gay Nineties concert band material. Long before Walt Disney premiered his Main Street U.S.A. at Disneyland, Robert Moses and his New York City Parks Department created a historic theme park based on the same concept. Between songs, audience members could stroll the street, get a shave or haircut, and listen to the main-street musical attractions, including organ grinders, harmonica bands, and an accordionist. A sign on the saloon advertised "Beer 5¢," making nostalgia out of something as simple as cheaper prices (and the ease of pre-Prohibition drinking only three years after the repeal of Prohibition!). The ballad contests concluded with a group sing involving all quartets and audience members. Typically, the group-sing commenced with "Sweet Adeline" and ended with "Auld Lang Syne."

In the 1937 competition (still a year before the founding of SPEBSQSA), the Green Brothers (Channel, Warren, Robert, and Peter), a "Negro quartet from Harlem," placed second behind the Tri-Boro Quartet (who had won the contest in 1936 as well). None of the press coverage made a great deal of the race of the singers, in part because popular memory still preserved a notion of the centrality of African Americans in the evolution of barbershop-style singing; some of the articles at the time alluded to James Weldon Johnson's comments on the matter. In New York, where so much sophisticated musical entertainment originated above 125th St., there was not yet a sense that secular close harmony had diverged into different, racially demarcated streams.

In another harbinger of the structure of the midwestern revival, the New York contests developed an adjudication system that balanced musical and extramusical performance features. The judging criteria for the second year of competition awarded 60 percent for musical criteria (tone, rhythm, technique, and harmony); 30 percent for interpretation, expression, and phrasing; and 10 percent for appearance and costuming.

The 1939 contest introduced a new element: "Gibson Girl trios" for performance of barbershop-era tunes. Gibson Girl trios were named after the drawings of women by the turn-of-the-century illustrator Charles Dana Gibson. Gibson specialized in late-Victorian female archetypes (also called "Coca-Cola women"), and the women he drew were portrayed as decoratively stylish but also active and "modern." Gibson's creations were first memorialized in a song titled "Why Do They Call Me a Gibson Girl?" The first Gibson Girl trio contest was won by the Gay Nineties Trio from Manhattan, followed by the Floradora Girls and the Sewing Circle Girls from the Bronx in second and third place. Women's trios were expected to sing from the same list of Gay Nineties hits required of the men.

In 1939, once again, the judges formed a spontaneous "Parks Tonsorial Quartet," with Al Smith singing lead on "The Bowery," followed by the requisite "Sweet Adeline." The contests, by the way, were broadcast nationally on the Mutual Radio Network, providing the barbershop revival with its first national audience and raising the possibility that some heartland revivalists may have heard and been influenced by the broadcasts of the New York contests.

The Heartland Revival

The barbershop revival society took root and matured in a wide swath of the American heartland stretching from Tulsa and Oklahoma City, Oklahoma, to St. Louis and Kansas City, Missouri; Wichita, Topeka, and Kansas City, Kansas; Chicago, Decatur, and Springfield, Illinois; Sheboygan, Wisconsin; Detroit, Michigan; and parts beyond. This same region was thought of as the "gateway to the west," a network of roads and railroads frequented by traveling salesmen moving goods through the heart of the country. The traveling salesmen from the Midwest circuit were typically only a generation removed from small-town rural roots, and they formed a population especially sympathetic to the residual beliefs of the late nineteenth century that I have characterized as neo-Victorian, especially after the depression had ravaged the Midwest with bank closings and farm and business foreclosures.

At the center of each of the heartland cities was a hotel or a few hotels preferred by traveling salesmen. The Muehlenbach Hotel in Kansas City is glorified in the lore and legend of SPEBSQSA as the site where in 1938 two traveling businessmen from Tulsa, Rupert Hall and O. C. Cash, stranded by canceled flights, struck up an acquaintance and began singing barbershop songs in the lounge, inviting other hotel guests to join in. Bill Lowe, a singer from Tulsa, claimed to have had a similar experience with Cash at the Rice Hotel in Houston in November the same year,: "he suggested we pick up a lead and bass somewhere. We tried all the negro [*sic*] bellboys, but the new war crop aren't up on their duties, so Cash thought we ought to try the snooty Empire Room just off the lobby. In less than ten minutes we had a fair quartet going and one of the birds turned out to be a lead Cash had found by phone [through random or "cold" calling] in Baton Rouge, La., a year before."[27]

SPEBSQSA's founder, O. C. Cash (1892–1953), was born near Keytesville, Missouri, and moved with his family in 1898 to homestead in the Cherokee Territory, in what would later become Oklahoma. In the town of Blue Jacket, Cash played in the Silver Cornet Band. He graduated from Bacone College in Oklahoma, passed the Oklahoma bar, and enrolled in the army soon before the end of World War I. Cash went to work as a tax lawyer for Stanolind, a pipeline subsidiary of Standard Oil of Indiana. He became involved in a host of professional and social organizations, including the National Tax Association, the Oil Industries Information Committee, the Mid-Continent Oil and Gas Association, the Tulsa Chamber of Commerce, the Oklahoma Public Expenditures Council, the Presbyterian Church, Sons of the American Revolution, and the Tulsa Farm Club. This civic activity prefigured his organizing efforts for a barbershop society.[28]

After their nostalgic singing encounter at the Muehlenbach, Cash and Hall brought their idea back with them to Tulsa, where they held an open singing session. Their initial organizing letter, sent to acquaintances, served as a tongue-in-cheek platform for the founder's distaste for big government of the Roosevelt era. Cash wrote:

In this age of Dictators and Government control of everything, about the only privilege guaranteed by the Bill of Rights not in some way supervised or directed is the art of Barber Shop Quartet Singing. Without doubt we still have the right of "peaceable assembly" which I am advised by competent legal authority includes quartet singing. The writers of this letter have for a long time thought that something should be done to encourage the enjoyment of this last remaining vestige of human liberty. Therefore we have decided to hold a songfest on the Roof Garden of the Tulsa Club on Monday April 11, at six-thirty P.M. . . .

As evidence of the work that your Committee has done in this connection, we inclose [*sic*] a compilation of most of the good old fashioned Barber Shop Quartet songs which we trust you will look over and familiarize yourself with. Bring this list with you. It is our purpose to start right away in at the first, sing every song, in numerical order, plow right down the middle, and let the chips fall there they will. What could be sweeter than ten or twelve perfectly synchronized male voices singing "Dear Old Girl!" Just thinking about it brought back to your Committee fond memories of a moonlight night, a hayride and the soft young blonde summer visitor from Kansas City we dated on that occasion years ago.

Do not forget the date, and make every effort to be present, telephone us if convenient. We will have a private room and so will not be embarrassed by the curiosity of the vulgar public. You may bring a fellow singer if you desire.

Harmoniously yours,

O. C. Cash, Third Assistant Temporary Vice Chairman
Stanolind Companies
Phone 2–3211
RUPERT HALL, Royal Keeper of the Minor Keys
Braniff Investment Company
Phone 2–9121[29]

Cash's title parodied bureaucratic rank while that of his co-founder played with a Masonic idea of a keeper of the keys to the temple. Although many attribute the lengthy and tongue-in-cheek organizational name to a travesty of government aid programs, its most obvious precedent is in the complex nomenclature of the men's secret fraternal orders to which many of the barbershoppers belonged.

The initial meeting of what was to become SPEBSQSA was held at the Roof Garden of the Tulsa Club on April 11, 1938. The first four who showed up woodshedded the tune "Down Mobile" and "I Had a Dream." By the end of the night, twenty-six men had participated, and they called a follow-up session for May 2. One person in attendance later recalled, perhaps mistakenly, a suggestion to apply for $1.1 million from the WPA to produce a directory of barbershoppers around the country so that travelers would never want for singing company. The highlight of the second meeting was the reunion of a quartet that had sung together during World War I and that was capable of singing credible quartet arrangements of the African American songs "Shine" and "Roll Away Jordan." As Cash said, this group "knocked the boys in the aisles."[30]

Cash wrote a letter to the participants in the first two meetings soliciting song contributions for a tune book, starting with eighty-four for which Cash already had the words. Incorporating additional submissions, Cash and a friend who owned a printing press printed and produced the book for the third meeting, held at the Alvin Hotel on May 31. This meeting attracted 150 singers and created a traffic jam in downtown Tulsa. A reporter for the *Tulsa World* noticed the commotion, called in a photographer, and filed a story for the Sunday paper that was picked up by the Associated Press (AP) and United Press International (UPI) and carried throughout the country. Cash remembers this story as the first nationwide publicity for the young organization, publicity that resulted in a flood of mail from interested singers.[31]

In late 1938 Cash incorporated the Society as a nonprofit fraternal organization. The organization was initially called the Society for the Preservation and Propagation of Barber Shop Quartet Singing in the United States, which would have generated the initials SPPBSQSUS. Soon "Propagation" became "Encouragement" and "United States" became America, to accommodate the possible entry of Canadian chapters. In retrospect, Tulsa was an especially fascinating location for the birth of this movement because of the city's convoluted racial history and politics. In the early 1920s, Oklahoma had more black municipalities than any state in the union, and it had a reputation for promoting land ownership among blacks. But its image of tolerance was shattered in 1923, only fifteen years before the emergence of SPEBSQSA, when Tulsa erupted in one of the worst race riots in American history, riots directed against the thriving, middle-class black neighborhood of Greenwood.[32]

Cash's movement reflected the resurgent interest in Victorian mores and nostalgia. He was quoted as saying, "What this country needs is some good old-fashioned barbershop singing. . . . If we're trying to get back to normalcy, let's go all the way back to handlebar mustaches, horsehair sofas, and bicycles built for two."[33] And a few years later he wrote, "Only at our Society conventions do I find the genuine, old-time, small-town, neighborly affection and fellowship so manifest when our bunch gets together."[34] In an anonymous tribute in the *Harmonizer* entitled "Apostle of Harmony," Cash was praised for having "offered opportunity in part to *relive* the more carefree days, to conjure up old associations and events through the magic of song, and in so doing escape joyously for a too brief period from the problems and pressure of modern life."[35]

Whereas the Tulsa-based organization shared with the New York barbershop contests an attraction to nostalgia and an approach that bordered on historical reenactment, the rhetoric was more Victorian in its advocacy of fellowship and character. Barbershoppers (still) advertise for new singers with the phrase "looking for men *of good character*." The Society Code of Ethics still states that "(4) We shall accept for membership only *congenial men of good character* who love harmony. . . . (5) We shall exhibit a spirit of good fellowship toward all members."

O. C. Cash was passionately committed to the sound of barbershop singing and to the thrill of swiping chords. As his daughter Betty Anne Cash recounted:

I knew my dad was nutty on this business, and really a radical, but I didn't realize that men were still moved to tears. . . . [Now] even when they hit one of these high bell-tone chords, the audience doesn't go [*gasps*]; but my dad used to break into "Oohs" and "Aahs" because of the harmonics—and would cry; get out his handkerchief over certain chords that a quartet would do. . . . Or he would go up to a quartet that he liked and have them sing "Sweet Roses of Morn" [or] . . . "A Rose that Grows in No-Man's Land." . . . There were several phrases in it, the particular harmonics he liked. And he'd have them sing it over and over. They'd finish and he's say, "Hot damn, that's good! Do it again!"[36]

The young organization set out to overturn the vaudeville- and burlesque-based images of out-of-tune, drunken carousers singing harmony in the moonlight outside a barroom or under a lamppost. An article called "Musical Revival" that ran in a Detroit newspaper spoke of the effort to clean up the image of barbershop harmony: "In recent times burlesque renditions of 'Sweet Adeline' have had a repressive influence. Men who might sometimes have sung a song have turned on the radio rather than resemble an inebriated fellow in a top hat hanging to a lamppost. [SPEBSQSA] has set out to plow under the burlesque version, and it is succeeding. However, 'Down by the Old Mill Stream' is still in good standing."[37] Similarly, *Time* magazine carried an article on barbershopping that claimed: "Many a U.S. citizen finds it difficult to disassociate barbershop singing from barroom. Not so the S.P.E.B.S.Q.S.A. which rarely mixes liquor with its lyrics, explains simply, 'A drunk can't sing.' Equally proud is the society of the propriety of its songs, not one of which 'you wouldn't sing in church.'"[38]

Barbershopping was spread in the early or charismatic period in part by publicity, but more potently by the organizing efforts of O. C. Cash. Standard Oil allowed him considerable leeway in his business travels to meet with potential barbershoppers, and quite often SPEBSQSA chapters resulted. He printed membership cards and distributed them to anyone who inquired about the group, asking them to form their own chapter. Original members of the midwestern chapters worked for companies such as Phillips Petroleum, Standard Oil, Pan-American Airways, and those in the insurance industry. Initial chapter meetings were often held in the hotels of the salesman circuit and in the lodges of midwestern fraternal societies: Elks, Lions, Masons (Scottish Rite, Templars, Shriners), Rotary, Kiwanis, Odd Fellows, and others. The considerable overlap with fraternal orders was in turn organizational, philosophic, and symbolic. The Freemason orders emphasized honor, duty, fellowship, and morality. As initiates progressed up the complex ladders of advancement, they received moral instruction. Freemasonry focused on idealized masculine roles (craftsman builder, soldier, fool or jester, and priest) and its mythology and liturgy lack any direct reference to family, women, and biological fatherhood. Still, the pursuit of leisure and recreation outside of work represented a departure from strict Calvinist models of rugged manhood based on work and discipline. Describing the entrance to a lodge, Mark C. Carnes discussed the role of play and fantasy in the fraternal world: "As if by magic, late-Victorian America gave way to an ancient and exotic realm."[39] This realm provided fantasy escapes for Victorian men, replete with secret rites, handshakes, "ancient and exotic" symbols and myths, recitations, costumes, and paraphernalia. By the early decades of the twentieth century, following in the footsteps of the Scottish Rite Masons, many orders had constructed proscenium stages on which to mount elaborate initiation rituals that were coming to more closely resemble theatrical productions.

American fraternal orders entered the period of their greatest growth and influence in the period that barbershoppers refer to as the "golden age of barbershop" (1890 to 1920 or so). S. Brent Morris, a historian of Freemasonry, estimates that by 1920, half of the adult male population of the United States belonged to one or more of the eight hundred or so secret fraternal organizations. Many of the most elaborate of the lodges, temples, and cathedrals erected by these orders were in heartland cities such as Wichita, St. Louis, Indianapolis, and Chicago, where their appeal to the white middle class proved nearly universal. In its infancy, SPEBSQSA grew in the shadow of these men's fraternal business and mystic societies. Calling itself a fraternal organization and drawing from the same initial membership pool as American middle-class fraternal orders, SPEBSQSA drew on the obvious affinity between these two forms of association. It is likely that most of the early barbershop leaders were also members of one or more fraternal orders, which amplified the similarities between the two.

Fraternal orders influenced the symbolism, organizational structure, and ideology of the barbershop revival. Barbershoppers often addressed each other with the fraternal title of "brother." The name of the Society, while ostensibly a travesty of New Deal "alphabet" projects, also captures some of the spirit of the arcane naming practices of the fraternal orders (e.g., International Order of Fools, Grand United Order of Odd Fellows, and A.A.O.N.M.S. Shrine). The symbol of the barbershop movement, a barber pole superimposed on an ancient lyre, resembles the arcane symbols of American Freemasonry or those of its more mundane businessmen's cousins such as the Rotary, with the lyre representing a connection to ancient musical practices. The barber pole itself, a descendant of guild symbols, has a striking similarity to the Masonic symbol of the (nonstructural) entry posts to the Temple of Solomon, which are likewise surmounted with an orb.[40] Trade unions of the American labor movement adopted similar names, initials, and symbols, perhaps to coopt the organic solidarity of preexisting fraternities.

Many fraternal orders organized subsidiary women's auxiliaries (e.g., the Oddfellows' Daughters of Rebekah Lodge and the Masons' Job's Daughters), a strategy that carved out separate realms of participation. This was an ongoing issue for SPEBSQSA as well (see chapter 4 for a discussion of women's participation in the barbershop revival). In fact, the obvious success of fraternalism and barbershopping in American life can be explained as reactions to the same factors, notably the advancement of women into previously all-male domains. The fraternal orders and the barbershop society provided respites for male socializing in male domains grounded in mythologies of the past. As Kenneth L. Ames has said of Freemasonry, "Here was order in a changing world, in a comfortable and predictable environment free from the challenges and unease generated by women."[41]

The theaters of fraternal orders proved to be excellent venues for the early parades of quartets. For example, the Oakland County (Detroit) chapter had its 1943 Parade of Quartets in the Detroit Masonic Temple. The 1944 Peoria chapter "Show of Shows" took place at the Shrine Mosque, and the

Society's 1944 Championship Contest Finals were at the Detroit Masonic Temple. Some fraternal organizations sponsored quartets—for example, the Lions Club Serenaders and the Shriners Quartet.

An early SPEBSQSA president, Caroll P. Adams, wrote, "We have something that the country needs and wants, namely, an outlet for pent-up emotions and repressed musical desires, and, as Joe Wolff so often says, 'a haven for physically and mentally tired men who seek wholesome relaxation' with other congenial souls, who share each other's love of spontaneous and original vocal harmony. Just think how many social and fraternal groups would gladly trade what *they* have for what *we* have in the way of 'ties that bind.'"[42] A 1943 *Harmonizer* article called "Tulsa's Initiation Ceremony" directly paraphrased (and travestied) fraternal order initiation rites. The article consisted of a dialogue among four characters—a barbershop initiate, his sponsor, the Grand Keeper of the Minor Keys (G.K.M.K.), and the Recording Pole Striker (R.P.S.)—that included the following in high-mannered and emphatically formal Masonic prose:

G.K.M.K.—Brother Recording Pole Striper is there in our midst any of the profane who has applied for membership in this society?

R.P.S.—There stands with us Brother _____ who represents himself as being endowed with the gift of close harmony.

G.K.M.K.—I shall proceed to propound the five indispensable interrogatories.[43]

Following the first national articles on SPEBSQSA, *Reader's Digest* claimed, "Americans Have a Club for It: S.P.E.B.S.Q.S.A, Inc." and *Time* magazine noted that "No mere anything-for-a-laugh organization, SPEBSQSA takes itself fairly seriously."[44] O. C. Cash's recitation of celebrity members (including "honorary" members) of his still largely fictional organization was one of the hooks for generating coverage of the organization. A *Reader's Digest* article concluded that "Celebrities and unknowns, rich men and poor, have been drawn together in one of the most democratic organizations America has ever had." To the contrary, the organization was quite undemocratic in its first year, run individually and rather idiosyncratically by Cash with input from Hall and a few other close associates. Among celebrity members mentioned were the crooner Bing Crosby, the comedian Groucho Marx, five southwestern governors (including Colorado's Governor Ralph Carr), the St. Louis Cardinals owner Sam Breedon, the actor Pat O'Brien, the Treasury Secretary James Farley, American music specialist and radio host Sigmund Spaeth, and Major Bowes, host of the popular radio show *Major Bowes' Amateur Hour* (on which, in 1935, appeared the Hoboken Four, a quartet featuring a twenty-year-old Frank Sinatra). Bing Crosby announced the existence of SPEBSQSA on a Los Angeles radio broadcast, helping to drum up support for a Hollywood chapter, and the comedians Bud Abbott and Lou Costello joined the Passaic County chapter of New Jersey a couple of years later.

The first SPEBSQSA convention in 1939 hosted a quartet competition. A hundred and fifty competitors, including men from seventeen cities in seven states, attended. At a short business meeting during the convention, the singers took steps to ratify an organizational structure and elected a president, Rupert Hall. Cash retired into his role as "Third Assistant Temporary Vice Chairman" and was never again terribly active in the organizational affairs of SPEBSQSA, although he spearheaded efforts to bring the convention to the World's Fair in New York in 1940.

The first Society championship quartet was a group from Bartlesville, Oklahoma, called the Barflies. The group formed when a transplanted Briton named Harry Hall was asked to organize a minstrel show for the town of Pawhuska, Oklahoma. Hall recruited a local tenor, George McCaslin, to put together a quartet, and Hall was drafted for the lead voice. The half-quartet picked up a minstrel show end man named Herman Kaiser as bass and recruited a bank employee as baritone. The resulting group was a hit, and they decided to continue singing as the Bartlesville American Legion Minstrel Quartet. When O. C. Cash booked the group for a state teachers' convention in Tulsa, he renamed the group the Bartlesville Barflies.

SPEBSQSA soon received some unwanted attention from ASCAP (the American Society of Composers, Authors, and Publishers), which had been founded in 1914 to secure royalties from performances and recordings for copyright holders. In 1938 O. P. Erickson, an early SPEBSQSA leader, had revised O. C. Cash's barbershop songbook and printed three thousand copies. ASCAP, when it got wind of the distribution of copyrighted song material, informed Erickson and Cash that they were liable for $150 per song multiplied by the number of copies distributed. By Erickson's accounting, this amounted to $2,218,605. Cash and Erickson quickly destroyed the remaining copies and opened up discussions with ASCAP about compliance. Sigmund Spaeth, a member of both SPEBSQSA and ASCAP, offered to mediate, and he emphasized the fraternal and nonprofit orientation of SPEBSQSA to the ASCAP representatives. ASCAP agreed to license to the Society the right to perform ASCAP material gratis at Society events (despite the fact that SPEBSQSA charged admission at most of its events)— a courtesy that remained in place for over twenty years. SPEBSQSA also refrained from issuing arrangements of protected songs unless royalties would be paid. As a result of the Society's newfound consciousness of copyright, the *Harmonizer* began listing classic barbershop songs whose copyright protection had expired. These were then considered fair game for Society arrangers. However, two years later, Sigmund Spaeth felt compelled to remind SPEBSQSA leaders that their continued distribution of the books could result in substantial fines.

The ASCAP controversy, although it ended well enough for SPEBSQSA, challenged the very nature of the revival movement. The "founders" had not conceived of the barbershop revival as a fan club for commercial, professionally composed Tin Pan Alley pop songs. Rather, they thought of the "old songs" as an inheritance, as the soundscape of their adolescence, and

Figure 3.3. The Bartlesville Barflies, winners of the first SPEBSQSA quartet competition, in Tulsa, Okla., 1939. They stand in front of a painted backdrop of a barbershop below an awning featuring the name of the cofounder of SPEBSQSA, O. C. Cash. *Left to right:* George McCaslin, tenor; Harry Hall, lead; Bob Durand, baritone; Heman Kaiser, lead. Heritage Hall Museum of Barber Shop Harmony. Used by permission, Society for the Preservation and Encouragement of Barber Shop Quartet Singing in America, Inc.

as collective cultural property—fair game for amateur singers. The ASCAP threat clarified that, at least in the eyes of the law, an arrangement of a favorite song from 1917—and its performance in public without permission and payment—constituted theft. Even after the settlement, many members were resistant to treating "the old songs" as private property and not a public commonwealth.

"The World of Tomorrow"

When Cash was informed about the activities of the New York group in 1939, he incorporated the New York organization (despite its non-membership nature) as SPEBSQSA Chapter no. 1, sent chapter cards to them, and appointed Fiorello H. La Guardia as chapter chairman and Moses and Smith as vice chairmen. With his vision of SPEBSQSA as the national umbrella organization for all amateur barbershop activity, Cash managed to persuade the New York group to fold its efforts under the wing of the Society, despite the Society's meager track record (only one competition versus five for the New Yorkers, and much smaller audiences for the Tulsa competition). Cash had in essence pulled off a corporate takeover of a much larger and better-funded counterpart.

The "coup" was especially fortunate for the Society because the New Yorkers (especially Robert Moses) would soon have privileged access to arguably the greatest spectacle of the first half of the century, the New York World's Fair, organized under the supervision of Robert Moses. Moses's long-term goal was to create an infrastructure in Flushing Meadows for a permanent park, financed with proceeds from the World's Fair. Unfortunately for his plans, the fair proved to be a terrible financial failure, and the funds for a permanent park never surfaced.[45]

Cash and the New York chapter leadership planned a World's Fair barbershop contest that would attract the two regional streams of barbershop revival. As host to the competition and chairman of the U.S. Conference of Mayors, La Guardia sent out the barbershop invitational letter to his counterparts in cities and towns across the country. La Guardia wrote that he was

> deeply conscious of the honor bestowed on my city by its selection for the annual convention and national championship. . . . We expect the greatest gathering of barbershop harmonizers in the history of the world. Sponsorship of such civic leaders as you, each in his own community will put this thing over in a big way. . . . We move at a fast speed today, and the strains of "Sweet Adeline" bring back those nostalgic memories. I think that in these troubled times a bit of harmonizing will do some good to all of us. I eagerly look forward to the pleasure of greeting you and your quartets at the World's Fair this Summer.[46]

La Guardia's letter touches on the themes of harmonizing as a balm for modernity's ills and as a nostalgic escape from economic and political troubles (the residue of the Great Depression and the looming conflict with European fascism and Japanese militarism). Barbershop harmony played a role within the symbolism of the World's Fair as a whole, balancing the fair's emphasis on technological promise with the reassurance that modernity was big enough to incorporate the reassuring qualities of the past. (The World's Fair grounds, ironically, were literally built on the refuse of the past; Moses effected this transformation on a mountainous garbage dump surrounded by swamp in the Flushing Meadows section of Queens with nine months of around-the-clock work and a budget of $50 million.) Calling the Fair the "World of Tomorrow" and promoting it with the modernist geometry of its featured buildings, the Trylon and Perisphere, organizers were conscious to not glorify simple machinery (that would have been too close to the Nazi glorification of the technology of war). Rather, they hoped to combine the display of modernist achievements with a celebration of democracy and community that would symbolize a perfectible, progressive culture of the future. It was to be, therefore, a theme park dedicated to the marriage of technology and democracy.

Along with his letter to the nation's mayors, La Guardia enclosed a copy of rules and guidelines for the contest. On a few important points, the Tulsa organizers clearly held sway in policy matters. For example, women (New York's Gibson Girl trios) were barred from competition; this was to be an all-male event. The barbershop contest structure, however, remained under the supervision of the parks department, and the judges included many New Yorkers: La Guardia chaired the group, which included Moses, Harry Armstrong (composer of "Sweet Adeline"), Jack Norworth (composer of "Take Me Out to the Ball Game" and "Shine On, Harvest Moon"), the orchestra leaders Douglas and Raymond Paige; George P. Rea (president of the New York Stock Exchange), Cesare Sodero (a choral conductor), Frank W. Smith (former president of Consolidated Edison), and Luther Seward.

O. C. Cash arrived in New York on March 10, 1940, to begin planning the event. The parks department greeted Cash with an open house at their headquarters in Central Park featuring the St. Mary's Horseshoers singing "The Sidewalks of New York" and "The Bowery." The former governor Al Smith, dressed in brown bowler and striped jacket, jumped into the center of the group as a classic "fifth-wheel" baritone. Smith is quoted as saying, "I'm no judge of singing, but I like these barbershop quartets. They're a national institution."[47] Small intimations of the cultural divide separating the Tulsa network and the New Yorkers surfaced in a *New York Times* commentary at the time of Cash's visit to New York: "Now there are two schools of barber shop singers: the school to which Mr. Cash belongs, exuberantly enthusiastic over their own talent and natural equipment, and the school of Mr. Al Smith, to which we are disposed to lean. Members of the Smith school feel just as strongly about their ability as does Mr. Cash of Tulsa, but they wear a *genial mask of diffidence*."[48]

The competitions took place on a stage adorned with the Parks Tonsorial Parlor set and ran for four days and nights, from July 22 to July 25. Over twenty-five hundred audience members showed up for the finals, far fewer than had been coming for the New York City events in the past five years. Nonetheless, a national broadcast of the finals carried barbershop harmony to an audience of tens of thousands. La Guardia presented the first prize to an Oklahoma City police quartet, the Flatfoot Four, outfitted in their police uniforms, for their renditions of "Shine," "Annie Laurie," and "Roll Dem Bones."[49] The Second Prize went to the previous SPEBSQSA contest winners from Bartlesville, Oklahoma, by then called the Phillips 66 Barflies, who performed "Mandy Lee," "Just a Dream of You," and a medley. The Four Barbers of New York, all commuting businessmen, took third wearing handlebar moustache masks, and the fourth place finishers were another police group, the Kansas City Police Quartet. Although New Yorkers judged the contest, Midwesterners took home three of the top four prizes. The Flatfoot Four won Crosley radio-phonograph sets with a home recording device. The other eight finalists received smaller packages of radios and phonographs.

According to reports, "Mayor La Guardia was by far the most enthusiastic man in the audience. With his glasses up over his forehead, the Mayor kept time with his hands and feet and frequently sang to himself as the quartets offered old tunes that appealed to him."[50] But Cash, too, reveled in the attention paid to barbershop harmony. He was quoted as saying that SPEBSQSA "is getting more publicity than the Townsend Plan and certainly makes more sense."[51]

The alliance between the New York barbershoppers and those based in Tulsa lasted only a year. The split was a result of first and second place finishes for African American quartets in the New York competition on June 26, 1941, before an audience estimated at fifteen thousand. According to the reviewer from the *New York Times,* the Grand Central Redcaps' fourteen-year-old lead singer "captured the musical imagination of the judges as well as the assemblage when he led the quartet through a group of spirituals. Winning first place also earned the group the distinction of representing New York City in the national barbershop quartet singing championships at St. Louis next month."[52] The Grand Central Redcaps consisted of two brothers, Robert and Owen Ward (second tenor and baritone), their nephew Jack Ward (lead), and William Bostic(k) (bass). The teenager was a replacement for an older member who got sick before the competition, but the three older singers worked as redcaps, or porters, on New York trains. There is some confusion as to whether this is the same group as a well-known New York area recording and concert quartet called the Grand Central Red Cap Quartet, which recorded four sides for Columbia in 1931.[53] However, the credits for the 1931 songs are given to "Cloud, Smith, Garrison, and William Robinson," presumably the singers, and it is unlikely that the same group ten years later would have no original members and would be instead a family quartet. It is much more likely that the

Figure 3.4. Former governor of New York State, Alfred E. Smith, and the St. Mary's Horseshoers at the elimination competition of the National Barber Shop Quartet Contest, held as part of the 1939–40 New York World's Fair. After the eliminations the Horseshoers and a quartet from Canton, Ill., were tied for first place. Heritage Hall Museum of Barber Shop Harmony. Used by permission, Society for the Preservation and Encouragement of Barber Shop Quartet Singing in America, Inc.

latter group took the same name as the more famous and earlier recording quartet, a very common practice at the time.

In response to the news that a black quartet would be representing New York, O. C. Cash sent a letter and telegram to James V. Mulholland on Stanolind Pile Line company stationery. The letter read in part:

> I sent you a letter today after talking to Dr. [Norman] Rathert of St. Louis. The question of allowing colored singers to compete with others in the contests has been discussed a number of times at our meetings, and last year the board came to the conclusion that to keep down any embarrassment we ought not to permit colored people to participate. I hope this rule will not seriously embarrass you, as any other sort of arrangement would seriously embarrass us. Many of our members and chapters are in the South, where the race question is rather a touchy subject. Neither Dr. Rathert or I are narrow about such matters, but I know from discussing the matter with Doc and the St. Louis brothers that they do not want to get involved in a question of this kind. I hope you will be in St. Louis with the other quartets. I

Figure 3.5. A visit to Tulsa, Okla., by the popular New York–based quartet the Southernaires (with pianist) involved members of SPEBSQSA in facilitating plans for the group to perform. Here the Southernaires are pictured with members of the Tulsa Chord Busters, 1939. Heritage Hall Museum of Barber Shop Harmony. Used by permission, Society for the Preservation and Encouragement of Barber Shop Quartet Singing in America, Inc.

would particularly like to hear the Police Department Quartet again, as I consider them one of the best I have heard.[54]

Cash's last comment was tantamount to a request to substitute the New York City Police Department Quartet for the Grand Central Redcaps. The New York response was equally quick. Robert Moses wrote to O. C. Cash:

The first and second quartets were composed of colored men. The judges took their duties seriously and even insisted that the four leading quartets sing a second time before the final decision was reached. We are now informed by your recent letter and telegram that colored quartets may not compete in the National Finals in St. Louis. If we had known this before we should immediately have dropped out of the national organization, a step which we are now compelled to take. It is difficult for me to see any difference between your national ballad contest and a national track meet in which colored men run in relays or compete individually. This is not a social event, but a competition, which should be open to everybody. Let me add that if American ballads of Negro origin are to be ruled out of barber shop singing, most of the best songs we have will be blacklisted. . . . Along with many others who found pleasure in the harmless amusement of American ballad contests, I am very sorry that this sour note has marred our pleasant harmonies.[55]

Al Smith also sent his resignation to Cash with a denunciation of racism. This was, of course, not Smith's first run-in with racism in Oklahoma. In his presidential campaign a little over a decade earlier, Smith had encountered, upon his arrival in Oklahoma, a line of burning crosses, signs left by the Ku Klux Klan protesting the "papist" candidate. In response to the Klan, Smith delivered his famous speech confronting religious intolerance the next day at the Oklahoma City Auditorium. The following night, the auditorium filled for an evangelist speaking on the theme of "Al Smith and the Forces of Hell."[56]

Cash was quoted in the *St. Louis Sun-Times* as having said, "I don't know why Brother Smith and Brother Moses raised the race issue except to embarrass us."[57] He argued that SPEBSQSA should be considered a public trust but rather a private social organization and should therefore be free to discriminate in issues of membership. He also argued that the more important issues were that the Redcaps were not members (of course, SPEB-SQSA rules prevented blacks from becoming members) and that they sang Negro spirituals rather than barbershop.[58]

A popular black radio jubilee quartet from New York, the Southernaires (Homer Smith, Lowell Peters, Jay Stone Toney, and William Edmonson), had visited Tulsa in 1939, the same year they first recorded for Decca. The Southernaires were the stars of a national weekly NBC radio broadcast, "The Little Weather-Beaten Whitewashed Church." A *Detroit Tribune* article from 1939 lists among the fans of the group "every loyal member and sympathizer of the Barbershop Quartet Singing Society of America [*sic*], who could no more resist the soft, close harmony of the four Negro singers than a swing addict could close his ears to Benny Goodman's clarinet."[59] Cash and his barbershop chapter hosted the group and appealed to a local hall to help secure their performance space (the appeal was necessary because the hall was being denied on the basis of race). SPEBSQSA was at that time a "separatist" organization with a charter requirement that members be "white men of good character." SPEBSQSA's support of the Southernaires and their extension of "honorary membership" to the group were cited as evidence that the movement was not racist, but SPEBSQSA members also insisted that the close-harmony arrangements of the Southernaires, other jubilee groups, and the Redcaps were not "barbershop." Soon after the Redcap incident, the Southernaires sent a letter of support to SPEBSQSA despite having received mail from fans asking that they distance themselves from the white barbershop organization.[60]

Moses, Mulholland, and the other organizers of the New York contests split from the Tulsa-based organization and continued their American Ballad Contests for Barber Shop Quartets as an unaffiliated event. SPEB-SQSA's divorce from the New York Chapter was at least partly mended after the war. In 1946 the Bronx chapter held a minstrel show advertised in the *Harmonizer*, and in intervening years the New York City Police Quartet competed at SPEBSQSA events.

The audiences declined in New York during wartime but were still significant (fifteen hundred in 1942, for example), and the parks department continued to hold the contests into the late 1960s. In 1942 the St. Mary's Horseshoers grabbed first place, a Bronx group called the Paramount Four took second (aided by a furlough for the group's drafted lead tenor), and a Bronx-based African American group, the Calliopes, took third. New York made its own concessions to the war effort, holding a parallel contest for the best military service quartets; it was won by a Coast Guard quartet stationed at Ellis Island.[61]

Not surprisingly, there is little mention of the independent New York contests (either before the founding of SPEBSQSA or after the "porter controversy") in SPEBSQSA publications, and New York was largely written out of the standard histories of barbershop revival, all of which begin institutionally with the founding of SPEBSQSA. The rise of these two tendencies in barbershopping, their mutual influence, their convergence at the 1939–40 World's Fair, and their separation over the issue of racism constitutes one of the defining social contests in the history of the American barbershop revival.

The improvements in the economy in the late 1930s led to a resumption of recordings of African American harmony quartets, both secular and gospel. The most popular jubilee quartet of the era was the Golden Gate Quartet,[62] which recorded for Bluebird in 1937 and continued recording until at least 1943 for a number of labels. They also released radio transcriptions (prerecorded programs) for the War Department during World War II. The Golden Gates were known as a spiritual quartet, but they also recorded many secular close-harmony songs such as "Sweet Adeline," "My Bonnie Lies Over the Ocean," and "Way Down upon the Swanee River."

Tag: Separate but Equal Harmony

An epidemic of nostalgia, neo-Victorianism, and nativism spread throughout America of the 1930s under conditions of a depression and the pervasive cultural and social changes of the Popular Front period. Growing out of a sustained interest in old songs and group harmony that percolated in networks of enthusiasts in the 1920s and 1930s, a movement for organized barbershop performance took hold in two geographical regions, and partisans of quartetting in both regions turned to competitions to focus interest in the form. The rapid efflorescence of barbershop quartet singing in the late 1930s and 1940s provided a cultural confirmation that the progressive politics associated with the Roosevelt reforms were encountering (and helping to engender) a widespread, simmering dissatisfaction and a longing for times of security, comfort, and privilege.

There were, in fact, significant symbolic differences between the two regional tendencies. The "heartland" revival hearkened back to small midwestern Victorian towns for the symbolism and visual iconography of the movement. The New Yorkers traded on images culled from vaudeville and from fondly remembered ethnic tenement neighborhoods. The quartet of Mulholland, Moses, Smith, and La Guardia provided this tendency with powerful patronage from the city's ethnic power brokers.

In its earliest years, SPEBSQSA was concerned with putting some distance between their brand of barbershop and the various African American barbershop-related forms. As a result, race became—at least to many of the heartland revivalists—a distinguishing factor in determining whether a performance actually was "barbershop." White groups might qualify even if they sang spirituals or songs that were not stylistically barbershop. It was certainly not possible to exclude an African American repertory or songs in a minstrel (blackvoice) style, for these formed a large part of the backbone of the barbershop canon. Black quartets, however, found themselves excluded from the genre as it was being defined and consolidated by the revivalists, even when singing material clearly in the barbershop mainstream. The social drama enacted by the New York chapter and the Society over the so-called porter issue provided a taste of the many conflicts over race that would roil the barbershop movement in the decades following World War II.

4

On Main Street, U.S.A.

In blissful dreams, sweetheart, it seems
One is never sad and never lonely
And if you'll come with me to stay
We'll live in dreamland night and day
—"Meet Me Tonight in Dreamland";
words by Beth Slater Whitson,
music by Leo Friedman, 1909

World War II intervened early in the life of this revival movement, transforming it in profound ways. This first section of this chapter chronicles the response of the barbershop movement to the military conflict, to the struggle against fascism, and to the emergent postwar global conflict between capitalism and communism. The second deals with issues of growth and conflict within the barbershop organizations. I close with a look at various treatments of barbershopping in popular culture, which include, among other things, close harmony's flirtation with the cowboy image and country music and its iconic status in radio, films, musicals, and theme parks.

War and the "Spirit of Harmony"

Barbershop adherents became noticeably more serious about barbershopping during World War II and the cold war. Edwin S. Smith, president of SPEBSQSA in 1953, noted that "the job of dignifying that somewhat frivolous title [SPEBSQSA] and making it a title of respect has been one of the fascinating and purposeful tasks of our Society. The name was the product of one era of American history. The effort to *recapture something American to the core* was suggestive of another era."[1]

Barbershoppers felt some need to defend the practice of singing barbershop harmony during a war, in a climate of military mobilization, rationing, and self-sacrifice. Society publications and sympathetic press portrayed barbershop quartet singing as a patriotic service, an example of the

115

kind of America that our troops were fighting to preserve. Following the Detroit Convention of 1942, the columnist George W. Stark wrote in the *Detroit News:*

> Skeptics may demand to know why, with the whole world at war, a great body of our citizens from coast to coast takes time out to converge on a given point and dedicate a whole week-end to singing. If you had been here, you would have found the answer. This is it: This is America. This is what the totalitarian viewpoint would consider a curious manifestation of the American way of life. This is the Rotary Club, the Board of Commerce, Broadway, Woodward Avenue and Main Street, singing out of its heart. This is the industrialist, the banker, the baker, the factory worker, the soldier and the sailor running the scale of human emotion for democracy. This is the *token of the essence of our country,* something that has been hard won and which will not be easily surrendered. This is something rare and precious that couldn't happen today in Germany or Italy, and there was a time when the little people of those countries could and did sing. They were happy then. But it can and does happen in America and it's a fine thing to put a special emphasis on it right now, because it dramatizes the very thing for which we fight.[2]

Stark's world of barbershop singing is sentimental ("singing out its heart") and non-classist ("the banker, the baker"). To Stark, barbershop harmony is neither disposable pop culture nor a simple leisure-time hobby, but something "hard-won and . . . [not] . . . easily surrendered," an "essence" of America. His view that barbershop is peculiarly American and fundamentally opposed to totalitarianism expands on older rhetoric about American values in barbershopping, yet the tone was a long way from Cash's awshucks, self-deprecatory, lighthearted moralizing of the early revival.

The Society passed patriotic proclamations and encouraged quartetting in the armed services. Quartets played for the troops stationed at home and for bond drives, parades, patriotic services, and war chest solicitations. Chapters were encouraged to recognize publicly those members in military service and to keep in touch with members overseas. Chapters were instructed to begin rehearsals with "America" and close with "The Star-Spangled Banner" while facing a "prominently-displayed flag." Society President Hal Staab urged barbershoppers to "do everything they can to stimulate among the people of our nation a proper spirit and morale during the tremendous emergency through which we are now passing."[3]

The 1942 Grand Rapids SPEBSQSA convention proclaimed in a telegram to President Roosevelt that "nothing stimulates patriotism so much as good singing." They pledged their "wholehearted and steadfast support in the prosecution of this war for liberty. We assure you of our continued effort to stimulate a proper spirit and morale among the people of this great country that we all love so well. We sang our way through the last war,

Figure 4.1. Many of the eleven finalist quartets of the St. Louis Convention, Kiel Auditorium, 1941. This convention was the subject of the well-publicized dispute with the New York Chapter over segregation. It was also the first convention to be held in wartime. The Tulsa Chord Busters, winners, stand in the center flanked by the Rice Brothers, the Four Harmonizers, the Capitol City Four, the Bartlesville Barflies, the Misfits, the Harmoneers, the Harmony Kings, the Kansas City Barberpole Cats, and either the Detroit Turners or the Sawdust 4. Heritage Hall Museum of Barber Shop Harmony. Used by permission, Society for the Preservation and Encouragement of Barber Shop Quartet Singing in America, Inc.

and we will do so through this one. God bless you." They then passed a resolution that "there will be no 'rationing' of Barbershop Harmony, that there will be no 'ceiling' on, or cessation of, barbershop quartet singing for the duration, and that a top 'Priority Rating' will be given to all singing which may, or even might, assist in keeping up the morale of the fighting forces, war workers and citizens of this good free Nation of Ours. Our Society intends to cooperate whole-heartedly and take its part in the War Effort."[4]

In 1944 the Society agreed to raise $1.2 million in the seventh war loan issue for the U.S. Treasury Department war bond campaign committee in order to finance the construction of two B-29 Superfortress bombers (the *Harmonizer* described them as "planes that are blasting the important cities and industrial centers of Japan quite off the map"). The two planes

Figure 4.2. Winners of the 1942 contest in Grand Rapids, Mich., the Elastic Four stand on a stage that combines SPEBSQSA's iconography with that of the war effort, including the Allied flags on top of the acoustic shell. *Left to right:* Herman Struble, tenor; Roy Frisbie, lead; Jim Doyle, baritone; Frank Thorne, bass and manager. Heritage Hall Museum of Barber Shop Harmony. Used by permission, Society for the Preservation and Encouragement of Barber Shop Quartet Singing in America, Inc.

were christened "The Spirit of Harmony" and "Close Harmony."[5] An issue of the *Harmonizer* was given over to the war bond drive, and the cover featured a full-color portrait of a B-29 tail assembly.

The last two SPEBSQSA barbershop quartet competitions of the war were held in Detroit at the Masonic Temple. Owing to crowded trains and the lack of motorcars, the war committee had limited conventions at this time to fifty people. Only twelve finalist quartets were permitted to emerge from four regional preliminary competitions so as to adhere to the overall limit on participants. The audience was restricted to 4,400 locals.

By war's end there was enough barbershop activity in the military to hold competitions in certain theaters of military operations, as evidenced by the MTOUSA (Mediterranean Theater of Operations United States Army) competition of 1945, won by the Dukes of Rhythm. Enthusiasm for quartetting could be found at all ranks. According to Bing Crosby, General Dwight Eisenhower, supreme Allied commander of the European theater, was a fan of barbershop harmony. As Crosby recalled, "We had luncheon with General 'Ike' and his staff, and since he liked to sing barbershop harmony, we got up a quartet. 'Ike' sang baritone."[6] Many African Americans participated in the armed forces quartets, and with one exception, the only African Americans appearing in the *Harmonizer* during the entire period covered by this chapter were in the photo spreads of armed forces quartets, some of which were black or integrated. (The exception was another nonmember quartet, a quartet of blind high school students, the Brailleroaders, with an African American tenor.)

In the aftermath of the war, with America's foreign policy increasingly dominated by a showdown with communism, the barbershop leader Deac Martin counterpoised barbershopping's balance of "rugged individualism" and "collective discipline" to Soviet culture:

> Impromptu part-singing characterizes much of the individualism which is so typical of the United States and Canada. When [singers disagree on harmony] . . . American individualism goes ragged as well as rugged, while listeners look for ear plugs. But, after everyone has had his say, we agree, "*That's* the chord," and we hope. . . . Good barbershopping requires self discipline so that no voice stands out. A protagonist of socialism might twist that to indicate that barbershopping is socialistic rather than "American." But, I said "self" discipline, tough though it is for the "American" temperament. Furthermore, anyone who would call barbershopping socialistic never attended a quartet rehearsal where each member of a foursome really takes his hair down, and democratically tells the other what he thinks. The way I see it men elsewhere have been shot for less.[7]

President Harry S. Truman had dabbled in barbershop quartet singing since his army days during World War I, and harmony singing was apparently his only musical activity other than his well-known piano playing. In 1946 Truman accepted an invitation to join SPEBSQSA as a paid member of the Kansas City Chapter.

At Truman's 1948 inaugural, the D.C. Singing Capital Chorus performed Frank H. Thorne's "Keep America Singing." The Society had adopted this to signal their dedication to homegrown singing as a nationalist and patriotic service. In 1949 the savings bond campaign committee and SPEBSQSA held a contest to generate a theme song for the bond campaign. Judges included the bandleader Fred Waring, the singer Perry Como, and the songwriter Oscar Hammerstein II. They selected a revision of "Keep America Singing" retitled "Keep America Saving."

With the occupations of Europe and Japan, the chief of the Army Recreational Service and the chief of the Music Section visited the 1949 SPEBSQSA International Convention in Buffalo and spoke to the international board.[8] Their proposal that SPEBSQSA assist the army in organizing quartets resulted in a joint "Operation Harmony" program to teach and disseminate quartet singing in the ranks. A SPEBSQSA trainer drilled thirty-five recreational officers in barbershop harmony, and the Society prepared barbershop harmony kits for the armed forces that included recordings, issues of the *Harmonizer*, songbooks, and barbershop memorabilia; these were distributed to over 750 military bases and posts. This initiative grew into the Armed Forces Collaboration Project.

Quartets began to tour Armed Forces posts in 1950, and within a couple of years the Harmony Halls had toured Germany and Austria, and the Buffalo Bills visited Germany, Japan, and Korea. Other quartets, including the Mid-States Four, the Cardinals (Madison, Wisconsin), the Schmitt Brothers (Manitowoc, Wisconsin), and the Clef Dwellers (Oakland county, Michigan), all participated in tours. Women's quartets toured as well.

Society members contributed to the program to compensate quartets for lost income, hoping that the touring program would spark quartet organizing in the ranks and bring many new barbershoppers into the Society's fold. SPEBSQSA's leadership resisted pressure from the military to subsume barbershop tours under the USO (United Servicemen's Organization) because they feared it would make their performances mere morale-building entertainment, similar to the vaudeville-like tours of comedians and pin-up girls. The military leadership did not understand the distinctions SPEBSQSA was making between participatory singing and spectator-oriented entertainment, and the two organizations eventually parted ways.

Radio and recordings introduced the barbershop revival to mass audiences during and after the war. By the early 1940s, Decca, Columbia, and Victor Records had produced albums of 78 rpm recordings. Decca released an album featuring the Bartlesville Barflies, the New York Police Department Quartet, the Commuters, the Beacon Four, and the Kansas City Police Quartet. Columbia's *Barber Shop Melodies* contained eight recordings of the Flat Foot Four of Oklahoma City, and Victor recorded the Springfield, Illinois, group the Capitol City Four.[9] In 1944 the Barber Pole Cats and the Chicago Harmonizers cut records for radio use only, to be distributed by World Wide.

The Frankenmuth Beer company (Frankenmuth, Michigan) sponsored a barbershop harmony program on WJR in Detroit to encourage listeners to recycle bottles during the war. The disc jockey began with recordings of the Fireside Quartet, but he eventually introduced close to three hundred barbershop recordings into rotation and brought Society quartets, including the championship Doctors of Harmony, to Detroit for live broadcasts.

The *Harmonizer*, launched in November 1941 under the short-lived title *Barber Shop Re-Chordings*, was the glue holding together the national movement. The quarterly publication carried arrangements, news about competitions and conventions, musical instruction ("The Barbershop Craft"), news from the chapters ("Swipes"), and running columns by key figures such as O. C. Cash ("The Founder's Column"), Deac Martin ("The Way I See It"), and Sigmund Spaeth ("The Old Songs").

Active chapters generated performances, which further popularized the Society. For example, the Manitowoc, Wisconsin, chapter boasted about the activity of one of its quartets: "We find them entertaining at the Lions Club in Brillion, the Manitowoc Grocers Association banquet, Chamber of

Commerce and wives in Kiel, Madison Parade, Kiwanis Ladies' Night Banquet Victory Bond Rally, Christmas broadcast over station WOMT, the Two Rivers Wisconsin Farmers' and Business Men's meeting and last, but by no means the least, the First Wisconsin State Contest in Milwaukee Auditorium . . . [where they] received bronze medallions awarded by the Kingsbury Brewery."[10] Multiply that level of activity by hundreds of quartets in scores of chapters over months and years to ascertain the impact of SPEBSQSA quartets and chapters on daily life in the United States and to understand the wide range of community-based contexts afforded quartets for performance.

The increasing seriousness of barbershopping also inspired Deac Martin to campaign against blue humor and the perpetuation of vaudeville-style racial and ethnic comedy. In his view, barbershopping was due for some "house cleaning" if it were to have a shot at mainstream acceptance. In a similar spirit, the 1948 SPEBSQSA Code of Ethics admonished quartets to "keep it clean and keep it sober."

As early as 1942 the Society promised that "we shall use our gift of barber-shop harmony as a means of rendering altruistic service in and to our communities." This marked a break with the movement's first few years, when the motivations of barbershoppers were by and large recreational. After the bond drives of the war years, the Society turned its attention to philanthropy. In this, they relied on a model established by the fraternal orders (such as the Shriners, Kiwanis, and Rotary). As the Society's president, Hal Staab, wrote, "The Society will be one of the most favorably known *Service Organizations* in the nation. Our Founder, O. C. Cash, will become as well known as is Harris of Rotary and Prince of Kiwanis."[11]

In 1949 SPEBSQSA raised over $50,000 and distributed it among various causes that included music scholarships and high school bands. By 1964 SPEBSQSA had revised its decentralized approach in favor of giving to a single, societywide charity, the Institute of Logopedics (a hearing loss and speech therapy organization), and SPEBSQSA adopted the slogan, "We sing that they shall speak."

Modernity and Its Dis-Chords

Early barbershop revivalists had sought to restore fellowship, community, and participatory music making in American life. To achieve organizational success in the decade after the start of World War II, however, Society officers enacted efficient staffing procedures, bookkeeping and budgeting, market analysis, public relations, advertising, newsletters, bylaws, budgets, a tiered system of competition, adjudication rules, educational programs, choruses, musical literacy programs, a headquarters, a staff, and a member benefits program—in other words, a full-blown modern American bureaucracy. The increasing emphasis on institutional growth and rationalism was anathema to some of the traditionalists. Much of the dissention in the ranks of the barbershop societies in the postwar years

had its roots in this fundamental debate over values—whether fully articulated or not.

In order to reach out to new members and to spread the word about
SPEBSQSA and barbershopping, SPEBSQSA initiated a collaborative program with the Music Educators National Conference to introduce barbershop harmony in the grade schools, and the Society developed a school-
friendly educational packet, "A Music Educator's Introduction to
Barbershop Harmony." For internal education, the Society produced two
"sound slidefilm" presentations in 1955–56 called *Balance and Blend* and
Voice Expression, using a short-lived technology that combined a 35-mm
projector and a 33⅓-rpm record player in a single piece of equipment.
SPEBSQSA published a series of books of arrangements called *Songs for
Men* and created an "Old Song Library" in 1947, asking members to donate
and bequeath collections of sheet music. A "Harmony Heritage Song Series" in the *Harmonizer* issued arrangements of songs that had recently
lost their copyright protection.

Internal education efforts met scattered resistance from singers who
longed for the simpler, more informal approach to singing. According to
the arranger and educator Val Hicks, "Too many of us, including myself,
have put a great deal of emphasis on barbershop craft when the average
chapter member didn't want it and doesn't need it. The most important
thing is that they're having fun with their singing and they feel a sense of
musical achievement within their own chorus or quartet."[12]

After 1939 the annual conventions emerged as the focal points of the
barbershop calendar. Competition, of course, is not a neutral practice; it
has profound consequences for the structure of the organization and for
the sound of the music.[13] Adjudication systems circumscribe style and rein
in departures, even while emphasizing the exceptional and virtuosic performances by which one group rises above the others. In other words, it is
seldom the normative or the average performance that succeeds in competition. In the social organization of expressive culture, competition provides transcendent goals, builds team cohesion, allows some performers to
achieve immortality by joining the list of champions, and gives certain performers the right to speak for a tradition. The degree of commitment to the
competitive model is one of those issues that perpetually divide the ranks
of barbershoppers.

An organization built on barbershop competitions departed from what
Deac Martin characterized as a "casual, free-wheeling, sheer fun-loving,
recreational hobby." The *Harmonizer* carried an exchange between Martin
and the arranger Frank H. Thorne about the merits of competition. According to Martin, "It should be evident that the parade of quartets heard
in Peoria did their best just for the love of it. I don't think any one of them
would have sung any better had a gold mug, a thousand dollar bill, and a
world's championship plaque been dangling before their vision. In other
words, in the case of a good quartet, they don't need any incentive to do
their best." Thorne demurred: "I refuse to admit that the same enthusiasm
can be maintained if no championship award is provided . . . [or] that we

can expect the same inspiration from a parade of quartets as we would get having a contest. . . . The American spirit is based on competition."[14] Some rank-and-file barbershoppers cherished the thrill of competition: "No one can taste the full flavor of the Society unless he has sung in a quartet and entered a contest. There's a heart-warming glow that spreads to the other three guys—for being 'on a team.' There's the thrill of locking a chord and hearing it ring. There's the feel that your singing is 'on' and that the audience is with you. There's the thrill of busting a song wide open after a long lay-off. There's the intolerable suspense of waiting to hear if your name will be called for the Finals."[15]

The first decade of Society competitions (1939–48) served as a shake-down cruise for the evolution of contest rules. At the 1942 convention in Grand Rapids, Michigan, sixty quartets competed, subject to the following adjudication criteria: harmony accuracy, 25 percent; song arrangement, 25 percent; voice expression, 30 percent; song selection, 10 percent; and stage appearance, 10 percent. In 1944 a Gay Nineties costume prize was added to the musical prizes. Contest preliminaries were held for the first time, and the fifteen highest point winners went on to the finals regardless of which preliminary they competed in. The Society dispensed with song selection as a judging category but forbade religious and patriotic songs and allowed judges to deduct points for inappropriate lyrics. Quartets had two songs or six minutes, whichever came first, to make their case. They were judged by eight specialist judges and four alternates. Two judges graded each major category: harmony accuracy, 300 points; voice expression (blend, etc.), 300 points; arrangement, 300 points; stage presence, 50 points; and costume (same judges as stage presence), 50 points.

The 1948 Oklahoma City Convention brought new rules. Modern harmony songs were forbidden, performances had to end on a major tonic chord, entrances and exits were to be included under stage presence, melodies could not be altered beyond recognition, and only very occasional chords without a high tenor melody could be countenanced. A five-point penalty would be assessed for every passage in which the melody was not fully harmonized, and the same penalty also applied to passages sung with simple humming accompaniment. Starting in 1948, the Society began to train judges and to screen them using a rigorous testing battery that included a Johnson Temperament Analysis Test (elsewhere used for employment screening and career counseling).

Despite their emphasis on fellowship, barbershoppers enshrined competition as a major feature of organizational life. As a result, barbershoppers have come to understand that the evaluative criteria for judging—rules, categories, and point systems—are the principal means of shaping barbershop performance and style. One persistent conflict revolves around the priority assigned to competition, and another around the criteria by which barbershop singing is to be judged.

The 1943 Chicago International Convention witnessed the debut of the Corn Belt Chorus, with 150 members from the Illinois chapters of Bloomington, Canton, and Peoria. By 1946 a SPEBSQSA survey revealed a surprising level of interest in the still relatively rare chapter choruses. Chorus proponents argued that choruses built confidence in inexperienced singers, sustained repertory, encouraged practice, developed public interest in barbershopping, and encouraged fellowship. In general, they provided the context for rapid growth, and they were thus the foci for a large portion of the Society's educational efforts.

SPEBSQSA had not been intended by the founders to be an organization of "mass sings" but of barbershop *quartets*, and many of the early or traditionalist members objected to this turn of events. Cy Perkins, a SPEBSQSA member since 1939 with the Misfits (the International Champion Quartet in 1945) lamented, "it seems to me that in the last several years the chorus movement has become so hefty that it is crowding out of the picture the singing unit that our founder, O. C. Cash, had in mind. I refer of course to the barbershop quartet . . . hasn't too much emphasis been placed on the chorus?"[16]

In 1952 SPEBSQSA initiated international competitions for choruses as well as quartets, although it debated reversing this decision owing to the expense of moving large choruses en masse to the international convention. Choruses helped to rapidly increase membership, providing a powerful argument in their favor among Society leaders. By 1953 SPEBSQSA membership had reached a plateau of 30,000, and for many years gains in new memberships were balanced by chapter dissolutions and lapsed individual memberships. Chorus proponents have, over the years, often advocated dropping the word "quartet" from the Society's name in order to publicize the organization's embrace of both quartets and choruses. Arguing that the phrase "barbershop quartet" had become a recognizable and valuable brand name for the Society, Deac Martin wrote that it was necessary to keep the "brand which sets this Society apart from all other singing associations."[17]

The woodshed, the place where cords (read "chords") were "chopped" (rehearsed or extemporized), gave its name to the informal ear singing of barbershop harmony. In the early days of the Society, quartets typically worked their way through songs with each singer finding an acceptable harmony for each melodic note, an approach dubbed "catch-as-catch-can." Although there were hundreds of sheet music arrangements available for quartets (and some books as well), most early members read little if any music notation. Many Society members maintained an attachment to the informal woodshedding approach of the early revival and opposed the introduction of sheet music.

In 1941 the arranger and bass singer Frank Thorne formed a quartet he called the Elastic Four for the stated purpose of winning the 1942 International Convention contest. The three additional singers were auditioned (using sight-read parts) and trained by Thorne, and the quartet performed Thorne's written arrangements. All four members had previous singing experience (church choirs, light musical comedy, college quartets, and vaudeville). The success of the Elastic Four at the 1942 contest sent shock waves through the organization. More-complex arrangements—by necessity written down and requiring more specialized arranging talent—looked to be the new competitive norm. Thorn also raised the pitch of his group's songs to intensify them, creating a new appreciation for high tessitura among barbershoppers. The group's other innovation was to stress the sonority of each chord, although this had the effect of further weakening barbershop harmony's reliance on more traditional and stepwise voice-leading. The Elastic Four's innovations were chalked up to the "Encouragement" side of the Society's mandate, elevating the level of barbershop singing rather than just preserving it.

Max Brandt has noted that some old-timers referred to the process of teaching fully formed arrangements (with no woodshedding possibilities) as "artificial insemination."[18] In 1943 Deac Martin waxed about the old days of "catch-as-catch-can" in which singers "thought of method and atmosphere as well as result," but he admitted that writing arrangements down helped to transmit them to future generations and could result in new "harmony that we just didn't know existed."[19] This controversy broke out in the President's Column in 1947 as the then-president Charles M. Merrill took the woodshedders' side, stating that his original idea of barbershopping was "four men in a corner working out harmony by ear and instinct: working it out as they went along. No audience; no distractions; no written arrangements. They sang it and worked it out the way it was *fun* to sing—not the way it was 'supposed to be sung.' . . . The source of its popularity—the reason for its revival by O. C. Cash—was its appeal as *participation* music, not as audience music."[20]

Woodshed advocates within the Society established an official "Woodshed" room with "no organized quartets allowed" at the annual convention in Buffalo (1949). The program became the responsibility of a group of ex-directors of the Society, who called themselves the Association of Discarded and Decrepit Board Members. For many old-timers, the woodshedders' room was a return to core barbershop values, but for the Society, it was a means of forestalling a split in the organization. Woodshedders eventually formed an interest group within *SPEBSQSA* called the Ancient and Harmonious Society of Woodshedders (AHSOW).

By 1949 over 30,000 barbershop singers belonged to two organizations (SPEBSQSA and the Sweet Adelines—see the following section). For serious barbershop quartets, the road to success now passed through the international competitions sponsored by the barbershop societies. Champion and medalist quartets moved to the top of a pyramid of sponsorship by barbershop enthusiasts, charging fees for appearances at local parades of quartets, civic clubs, and men's fraternal lodges. After 1953 medalist performances were released by Decca Records, and winning quartets might find work in radio and television commercials.

The Society ethics statement declared, "We shall not permit or tolerate the commercialization of the Society in any manner whatsoever," yet competitive success for the elite quartets in the amateur barbershop societies created the conditions for professional or semiprofessional employment. Barbershop revivalists were forced to consider how their amateur activities could coexist with professional and semiprofessional quartets. The Society determined that professional quartets could be members of the Society, but that the title "society quartet" would be reserved for amateur groups (defined as having at least three members for each of whom vocal performance generated no more than 50 percent of income). Non-society quartets were prohibited from participating in contests and from using the Society's name in performances.

Many of the conflicts that have stirred the men's barbershop society have been rooted in tensions between authenticity and expediency. The support for "authentic" forms of barbershop singing mirrored a dynamic prevalent in music cultures throughout the world—especially those that had been heavily impacted by modernity and commercialism—in which various criteria for success (appeal to the greatest numbers, standardization, improved audio quality, etc.) are counterpoised to authenticity, requiring "grittiness," a close connection to the community of origin, and a connection to the past. In modernizing musics all over the globe, fans argue about "selling out," "crossing over," and authenticity. Discussions over barbershop authenticity continued to cycle back to the image of impromptu, informal quartets singing in mythologized barbershops and street corners. All of these controversies in the barbershop movement were articulated and on the table by the early 1960s, but they have continued to pull barbershop enthusiasts in conflicting directions ever since.

In 1957 the Society negotiated the purchase of a building to serve as the international headquarters in a lakeside mansion in Kenosha, Wisconsin, for $75,000. Eventually named Harmony Hall, it housed the Old Songs Library (at the time the second largest collection of pre–World War I popular music), offices, meeting spaces, and the Barbershop Museum. The purchase of Harmony Hall allowed SPEBSQSA to centralize education efforts, bringing groups together for leadership training, judges' clinics, choral workshops, and arrangers' workshops.

A Foursome of Her Own

World War Two introduced a vast number of women into the workforce and into public life, and male exclusivity was becoming more difficult to police, even in bastions of traditional values such as in the barbershop revival. During the war a handful of women's quartets appeared as featured performers at SPEBSQSA parades of quartets and conventions. A performance by the Barberettes of Peoria, Illinois, and the Johnson Sisters of Chicago at the SPEBSQSA Chicago chapter in 1942 caused members of the Peoria chapter to protest the (rumored) admission of women to the chapter, as reported in the Associated Press. The same two women's barbershop quartets performed at the 1943 Chicago Society convention. The Barberettes, the Johnson Sisters, the Blendettes (from Muskegon, Michigan), and the Charmerettes (from Jackson, Illinois) all entertained at the 1944 men's convention. Although the Barberettes were of recent origin, the

Johnson Sisters had been singing barbershop since 1928 (at which point the sisters ranged from twelve to fifteen years of age), when they learned their first song, "Sweet Kitty Dooley." The Barberettes all worked during World War II—two in defense, one in a department store, and one in wholesale jobbing. One was the daughter of a prominent male barber-shopper (most women in early barbershop quartets had at least one male relative in SPEBSQSA).

For all of the discomfort evident in the men's reaction to the female quartets, many men considered the early women's quartets to be talented and entertaining, and the women's quartets performed actively on the men's parade-of-quartets circuit. One advertisement in the *Harmonizer* designated the Johnson Sisters as the "*mascots* of the Chicago Chapter," linking or claiming them while at the same time distancing them from the men. In advertising the appearance at the Chicago Convention of the Johnson Sisters and the Barberettes, the *Harmonizer* proclaimed that the two groups were "still shopping—BARBER shopping, youse guys!"[21]

The women's quartets occasioned spirited debates. Should the women's groups be allowed to join SPEBSQSA? And if not, what should be their relationship to the men's Society? Among women barbershoppers, there was as yet no clear consensus about whether to try for: SPEBSQSA membership, affiliation with SPEBSQSA as a women's auxiliary similar to those of the men's fraternal orders, or a separate organization. A few men supported outright integration of the organization, but most male barbershoppers' reactions to female barbershopping ranged from patronizing support for a separate organization to outright disdain and opposition to the very notion of female barbershop singing. Opponents of women's membership in SPEBSQSA cited the necessity to perform close harmony in single-sex quartets as the primary musical rationale for separate societies, but most were also openly protective of the space SPEBSQSA sanctioned for all-male socializing.

At the 1945 SPEBSQSA Convention, Edna Mae Anderson approached many of the wives of barbershoppers to inquire about their interest in singing. She elected to start a women's society in her hometown of Tulsa, the same city that had nurtured the men's Society. On Friday, July 13, 1945, just about a month before the end of World War II, Anderson called an organizational meeting in her home, where she and the others planned a group sing and chapter inauguration for July 23 at the Hotel Tulsa (the birthplace of the men's group).

O. C. Cash supported the move (indeed, his daughter was involved in it), but his support of a separate women's organization was simultaneously a defense of his own all-male organization. Cash wrote a description of the women's early efforts—playing with derogatory stereotypes (tongue, as always, firmly in cheek)—in his Founder's Column of August 1945:

It's the wimmin again! For some time we have heard rumblings of a proposed women's auxiliary to our Society. In Detroit this June, I am told, misguided women of Michigan, Illinois, Indiana and Ohio, probably others, ribbed up the Oklahoma girls to start the movement in Tulsa and I'm damned if they ain't done it. With little or no publicity they called a meeting at which about 75 gals showed up—just twice the number we had here in Tulsa at our first get-together. . . . So I am going to ask all you brothers to write me suggesting names for the girls' organization. They won't ever be able to agree on that. So we must help them. Hal has suggested "The Bustleers" and "The Corse-teers." I think "Sweet Adelines, Ltd." or "Floradoras, Inc." would be more appropriate. After we get them named, we'll start naming their quartets. They will have trouble with that too. Now we have had so much fun during the past seven years and our Society has been such a joyous, happy one that it is a shame this had to come up just when we were getting along so peacefully. I am bewildered, confused, and all messed up, besides being upset. Hoping you are the same, I am [signed] O. C.[22]

Cash's suggestion just slightly preceded the adoption of the name "Sweet Adelines" by the women's group. As a result of the name choice, the women's barbershop movement was named for the classic object of men's affection in the most famous barbershop tune of all time. Cash's alternate name for the women's group came from an early (1900–1902) Broadway revue, *Floradora*, which featured a women's vocal sextet called the "Flo-radora Girls" on the hit song, "Tell Me Pretty Maiden, Are There Any More at Home like You?"[23] The original Floradora singing was not in four-part harmony, so it can be inferred that it was the elegant, late Victorian fash-ions of the Floradora girls that helped to make them an archetype for women's barbershoppers (see the material on the "Gibson Girl Trios" in chapter 3). After the revue closed on Broadway in 1902, it traveled around the country as a touring show. The first logo for the new women's harmony organization was a rendering of four of these Floradora Girls.

On August 15, 1945, just days after the atomic bombs fell first on Hi-roshima and then on Nagasaki, the Tulsa women formed the Atomaton Chapter of a still-hypothetical national organization, Sweet Adelines in America. Edna Mae claimed that the chapter name came from the "atom" of energy that the women brought to singing. For many years afterward there were rumors that Sweet Adelines would become a women's auxiliary of SPEBSQSA, but there was little support for this within SPEBSQSA. The first performance of a Sweet Adeline quartet was the appearance by the Floradora Girls (quartet) at the Tulsa Hi-Twelve Club luncheon on Sep-tember 18, 1945.

Membership in the chapter grew quickly to eighty-five members by the end of 1945. By 1950 Sweet Adelines had over fifteen hundred members in thirty-five chapters (which included sixty quartets) in fourteen states. Most of the group's attributes—national competitions, education, service, and chapter organization—followed the model established by SPEBSQSA. Sweet Adelines held their first national convention and contest in Tulsa in October 1947, attracting quartets from Tulsa and Bartlesville (Oklahoma);

Figure 4.3. The original logo of Sweet Adelines Inc. Used by permission.

Chicago, Decatur, and Peoria (Illinois); and Kansas City (Missouri)—a geographical range similar to that of the early men's Society. Helen Seevers, a newspaper reporter from St. Louis, was elected president. As legend has it, Seevers scoured the audience for judges fifteen minutes before the competition, recruiting three members of Sweet Adelines and two members of SPEBSQSA. The first convention's medalists were the Decaturettes (Decatur, Illinois); the Johnson Sisters (Chicago); the Keystone Barberettes (Peoria); the Voca-Lizas (Bartlesville); and the Floradora Girls (Tulsa). The 1948 convention took place in Topeka, Kansas, with the Johnson Sisters taking first place, and in 1949, Sweet Adelines launched their own national newsletter, the *Pitch Pipe*, which is still published.

The existence of a women's organization did not forestall all efforts to integrate SPEBSQSA by gender. In 1948 a Chicagoan, Patricia Vance, sued SPEBSQSA over its policy of not admitting women. The suit petitioned the court to order SPEBSQSA to "associate women in its activities and thereby add dignity, charm and good singing, necessary in the perpetuation and development of quartet singing."[24] The suit was dismissed "for want of equity."

Between 1946 and 1957 the women's organization garnered significant national media attention. The Floradora Girls were flown by CBS to New York to perform on the radio show *We the People* in 1946, and *She* magazine featured the Sunbonnet Sues. The Charmerettes issued a three-record album in 1947 on Wolverine Records ("Specializing in barbershop quartet recordings"). The Nota-Belles joined a U.S. State Department tour of Korea, and an article in *American Family* magazine featured the Tune Twisters. Outside of the Chordettes, who were not affiliated with Sweet Adelines, the most visible women's barbershop group in the 1950s was the Big Four (Chillicothe, Illinois), winners of the 1953 championship. Their media and concert credits include twelve weeks on the Arthur Godfrey Show, appearances on shows hosted by Jack Paar, Steve Allen, and Dave Garroway, and a performance with Liberace at the Chicagoland Music Festival. Recordings of Sweet Adelines medalist quartets in 1955 and 1956 were issued by Decca, but Archie Blyer's Cadence Records picked up the series starting in 1957.

The organization—and women's barbershopping in general—got a boost from a 1963 episode of *The Lucy Show*, a successor to *I Love Lucy*. In the episode, Lucille Ball convinces her friend Vivian Vance and her Women's Volunteer Fire Department barbershop quartet (called the Four Alarms) to allow Lucy to replace the group's former lead. With regional finals scheduled for a week away, Lucy engages a voice coach, Dr. Gitterman (the character and comedic actor Hans Conreid) to help with her breathing, posture, vowel formation, and projection—with vaudevillelike slapstick results. Lucy's voice (really an alto) is weak, but their old-fashioned arrangement of "By the Light of the Silvery Moon" requires her only to half-speak the verses and to sing the "call" lines in the chorus to which the other three voices respond. Overcoming debilitating stage fright, Lucy and her Four Alarms stage a winning performance with a nice trio swipe and a dramatic tag. To Lucy's horror, their prize is the right to sing in the finals in New York City "televised from coast-to-coast and seen by the entire nation"! The real organization was not mentioned by name, but the contest structure made clear that Sweet Adelines was indeed the model.

Sigmund Spaeth's arrangement of "Sweet Adeline," adapted for women's voices by Floyd Connett and Bob "Buzz" Haeger, became the official theme song of the organization in 1955. Many other men, such as the arrangers and directors Ozzie Westley and Floyd Connett, played important roles in the first decades of the organization (when male directors of women's groups were the norm), and it was decades before Sweet Adelines jettisoned the expectation of being coached and directed by men. Another residue of the male origins of the revival is the use of the TTBB designation for women's voices. In the women's barbershop organizations, sopranos and altos—although singing in women's ranges—classify their voices using the men's terms, and, as in the arrangements for male voices, the second tenor (second soprano) generally sings the melody.

Although gender issues were not often made explicit, many Sweet Adelines recognized that participation in barbershopping generated certain contradictions for women. The barbershop canon comprised songs written primarily from a male subject position, reflected in the choice of pronouns, women's names, and the nature of the situations described in the narrative. What were the choices possible for women barbershoppers? They could avoid songs with an obvious male subjectivity and restrict the repertory to songs that were not gender specific;they could perform songs such as "I Want a Girl Just like the Girl That Married Dear Old Dad" with a sense of irony, claiming the men's songs for women's public performance; they could perform the same songs without a hint of irony in a straight-ahead homage to the "old songs"; they could change the lyrics to reflect a female subjectivity (replacing pronouns, names, and even plots); or they could write, commission, or arrange new songs more appropriate for women or borrow them from contemporary popular music.

Over the first few decades of its existence, Sweet Adelines chapters and quartets tried all of these approaches. As a result of the "pronoun problem" (my term, not theirs—really a much larger issue of female subjectivity and male-oriented texts), Sweet Adelines has always exhibited a greater willingness to experiment with repertory and to admit songs and arrangements that are less obviously "barbershop" than those allowed for competition by SPEBSQSA. Although Sweet Adelines International grew to a peak of over 35,000 members by 1985, expanded to many foreign countries (Netherlands, Japan, Canada, and others), and instituted many educational efforts, they were never able to fundamentally alter the public perception of barbershopping as a normatively male activity. Articles about the organization still often proceed from the angle that "it's not just men who sing barbershop."

Close(d) Harmony: Boundaries, Margins, and Diversity

In the first few decades of the barbershop revival, the issue of race surfaced in conflicts over membership, repertory, historiography, and the continuing penchant for minstrel-style performances. The controversy over the Redcap Porters quartet and the subsequent emphasis on an all-white organization exposed an undercurrent of racism in the Society. SPEBSQSA was certainly not alone in its segregationist stance (at first formalized in chapter charters and later de facto), but it did retain a segregated posture for some years into the 1960s.

Throughout the 1940s and 1950s, some SPEBSQSA chapters continued to perform minstrel shows in blackface. For example, the Wilmington, Delaware, chapter presented annual blackface minstrel shows starting in 1941 called "Minstrelsy as It Used to Be." The show featured a traditional semicircle of performers with six "end men," a bones player, and a tambourine player, and it included contortionists, tap dancers, two barbershop quartets, and an interlocutor. In 1942 the SPEBSQSA National Committee on Chapter Means and Ways released a fundraising primer suggesting thirteen ways to raise funds, including minstrel shows.[25] In 1946 the *Harmonizer* advertised minstrel shows in Michigan and Kansas. A chapter in Minnesota mentioned its "forthcoming Black Minstrel show, which will be presented in the high school auditorium on January 11 in cooperation with the Junior Chamber of Commerce. Much publicity is being given through the press, radio, and movie shorts and a packed house is expected on 'Jubilee' night."[26] For the Hutchinson, Kansas, chapter's "mammoth minstrel show" in 1946, scores of blackface chorus members lined up on stage underneath a giant, broadly smiling black minstrel caricature framed by giant dice (props drawn from the "coon" gambler and layabout image in the song "Roll Dem Bones").

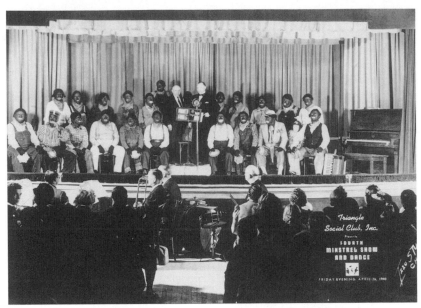

Figure 4.4. Fourth Annual Logan Square Minstrel Show, featuring
the Logan Square Quartet, in Chicago, 1940. This performance was produced
by the Triangle Social Club and may have taken place at the Logan Square
Theater on North Milwaukee Avenue. Heritage Hall Museum of Barber
Shop Harmony. Used by permission, Society for the Preservation and
Encouragement of Barber Shop Quartet Singing in America, Inc.

Just as SPEBSQSA debated the question of race from the 1940s until the
1970s, so did Sweet Adelines. Apart from the "race question," Sweet Adelines had experienced many of the same tensions over centralization and
choruses that SPEBSQSA had. The board of directors was self-electing,
and some disgruntled members campaigned to democratize the organization. The split occurred after the 1957 convention in Miami, at which the
outgoing board introduced a resolution to restrict membership to Cau-
casian women. Sweet Adelines had no black members, and no one was
aware of any black singers who had petitioned to join the organization.
Still, the board argued that there had always been a tacit agreement about
racial exclusion and that it was time to formalize this policy by writing it
into the by-laws. In the aftermath of the convention, chapters split, quartets broke up, members resigned, and arguments ensued at all levels of the
organization.[27]

A gag order was imposed by the board, barring any further discussion of
the issue. Unable to address their dissatisfactions within the organization,
starting in July 1958 a number of northern chapters dropped out of Sweet
Adelines, including chapters in Rhode Island, Massachusetts, and Ontario.
Representatives from these chapters met in Providence, Rhode Island, to
start a new women's barbershop society that would be more democratic in

nature and unrestricted by race. They founded Harmony Incorporated, incorporating in February 26, 1959, with Peggy Rigbie, a former director of Sweet Adelines, as president. The group adopted the motto "A blend with friendship" soon thereafter and introduced a newsletter called *The Key-Note*. By 1962 chapters had formed (or converted from Sweet Adelines) in Vermont, Illinois, and Wisconsin. In 1963 an Ottawa, Ontarios, chapter of Sweet Adelines accepted a black member and was threatened with expulsion. Harmony Incorporated held its midyear meeting in Toronto and recruited the chapter, attracting a great deal of Canadian publicity along the way. In addition to their stand on race, Harmony Incorporated also developed a reputation for stressing a more traditional barbershop repertory. Two other competing organizations formed from the ranks of Sweet Adelines: a short-lived Society of Women Barber Shop Quartet Singers in America (SWBSQSA) and an unaffiliated British group, the Ladies Association of British Barbershop Singers (LABBS), which is still in existence.

In 1963 the racial question in SPEBSQSA was relegated to "chapter option" status, meaning that chapters were free to do as they pleased. Performing in blackface was banned by SPEBSQSA by the 1970s, but elements of the minstrel legacy persisted. The repertory still contains the bulk of blackvoice southern pastoral or Dixie songs and most of the early ragtime and coon songs. These songs may have their texts expunged of their most objectionable terms (such as "coon," "darky," and "nigger") but many contain references to "mammies" and "strummin' banjos" and other conventions of the minstrel and coon songs. A recent barbershop convention featured a competition medley of "Darktown Strutters' Ball" and "Bill Bailey, Won't You Please Come Home?" in which the quartet enacted all of the gestural and choreographic conventions of Al Jolson's blackface minstrel act without the blackface. This one performance included exaggerated cross-legged stepping with hands cocked downward and out in front of the body or hands held palms forward on either side of the head and shaken back and forth (watch old footage of Jolson in blackface and you will understand what I mean). Many in the audience may have missed the connection, but these gestures were part of a deeply rooted minstrel tradition.

Minstrelsy presents an enduring challenge to the "preservation" mission of the barbershop societies because so many songs of the era were products of a culture industry that demeaned, infantilized, and stereotyped blacks. It is not an accident that oppressive racial laws were named for the minstrel character Jim Crow or that some anti-black riots were blamed on minstrelsy. And yet, much of America's enduring popular music was formed in this cradle of racial intolerance. How then can barbershoppers preserve the old songs and not preserve the old racism? This is a question to which I will return in the conclusion of this book.

Throughout the late 1940s and 1950s, a renaissance of harmony singing in America was spurred on by gospel, rhythm and blues, and jazz vocal groups. One of the leading groups, the Mills Brothers, had deep roots in barbershop music. John Mills Sr. was a barber with his own barbershop in Piqua, Ohio. He was also an accomplished quartet singer, performing for many years with the Four Kings of Harmony. His four sons, Herbert, Donald, Harry, and John Jr., born between 1911 and 1915, showed early promise as vocalists and started their own harmony quartet, Four Boys and a Kazoo, when the smallest was only three years old. They were contracted to perform on two local sister radio stations, WSAI and WLW. A year later, playing their debut at the Piqua Opera House, John Jr. realized on stage that he had forgotten the kazoo. Trying to rescue the situation, he improvised a kazoo sound with his voice. The popularity of the imitation convinced the brothers to experiment with other instrument sounds, and this quickly became a trademark of the quartet, as on their 1938 recording "Caravan." The group also popularized an active bass part dubbed the "talking bass," which can be heard clearly on their 1932 recording of "Rocking Chair" for Brunswick Records.

The brothers sang on radio under a number of aliases for different sponsors, leaving for the CBS radio network around 1930. They were the first African American group to make a national network commercial program (for a product called Vapex) and later sang on programs sponsored by Crisco and Elgin Watch. By late 1931 they were recording for Brunswick, which released their first big hit, "Tiger Rag," in 1931, with Bing Crosby (the reverse side was the barbershop favorite "Nobody's Sweetheart"). They traveled for an extended series of performances in Great Britain at the Palladium, including a royal command performance. John Jr. died while in Great Britain, at which point the remaining brothers considered breaking up. Then John Sr. stepped in to replace his son.

The Mills Brothers always kept a stable of barbershop songs in their repertory—songs such as "Put on Your Old Grey Bonnet," "Sweet Roses of Morn," "Peg o' My Heart," "Sweet Adeline," "Ida, Sweet as Apple Cider," "You Tell Me Your Dreams, I'll Tell You Mine," "When I Wore My Daddy's Brown Derby," and others. However, their two-volume set of barbershop ballads for Decca in 1949, *The Mills Brothers Famous Barbershop Ballads* (D 9–49), made their affinity for barbershop a public affair. They followed this up in 1957 with an LP called *The Mills Brothers in Hi-Fi: Barbershop Ballads* (DL 8664). The Mills Brothers sang a consistently mellow and low-key close harmony on their barbershop recordings, accompanied by a plucked or strummed guitar. Their crooning style, frequent use of humming accompaniment, and solo verses skirted the emergent definitions of barbershop popularized by SPEBSQSA, yet their full four-part harmonies on choruses lay well within the bounds of barbershop—Jay Warner aptly describes their style as "pop-barbershop." *Barbershop Ballads* even contained a tribute song to SPEBSQSA called "The Barbershop Quartet," by D. Manning. While they did not "bust tags" in the same fashion as Society quartets were beginning to do, they did include many subtle swipes, such as at the end of the first and last lines of "Down in the Old Neighborhood" by William J. McKenna, a nostalgic ode to "neighborly neighbors and pals" and "the old neighborhood."

Neither of the Mills Brothers' barbershop albums was mentioned in Society publications except in advertisements placed by the recording com-

Figure 4.5. Cover to the long-playing record *Barbershop Ballads*, by the Mills Brothers. Decca Records. Used by permission, Universal Music Group.

panies, and the dominant perspective in SPEBSQSA appears to be that the group did not sing "barbershop." Deac Martin said, "I like the harmony of the Andrews Sisters, DiMarco Sisters, Mills Brothers, and the Ink Spots, but it is not 'barbershop' even though it is close harmony."[28]

The Mills Brothers were one of the most often cited influences by early rhythm and blues (and doo-wop) vocal harmony groups. Another example of an African American quartet with a barbershop sound was the Four Fellows, a 1950s-era group from Brooklyn that patterned its sound originally on the Mills Brothers. The group's leader learned to sing barbershop harmony from his father, who sang with the Dunbar Barbershop Quartet. The Four Fellows were known for a mellow style of vocals, in evidence on their 1955 hit "Soldier Boy," with its audible connection to barbershop. Other 1950s and 1960s rhythm and blues vocal groups with roots in barbershop included the Hilltoppers, who started out singing barbershop harmony at Western Kentucky State College, and the world-famous Jordanaires (a black gospel and barbershop quartet, best known as the back-up vocalists for Elvis Presley on recordings, in movies, and on television until around 1970).

Of the many twists and turns taken by close harmony in the twentieth century, a few led to the singing of the southern mountains and the western plains. Exposed to the currents of close harmony throughout the nineteenth century, the rural South was home not only to shape-note singing conventions but to quartet tours sponsored by gospel publishing companies such as J. D. Vaughan (Lawrenceburg, Tennessee), the Hartford Company (Arkansas), and the Trio Music Company of Texas.[29] Family harmony singing for gospel and country songs proliferated throughout the region, especially a "brother" style of close and high harmony. Bill and Charlie Monroe, Ira and Charlie Louvin, Ralph and Carter Stanley, Jim and Jesse McReynolds, and many others carried this "high lonesome" harmony tradition into what would become known as bluegrass music, following the ensemble model of Bill Monroe's Blue Grass Boys. Bill Monroe sang many lead verses with his group, but usually took the high harmony on the choruses. Most of these harmonies featured a high and reedy lead voice harmonized still higher by the first tenor, and often supported below by a baritone or (more rarely) a baritone and bass. In general, this was a duet and trio close-harmony style.

Many country singers of the rural South were aware of the fad for the myth and lore of the American west in the 1930s and followed Jimmie Rogers in reshaping their images as "western" singers. Close-harmony singers were not far behind. In particular, many were engaged in the Hollywood western films of the 1930s through the 1950s. Two Illinois farm girls who sang close harmony, Molly and Dolly Good, were repackaged as the Girls of the Golden West.[30] Gene Autry, the "Singing Cowboy," was accompanied in some of his films by barbershop-style quartets. The Ohio-born Leonard Slye (better known as Roy Rogers) formed a close-harmony vocal trio called the Pioneer Trio, which in 1934 was renamed the Sons of the Pioneers. The trio grew into a quartet with the addition of the bass singer and fiddler Hugh Farr. The tenor Lloyd Perryman replaced Rogers when the latter embarked on his solo movie career. "Cool Water," "Tumbling Tumbleweeds," and other Sons of the Pioneers hits demonstrate a smooth close-harmony style tinged with jazz stylings and a "western ambience" accompaniment. The Sons of the Pioneers and the Riders of the Purple Sage convinced moviegoers that cowboys were natural harmonists, at home with close-harmony singing on the range around a campfire.

By the 1950s barbershoppers recognized a number of subgenres of close harmony. Barbershoppers spoke of "modern" (jazz and pop), "glee club" (triadic harmonies and melodies harmonized below the lead), "spiritual" (black), and, of course, barbershop quartets. Traditionalist barbershoppers, such as Maurice "Molly" Reagan, advocated vigilance to ward off modernizing influences. Reagan wrote, "There is a third group—the Modernists—who persist in trying to force their dissonant harmonies into our singing activities. They are no Barbershoppers in any sense of the word. We in the society must be constantly on the alert to stamp it out as soon as it appears. 'Eternal vigilance is the price of keeping our "P" in 'Preservation.'"[31] It may be of some interest to barbershoppers that a number of pop, jazz, and rhythm and blues vocal groups, especially those most respected for their revolutionary impact on harmony, had roots in the barbershop sound.

One of the most influential vocal group harmony pioneers in the 1950s was the Four Freshmen, a (white) group from Indianathat started out as a barbershop quartet called Hal's Harmonizers. "Decked out in Gay '90s apparel (arm bands, exaggerated false moustaches, and waiters' aprons) the quartet began singing 'Sweet Adeline' at fairs and conventions until they became bored with the confinement of barbershop chords. Not wanting to give up the income base they became a second group, the Toppers. As fans of Stan Kenton they began using diminished and augmented chords, creating a jazz vocal style, and sang at local malt shops near the school."[32] In other words, the quartet imitated extended chords, despite being able to muster only four singers. The group experimented with voicing chords in various inversions and with octave displacement so as to spread the formerly close harmony out widely. The result was a very jazzy harmony, which could be described as a barbershop-meets–Stan Kenton sound.

The Four Freshmen were a seminal harmony group not because of their few hits but because of their influence on such popular groups as the Hi-Los, the Modernaires, Manhattan Transfer, the Beach Boys, the Lettermen ("Goin' Out of My Head"/"Can't Take My Eyes off of You" medley), the Mamas and the Papas, Frankie Valli and the Four Seasons ("Cherie," "Rag Doll,"), the Chaperones, and the Happenings ("See You in September," "Go Away, Little Girl"). In short, groups indebted to the Four Freshmen contributed some of the most attention-grabbing and distinctive harmonies in all of pop music over two decades. Admittedly, it was often the departures from close harmony that helped to mark these arrangements as revolutionary and arresting; nonetheless, barbershop provided the ground or foundation from which these innovations sprouted.

Barberpop (Four Case Studies)

The postwar era, between 1946 and 1960, represented a zenith of visibility for the barbershop revival movement and the period in which barbershop quartets became a trope or a rhetorical device in the media and culture industries. As a result, one can speak of the emergence of barberpop (a pop-cultural manifestation of barbershopping used to signify Gay Nineties nostalgia). In 1946 the *Fibber McGee and Molly Show* devoted an entire broadcast to barbershop harmony. Starting in 1947 the Mutual Broadcasting Network carried the Society's international competitions, and in 1954 they were picked up by CBS and heard by an estimated one million listeners. Winning quartets from the conventions appeared on *Arthur Godfrey and His Friends*, Ed Sullivan's *Talk of the Town*, the *Lawrence Welk Show*, *Ted Mack's Amateur Hour*, and in newsreels shown in movie theaters before feature presentations.

In 1948 the cartoonist Chester Gould added a "Mumbles Quartet" to his Dick Tracy strip. In this sequence, the notorious (and speech-challenged) criminal Mumbles created a sham quartet to entertain at parties. The group entertained the rich and absconded with their valuables. SPEBSQSA members objected, with one noting that "Mumbles and his pals are an obnoxious reflection on the institution of barber shop quartet singing. . . . He is a villain who runs his words together."[33] After all, this was a singing society that prided itself on precise articulation and that would later adopt the slogan, "We sing that they may speak."

The Flying L Ranch Quartet in Hereford Heaven

The Flying L Ranch Quartet began as the Bartlesville American Legion Minstrel Quartet, which O. C. Cash renamed the Bartlesville Barflies (see Chapter 3). The Barflies took first prize in the inaugural Society competition in 1939 and later picked up a sponsor, changing their name to the Phillips 66 Quartet (under which name they placed third in both the 1941 and 1942 championships).[34]

In 1943 two members of the quartet went into the armed services. The remaining two, George McCaslin (tenor) and Harry Hall (lead), were asked to form a quartet for a Wichita barbershop show by the baritone Bill Palmer, who also recruited the bass Fred Graves of the Okie Four (a group that had included SPEBSQSA's founder, O. C. Cash). The reconfigured quartet performed in Wichita as the Mystic Four (note the Masonic reference), but on the way to perform at the Chicago SPEBSQSA International Convention in 1943, they adopted the name The Mainstreeters (they placed third once again in the competition).

From a spot on a radio show called *Hey Rube*, the Mainstreeters launched their own weekly Tulsa-based radio show on KTUL, which could be picked up hundreds of miles away. The quartet was asked to play a Red Skelton bond drive show in Hollywood in early 1944, and in two consecutive programs at the Convention Hall and the Coliseum Hall, they preceded Skelton, entertaining a combined audience of 10,000.

Soon after this they were "discovered" by Governor Roy Turner of Oklahoma while they were singing at the Tulsa Club. A rancher by profession, Turner and his close friend (and fellow rancher) Bill Likins adopted the group. Likins took over as manager and renamed the group the Flying L Ranch Quartet after his own ranch in the cattle-rich region of southern Oklahoma called "Hereford Heaven." Both Turner and Likins were prominent members of the breeders group the Hereford Heaven Association. In September 1945 Victor Records released the group's four-record album, which included their theme song, written by Governor Turner, "Hereford Heaven," and another Turner homage to Hereford cattle called "Beau Blanc Visage" (Beautiful White Face). Backed by the powerful governor, the members of the Flying L Ranch Quartet found themselves acting as musical ambassadors for the Hereford Heaven Association, the governor, and the state.

The connection to the governor paid off handsomely during the next summer (1946) as western movie star and singing cowboy Roy Rogers prepared to shoot the movie *Home in Oklahoma* and agreed to feature the quartet. Rogers invited the quartet to sing at his wedding to Dale Evans,

Figure 4.6. The Flying L Ranch Quartet in 1946 with Roy Rogers and co-managers Governor Ray Turner and Bill Likins. *Front row (left to right):* George McCaslin, tenor; Roy Rogers; Bob McCullough, lead. *Back row (left to right):* Bill Likins; Bill Palmer, baritone; Fred Graves, bass; Governor Ray Turner of Oklahoma. Heritage Hall Museum of Barber Shop Harmony. Used by permission, Society for the Preservation and Encouragement of Barber Shop Quartet Singing in America, Inc.

which took place at Likins's Flying L Ranch. In April 1947 the Oklahoma City chapter of SPEBSQSA held a parade of quartets and invited barbershoppers from across the nation to a "ranch frolic and barbecue" hosted at the ranches owned by the governor and Likins in the "Heart of Hereford Heaven."

The Flying L Ranch Quartet subsequently played at campaign stops for the governor's successful reelection campaign. They sang at the inauguration ceremony in January on the steps of the state capitol and at the inaugural reception, where the governor sang with them. The group's second shot at national exposure was at the inauguration of President Harry Truman in 1949, where the Flying L Ranch Quartet represented Oklahoma, sang at inaugural banquets and balls, and rode in the inaugural parade on the Oklahoma state float.

Hereford Heaven was the first of a group of postwar films featuring barbershop quartets that culminated in 1962 in the film version of *The Music Man.* In 1952 the famed vaudevillian George Jessel produced a misty-eyed film called *Wait till the Sun Shines, Nellie,* about a small-town barber whose personal tragedies mirror the loss of innocence in twentieth-century America.[35] The protagonist is deserted by his wife, who moves to the big city, and his son joins a vaudeville troupe only to wind up a gangster. The barber later fights in the Spanish-American War and after returning home succumbs to the temptations of alcohol. Eventually he modernizes his barbershop to keep up with the competition. In part because of his modernization, he ends up consumed with memories of simpler times. As a reviewer noted, "the wholesomeness of the small town is indicated in neighborly deeds and the occasional harmonizing of a barber-shop quartet."[36]

The Chordettes on The Arthur Godfrey Show

The Chordettes may have been the last quartet whose origins lay in barbershop harmony to have become pop stars with top-ten hits, although its major hits were not strictly in barbershop style. It was certainly the best known of all of the women's barbershop groups and was one of the first artists of any genre to capitalize on the new medium of television to launch a successful recording career.

The quartet was organized in 1946 by Jinny Cole Osborn, the daughter of the SPEBSQSA president "King Cole" (also president of the Kingsbury Brewery in Sheboygan, Wisconsin). Raised on barbershop harmony, Jinny recruited her high school friend Janet Buschman Ertel on bass, Dorothy Hummitzsch as lead, and (after Janet's sister served for a short time) Carol Hagedorn as baritone (after she married Janet's brother, Carol used the name Carol Hagedorn Buschman). Two other singers played important roles in the group (replacing the original members for tours or recordings): the tenor Margie Needham and the bass Nancy Overton.[37]

The group polished their harmonies and rhythms adapting "King" Cole's male quartet arrangements to the needs of a female quartet. With promotional help from the elder Cole, they were soon playing weekends on the barbershop circuit from Chicago to Oklahoma. Carol Hagedorn Buschman remembered: "We did all the barbershop shows. And since we began, everything was always very nice. We never had to come up the hard way. We were only exposed to nice people. We were treated royally in barbershop."[38]

Their break came while they were performing at a private party in Rhode Island attended by Henry Ford (founder of the Ford Motor Company) and Harvey Firestone, the tire magnate. A guest at the party recommended them to Arthur Godfrey, who invited them on to his hit radio and television show, *Arthur Godfrey's Talent Scouts*. Godfrey's first major national network radio show, a CBS production called *Arthur Godfrey Time*, went on the air in 1941. In auditions for the show, Godfrey was already looking for a quartet to handle "traditional material like gospel and barbershop." In a move that was controversial at the time, he hired a black quartet called the Jubilaires. Godfrey hired Archie Bleyer as his orchestra arranger and conductor. Godfrey's second national show was the Monday night radio version of his audition show, *Arthur Godfrey's Talent Scouts*, a prized venue for up-and-coming performers. Winners of the applause-meter decision were invited to perform Tuesday through Friday of the same week on Godfrey's morning radio show. From 1948 on *Talent Scouts* was simulcast on radio and television. By 1950 Godfrey's *Talent Scouts* had bumped Milton Berle's show from its perch as the most popular television show, and Godfrey had a strong claim on the title of the most popular entertainer in America.

On September 27, 1949, Godfrey, just back from a month's vacation, invited the Chordettes to perform and interviewed SPEBSQSA's Ted Rauh of Hasbrouck Heights, New Jersey. Godfrey reminded him that Hasbrouck Heights was Godfrey's hometown.

TR: Everyone talks about it, Arthur.

AG: Why? I paid off the bills. They don't have to talk anymore. Any hobbies?

TR: Barbershop singing. I'm president of SPEBSQSA, Incorporated.

AG: I'm a member of that group too! The Manhattan Chapter. Never been to any meetings though. What did you bring for talent? Not a barbershop quartet? [They look over at the Chordettes.]

TR: Not a men's, a ladies'. Ginny's father is [past] president of the SPEBSQSA.

AG: [Have they] done anything professionally?

TR: Traveled around the country.

Then Godfrey introduced the Chordettes and they sang a pop song, "Ballin' the Jack."[39] At the end of the night, the Chordettes edged out the comedian Wally Cox on the applause meter, and they were soon invited to join the cast of Godfrey's morning show, on which they reigned as one of the most popular performers for five years. This was a big move up for the women's quartet from Sheboygan. As regulars on the Godfrey show, the Chordettes became part of what Godfrey called his "Little Godfreys," his stable of on-air talent, from whom Godfrey demanded flexibility, hard work, absolute dedication, a wide-ranging expertise, and suppression of personal ambition. Later in 1949, Godfrey was given another nighttime television show to host, *Arthur Godfrey and His Friends,* and he signed up his entire *Arthur Godfrey Time* cast to star in the show, including the Chordettes.

For years to come, the Chordettes's career was shaped by Godfrey and two of his arrangers, Walter Latzko and Archie Bleyer. Latzko arranged barbershop pieces for the Chordettes to perform on a week-to-week basis. Godfrey went into the studio as a soloist with the Chordettes to record many of Latzko's arrangements tunes, including "Candy and Cake," "Dear Old Girl," "I Like the Wide Open Spaces," "Love Is the Reason," "Dance Me Loose," and "Slow Poke." These were issued as 78-rpm records on Columbia Records between 1950 and 1952. At the same time, Columbia released a set of four Chordettes albums in barbershop style, followed by another four-album set (*Harmony Time,* vols. 1 and 2). A published book of arrangements from their first Columbia albums became a primer for hundreds of women's barbershop quartets around the country. Their recording of "Down by the Old Mill Stream" with Godfrey is typical of their collaborations. In it, Godfrey's likable baritone carries the tune, with echo lines and shimmering close harmonies arranged by Latzko. Several well-placed swipes, especially in the tag, make this arrangement a wonderful example of barbershop styling for the period, despite the unorthodox pairing of a baritone with a women's quartet.

As a member of SPEBSQSA, Godfrey promoted many quartets over the years on his various shows. Another of his featured quartets was an integrated group of former Coast Guard servicemen called the Mariners. Primarily a pop and spiritual quartet, the Mariners often crossed over into barbershop arrangements, as in their 1953 hit "I See the Moon," which was called "a cross between barbershop harmony and a beer-hall song."[40] The 1951 SPEBSQSA champions, the Schmitt Brothers, from Two Rivers, Wisconsin, appeared on Godfrey's morning radio show in July 1951 following a guest spot on Godfrey's main competition, Ed Sullivan's *Talk of the Town* television show, the night before. Godfrey also hosted a children's quartet called the Four Chips, which had recently made the rounds of SPEBSQSA parades of quartets and the Society's convention. *Arthur Godfrey's Talent Scouts* regularly featured barbershop quartets in the weekly competitions. In 1954 the Easternaires performed "Trees" on the talent show to take the weekly honors and was rewarded with the standard performances on Godfrey's morning radio show.

In 1952 the lead, Dorothy Hummitzsch, married, became pregnant, and decided to leave the Chordettes. Although the quartet held try-outs for replacements, they did not bring anyone on board until the men's barbershop conference in Youngstown, Ohio, where a fan, Lynn Evans, was assigned to provide hospitality for the group and joined them for a few songs in rehearsal. Lynn was recruited on the spot and left with the quartet the following day for New York.

Their troubles with Godfrey occurred after Archie Bleyer started his own record company in 1953 and offered his first recording contract to Godfrey's biggest singing star, Julius LaRosa. Miffed at LaRosa's skyrocketing career, at his contract with an outside manager, and at the extracurricular business arrangements among his own crew, Godfrey fired LaRosa publicly—and without advance notice—at the end of a television broadcast on October 19, 1953, with the now-famous line, "That was Julie's swan song with us." Bleyer was fired at the same time, although he continued with Godfrey's Monday evening *Talent Scouts* show for a few weeks. The show's conflicts produced some of the choicest gossip of the year in American entertainment, and audiences debated whether the Godfrey show could survive the loss of its top talent.[41] Having joined Bleyer's Cadence label (Jan Ertel of the Chordettes had married Bleyer) along with the Mariners, the Chordettes fell out of favor with Godfrey. In October 1953

Figure 4.7. The original Chordettes. *Left to right:* Jinny Osborn, tenor; Carol Buschman, baritone; Lynn Evans, lead; and Janet Buschman Ertel, bass. Heritage Hall Museum of Barber Shop Harmony. Used by permission, Society for the Preservation and Encouragement of Barber Shop Quartet Singing in America, Inc.

they performed on the *Eddie Fisher Coca-Cola Show* on NBC (the chief rival of their CBS patrons) and sought increased exposure outside of the Godfrey orbit. They also finished out their recording contract with Columbia, which included their last identifiably barbershop album, *The Chordettes Sing Your Requests* (1953). Godfrey responded by inviting a competing group, the McGuire Sisters (a trio), onto the show. Once the Chordettes' nominal replacements had adjusted to the show, Godfrey called Jinny Osborn to tell her he was letting the group go in order to not "stand in the way of their success."

The Chordettes joined a lesser-known radio show, *The Robert Q. Lewis Show,* in 1954, and from that time on the group was essentially a women's pop quartet. Their arrangements were written or approved by Bleyer, who was convinced that barbershop harmony did not record well, and he refused to release the one purely barbershop album that the Chordettes recorded for his label. Nevertheless, Bleyer continued to make use of barbershop arranging devices, like the famous staggered-entry "chime" or "bell" chord that graced the group's first hit, "Mister Sandman." "Mister

Sandman" climbed into the number-one spot on the charts (it reached number eleven in England), stayed at the top for seven weeks, and continued to chart for twenty weeks between 1954 and 1955.

The Chordettes suffered a two-year drought in hit recordings but again scored with a cover of a black rhythm and blues tune, "Eddie My Love," in 1956–57; they went to number five soon after with "Born to Be with You." "Lollipop" (1958) also climbed into the top ten. Their last recorded dalliance with barbershop was captured on the Cadence LP called *Close Harmony* (January 1955), an album that featured mostly postwar pop songs but that nonetheless—in Walter O. Latzko's arrangements—evoked barbershop style.

During the late 1950s, the Chordettes appeared often on *American Bandstand* and *The Ed Sullivan Show*, and they sometimes performed rhythm and blues or rock and roll material before their retirement in 1961. The Chordettes inspired many women to form close-harmony quartets and even to join Sweet Adelines. Their success, along with that of the Buffalo Bills, helped to make the 1950s a banner decade for the popularization of the barbershop style in the media.

The Dapper Dans on Walt Disney's "Main Street, U.S.A."

Millions of visitors from all over the world have experienced a live barbershop quartet on two quaint little Main Streets, one in Anaheim, California, and the other near Orlando, Florida, both emanating from the imagination of Walt Disney and his passion for Americana. During a sabbatical from his animated movies in the 1940s, Walt Disney installed a ridable, three-quarter-sized, historical reproduction of a train on his property near Los Angeles. His enjoyment in riding the train around his property led him to propose building an all-ages park of historical theme attractions on the edge of the property where his Burbank, California, studios stood.[42] He first proposed that the park be called "Mickey Mouse Park." Disney imagined his park fronted by a replica of a "Main Village," complete with village green and bandstand. Early on in this secretive project, Disney brought in a well-known illustrator of Americana, Harper Goff, to further the project.

Meanwhile, Disney was also beginning work on a traveling exhibit of historical tableaux devoted to small-town images and sounds and populated by animated figures that he intended to call "Disneylandia." Disney himself carved the first few sets, based on drawings by illustrator Ken Anderson. When Harper Goff came over to work on this second project, Disney had Goff design a barbershop quartet "in which all four figures were to break into harmonious song" singing "Sweet Adeline."[43] Disney himself sculpted the figures, which were equipped for mechanical motion in Disney's machine shop. The machine shop was able to get Disney's barbershop figures to perform a full minute-and-a-half routine, but Disney's moving-figure ideal for Disneylandia outstripped the available technology and appeared to be too costly. (His concept for robotic characters was later realized by Disney's patented Audio-Animatronics system, which had its national debut at the 1964–65 New York World's Fair.) As a result, Disney reconceptualized his pet project as a stationary exhibit, combined it with his "Mickey Mouse Park," and shortened the name to "Disneyland." Nevertheless, a barbershop quartet was always part of Disney's vision of a theme park.

As Disney developed his idea, he insisted that the park have one entrance and that entrance be Main Street, U.S.A., a recreated, idealized, turn-of-the-century Victorian town. Main Street was—as Disney's daughter later insisted—Walt Disney's tribute to his childhood home of Marceline, Missouri. Disney's parents moved to Marceline (population 5,000) in 1906 to escape crime in Chicago, where his father had worked as a carpenter for the 1893 World Columbian Exposition. The Disneys lived on a farm in Marceline for four years until, owing to Walt's father's illness and mounting farm losses, they lost the farm to foreclosure. The vision of the small midwestern home that they lost stuck with Disney throughout his life. After Disneyland Park opened in 1955, Disney occasionally spent the night in a tiny apartment on Main Street, U.S.A., that he commissioned for himself over the firehouse, and he placed a sign for his father's failed contracting business ("Elias Disney, contractor, est. 1895") in a second-story window. The buildings of Disney's Main Street were reduced in scale and designed in an exaggerated perspective that visually enhanced their size. According to one of Disney's biographers,

> the designers of Disneyland were movie-studio art directors—artists who knew the technique of creating sets and backdrops to provide a storytelling experience. Their Main Street was unlike any small-town Main Street that ever existed. At Disneyland, all the shops and emporiums complemented each other; even the signs and paint colors were in harmony. The result was pleasingly believable to the visitor. They thought, "'That's the way Main Street must have been in the old days!'" But that's [only] the way it *should* have been.[44]

The brochure drafted to obtain financing from ABC for Disneyland noted that "here the older generation can recapture the nostalgia of days gone by, and the younger generation can savor the challenge of the future."[45] (The deal with ABC Television provided for a weekly television special focusing on the park in return for funding.) The opening of Disneyland Park was covered by the largest assemblage of crew, cameras, and television cable in the history of broadcast television, and its three ABC hosts included the future president Ronald Reagan, whose own vision of America as a "shining city on the hill" often seemed to have been drawn from the same nostalgic trove that produced Disney's Main Street, U.S.A. The Disney biographer Richard Schickel's comment about his subject might just have as easily described the future president: "When, in a time of deep inner stress, we demanded another kind of unifying vision, he gave us a simplified and rosy-hued version of the small town and rural America that may have formed our institutions and our heritage but no longer forms us as individuals."[46]

Disney finally had the venue in which to install his quartet, but he decided to go with live performers. The Dapper Dans of Disneyland were contracted to perform long hours six days a week. Still, all four members pursued their outside music careers and studies in their spare time (the group consisted of three music teachers and one music student). The original Dapper Dans of Disneyland were Ron Browne, Fred Frank, Tom Knox, and Jim Schamp. In 1957 SPEBSQSA held its international convention in Los Angeles and included in the itinerary a trip to Disney's Main Street, U.S.A., with its new barbershop quartet.

The Dans were contracted for a series of broadcasts on *The Mickey Finn Show*, and when Finn booked performances in Las Vegas and Reno, he offered to bring the Dans along. Attempting to fly back to their day jobs after a concert, the group crash-landed on Route 66 in California, at which point they gave up their jobs and their Disney contracts to pursue quartet singing as a career on *The Mickey Finn Show*. Having left Disney, the group took the name the Dapper Four, since Disney had a trademark on the original name.

Disneyland recruited a new set of Dans: Dick Kneeland, Bob Mathis, "Bub" Thomas, and Jerry Siggins, and in September 1972 Tom Howe joined the group as a fill-in fourth to enable to group to fulfill their seven-days-per-week schedule. The new group joined the cast at Walt Disney World Resort near Orlando, Florida, performing on Disney's new Main-Street, U.S.A. (a new quartet was formed to replace them in Anaheim). The barbershop that they fronted at Walt Disney World Resort was named the Harmony Barbershop. In the process of transplantation, the quartet became the Dapper Dans of Walt Disney World Resort. They planned to teach other Disneyland employees how to sing barbershop harmony and even considered forming a SPEBSQSA-affiliated Disney chorus. All the Dans were from the SPEBSQSA far western district at the start but switched to the Orlando chapter. By 1986 the group was a sextet from which four sang at any given moment. The Dans pioneered this practical strategy of having six flexible voices on call—three of the singers could sing any of the four parts—and this helped them meet the demands of their Disney contract.

The Dapper Dans of Disneyland and the Dapper Dans of Walt Disney World Resort have maintained the Disney barbershopping franchise for decades. In 1994 the Disneyland quartet provided the voices of the barbershop quartet, the B-Sharps, on the cartoon show *The Simpsons* (the "Homer's Barbershop Quartet" episode). They sang "Goodbye, My Coney Island Baby" in front of the Statue of Liberty for an Independence Day celebration attended by a cartoon version of the president and first lady, Ronald and Nancy Reagan. The Dans' rendition of the song for the B-Sharps was the same one they had sung for years at Disneyland.

The original Disney quartet helped launch the career of the Osmond Brothers (Alan, Wayne, Merrill, and Jay, older brothers of Donny and

Figure 4.8. The Dapper Dans performing at Disneyland Park. Used by permission, © Disney Enterprises, Inc.

Marie). They began singing during family gatherings on Friday nights, and when the youngest of the four was three years old, they sang four-part harmony in Mormon church services. They learned their first barbershop songs from their father before encountering contemporary barbershop singing via the radio broadcasts from the SPEBSQSA convention in Chicago in 1960. Their father then hired the Society arranger Val Hicks to teach the elements of barbershop harmony and singing to the boys. On a visit to Disneyland, the brothers encountered the Dapper Dans. After hearing the boys sing, the Dans introduced them to Disney's television producer, Tommy Walker, and the Osmond Brothers were invited to perform on the *Disneyland after Dark* television show and in live performances at Disneyland's Golden Horseshoe Theater. The brothers next heard from *The Andy Williams Show* and were invited first as guests before being signed to a five-year contract. The Osmond Brothers found widespread public exposure on occasional Disney television specials and in weekly appearances on *The Andy Williams Show*, but like the Chordettes they were soon considered more of a pop vocal group than a barbershop quartet.

The Buffalo Bills in The Music Man

The Broadway musical (and film) *The Music Man* did more to fix an image of barbershopping in the public's mind than did any other book, photograph, movie, play, or recording. It made stars out of the 1950 SPEBSQSA contest–winning Buffalo Bills, who were featured in both the Broadway and Hollywood versions, and the musical's touring companies offered steady employment for many quartets during the late 1950s and 1960s.

The Bills—Vernon Reed (tenor, an executive with the Tonawanda Boys Club), Al Shea (lead, a Buffalo policeman), Hersh Smith (baritone, replaced in 1950 by Dick Grapes, who worked at a paper company), and Bill Spangenberg (bass, truck driver)—met in 1947 to form a quartet. The nameless quartet was hired to perform for the Monday Morning Quarterback Club, a booster organization for the first incarnation of the Buffalo Bills football team (of the soon defunct All-America Conference). The team's treasurer proposed to call the quartet "The Buffalo Bills" just for the day, but the name stuck. (After the football team failed and the group had registered their name, the new Buffalo football franchise had to obtain the permission of the quartet to use the name!)

The Buffalo Bills competed in the 1948 and 1949 SPEBSQSA International Quartet Contest, placing sixteenth and sixth, respectively. At the 1950 international conference, held in Omaha, Nebraska, at the Aksarben Theater (the name is "Nebraska" spelled backward), they took first place and amassed the largest point tally in barbershop history for their rendition of two southern-oriented songs, "Goin' South," and "When I'm Walkin' with My Sugar down among the Sugar Cane." They also sang a competition medley called "Goodbye, Old Dixie, Goodbye" consisting of "Way Down Home Where the Swanee River Flows" and "Swanee River." Dick Grapes confessed that soon after winning, he feared the effects of being in a Society championship quartet on his Tonawanda job. After the contest, he ran into a wealthy industrialist, Bob McFerrin. On hearing of Grapes's anxiety about work, McFerrin contacted Grapes's boss, placed an order "that would choke a cow" with the company, and suggested that Grapes be given all the time off he needed to represent the Society.[47]

The Bills' victory helped to popularize a sound for barbershop quartets that many barbershop enthusiasts called "big" or "robust" sound. "Big" refers first of all to intensity; all four singers possessed strong, youthful voices with a dynamic range from soft to overpoweringly loud, and their voices blended strikingly well. Their early arrangements, most of which were written by the past SPEBSQSA international president Phil Embury (the "fifth Bill"), emphasized drama and vigor.

Soon after their SPEBSQSA victory, they appeared on the national radio show *We the People* and were feted by the Manhattan and Buffalo chapters on their return trip to their hometown. The discussion topic on *We the People* was the ban that SPEBSQSA had enacted on performances of the song "Sweet Adeline" in the belief that it was too closely associated with inebriated singing. Harry Armstrong, the composer of "Sweet Adeline," was on the show, and the Buffalo Bills represented the Society. After the show aired, SPEBSQSA lifted its ban. The Bills soon shared a bill with the Washington, D.C., chapter chorus at a "Barbershop Harmony" concert in front of the Capitol at the Washington, D.C., sesquicentennial celebration. Their first national television appearance was on *The Faye Emerson Pepsi-Cola Show* in a made-for-television movie in April 1951.

Figure 4.9. The Buffalo Bills with their first-place quartet trophy from the 1950 convention in Omaha, Neb. *Left to right:* Vernon Reed, tenor; Albert Shea, lead; Dick Grapes, baritone; Bill Spangenberg, bass. Heritage Hall Museum of Barber Shop Harmony. Used by permission, Society for the Preservation and Encouragement of Barber Shop Quartet Singing in America, Inc.

In 1951 the Bills released an album of four records (eight sides) on Decca (*Barbershop Gems,* Decca DL 5361). This is the album that Meredith Willson, the composer of *The Music Man,* first heard in a local record shop, and that converted him into an admirer of the group. Willson, an arranger, composer, and orchestra director, hosted a radio show (*Music Today*) with his wife, and they began to include the Bills' material on frequent rotation. In 1954 Willson and his wife traveled to Buffalo to meet the Bills and to hold a jam session with them in the studios of WBEN. Thereafter the Bills became frequent guests on Willson's show.

The Bills competed on *Arthur Godfrey's Talent Scouts* in February 1957, won first honors, and received the requisite invitation to perform on Godfrey's morning radio show for the rest of the week. Their competition number was "In the Blue Ridge Mountains of Virginia." In March 1958 the subsequent SPEBSQSA champions (who won at the 1951 convention), the Schmitt Brothers, performed on the *Lawrence Welk Top Tunes and New Talent Show.* Lawrence Welk's various television shows, along with those of Ed Sullivan and Arthur Godfrey, were high-visibility platforms for the promotion of barbershop quartets in the late 1950s and 1960s. Welk even recruited a quartet for regular appearances on his show (around 1958). The

Bills and the Schmitt Brothers were also regular headliners at an annual barbershop show at the Chautauqua Institute in upstate New York that began in 1954. With nearly 10,000 in attendance, the Chautauqua show claimed honors for the world's largest barbershop concert, but the New York City contests in Central Park (see chapter 3) were at this time still drawing a larger audience, estimated at 18,000.

In 1956 Meredith Willson was nearing completion of his Broadway musical *The Music Man,* adapted from his own book. The music and the script were supplied by Willson, but Willson shared libretto credits with Franklin Lacey. Like Disney, Willson was a son of the Midwest (Iowa, in his case) and *The Music Man* was his sentimental paean to his childhood home, complete with allusions to the importance of John Philip Sousa, in whose band Willson had played flute for a few years during the 1920s.

The story takes place in the fictional town of River City, Indiana, around 1912, with the arrival of Harold Hill, a traveling salesman and confidence man. Hill plans to defraud the locals by convincing them that they need a Sousa-style marching band to maintain the morals and innocence of the town's younger generation. Hill plans to sell band instruments and outfits to the town, make a quick profit, and skip town before his lack of musical expertise is exposed. But Hill falls in love with the local librarian, and in the end, well, everything turns out fine.

In the musical, the barbershop quartet singers are the cantankerous members of the board of education. Their three songs were "Lida Rose" (sung three times), "It's You," and "Sincere"; the quartet was also asked to woodshed "Good Night, Ladies" as musical counterpoint to a song sung by a group of female characters. Willson sought to interject "genuine" barbershop harmony within the limitations of the plot (and despite orchestral accompaniment), and the songs' structures and key modulations were designed to fit into the overall musical flow.

Willson recommended the Bills to his producer, Kermit Bloomgarden, who contacted the group in March 1957. Kermit interviewed the Bills and auditioned them at the Imperial Theater in New York in front of the producer and the musical director. They started with "Alexander's Ragtime Band" and, when asked for a ballad, followed with "Love Me and the World Is Mine." Finally they were given a script to read, to make sure they could handle the combination of acting and singing; they were offered the roles on the spot.

On the way home they discussed the offer. Two of the Bills could get a year's leave from work to join the production: Al Shea could opt for unpaid leave from the police force, and Bill Spangenberg could pay union dues for a year and maintain his membership in the Teamsters. If *The Music Man* bombed, they could return to Buffalo and to their jobs with seniority. Vernon Reed and Dick Grapes, however, would have had to quit work to join the cast, and Grapes decided that he could not risk his family's security on an unsure proposition. Grapes released the group from an agreement they had made that either all or none would go, and the Buffalo Bills set out to replace their baritone in early summer of 1957. They recruited Wayne

"Scotty" Ward of the Great Scots Quartet of Stubenville, Ohio, as Grapes's replacement. The now-complete quartet joined Actors' Equity, took one-year leaves from their jobs, and moved with their families to New York. The one-year leaves became permanent, and this quartet, comprising two salesmen, a police officer, and a truck driver, cast their lot with show business.

The Music Man opened at the Shubert Theater in Philadelphia on November 18, 1957, and then on Broadway at the Majestic on December 19. Reviews of the musical were mixed, although only Dorothy Kilgallen panned it entirely. Reviews of the movie version of a few years later called it "a classic of corn, smalltown nostalgia and American love of a parade," "overacted, overcute, overloud, and overlong," "pure corn. But it is high grade Iowa corn," and "full of the innocent merriment that we associate with the Middle West when our century was young."[48] Willson himself claims to have taken the characters and situations right out of his boyhood hometown in Iowa, patterning his quartet on a group called the Rusty Hinges that had a busybody or meddlesome reputation in his hometown. However, Willson's own memories, and his attempts at staging them, seemed to draw from the stock characters (rubes, city slickers, traveling salesmen, etc.) of vaudeville skit comedy.

The Buffalo Bills continued on the roster of Arthur Godfrey's morning television show during the early months of their Broadway success, and they maintained an active concert career on Sundays, when they had a day off from the production. A second cast was assembled to tour *The Music Man* on the West Coast, and the Frisco Four of San Francisco was offered the quartet part in this touring production, which shortly became the national touring company. The Frisco Four appeared on national television, including a spot on Ed Sullivan's Sunday evening show in July 1958. Van Johnson, the actor who played Professor Hill in the touring production, in 1952 joined SPEBSQSA's southern California chapter, which had named itself "The Music Men."

The Buffalo Bills stuck with the Broadway production until the summer of 1961, when they left for Hollywood to film the movie version. The Broadway musical and the Warner Brothers movie, which premiered in July of 1962, had a number of SPEBSQSA tie-ins. The publishers of the sheet music for *The Music Man* invited SPEBSQSA arrangers to contribute additional quartet arrangements of the musical's songs. Warner Brothers and SPEBSQSA sponsored a joint "Music Man Quartet Contest" in conjunction with the film's premiere. Prizes included an award from Meredith Willson and the chance to sing at the local opening of the movie. SPEBSQSA declared April 9–16, 1960, to be National Barbershop Harmony Week (an outgrowth of the former Founder's Week in honor of O. C. Cash). In 1963 President John F. Kennedy declared the same week to be National Harmony Week.

The Bills experienced the most dramatic arc of success in barbershop revival history, leading from a SPEBSQSA championship to a prominent spot in all of the major media (film, radio, recording, and television). By the time the Bills retired in 1967, they had logged a now-legendary 728 concerts, 216 television shows, 1,510 theatrical shows, 626 corporate conventions, 675 radio shows, 672 nightclub performances, 137 state fairs, and a major motion picture.[49]

Tag: Down by the Old Maelstrom

The barbershop revival, dedicated to the musical evocation of more placid times, weathered the storms of World War II and the cold war, becoming more firmly institutionalized in one, then two, and eventually three barbershop revival organizations. In the context of this era, the barbershop movement got serious, arguing for a peculiarly American, patriotic, and antitotalitarian character of barbershop harmony. During this period, and under the impact of the competition system, revivalists increasingly codified their notion of barbershop harmony. But to say that its forms and meanings became more clearly defined is not to say that this occurred without sustained debate or institutional conflict. Rather, the barbershop revival movement was caught in torrents of controversy over musical literacy, choruses, professionalism, and issues of inclusion and bias.

In this same period, barbershop harmony became even more firmly rooted in the public's mediated, pseudohistorical notion of turn-of-the-century American life. For this, one can give partial credit to popular-culture entrepreneurs such as Meredith Willson, Arthur Godfrey, George Jessel, Lawrence Welk, Roy Rogers, Lucille Ball, and Walt Disney (and of course Norman Rockwell and Robert Moses). Their dalliance in Gay Nineties nostalgia was projected out through their expansive cultural productions. The revival barbershop quartets became fixtures on theme floats in local parades, in competitions at county fairs, in historical theme parks, in movies, on television and radio programs, in recordings, and in innumerable local and high school productions of *The Music Man*. This circulation of the barbershop iconography in the electronic and print media and in popular culture in general is what I mean by the term "barberpop."

Barbershoppers lament that the subsequent decades never again presented barbershoppers with the same opportunities to reach mass audiences and to control the representation of barbershopping, and that public impressions of barbershop harmony remain stuck in the early decades of the revival. During recent decades, the public has been almost entirely oblivious to the increasingly sophisticated styles of barbershop singing in society competitions and unaware of the less cartoonish costuming and staging in contemporary barbershop. A stark divide has developed between the barberpop of public consciousness and the experience of barbershopping among its adherents in the barbershop societies. The image of barbershopping carried by millions is still one of four guys in striped jackets singing "Down by the Old Mill Stream" who step out of a parallel Norman Rockwell universe and into our dimension when we need to conjure up a simpler and less stormy time in American history.

5

Romancing the Tone
Song, Sound, and Significance in Barbershop Harmony

The old songs, the old songs
The good old songs for me
I love to hear those minor chords
And good close harmony
—Geoffrey O'Hara,
"A Little Close Harmony
(The Old Songs)" (1921)

A t the 1990 Evergreen District **SPEBSQSA** Quartet Preliminaries, I saw Premium Blend take the stage dressed collectively as Norman Rockwell's "Barbershop Quartet." During the first song, "Oh! You Beautiful Doll," one member of the group was on the receiving end of a simulated shave. Then they struck the Rockwell pose to deliver "Naughty, Naughty Nineties." Premium Blend was putting into practice the **SPEBSQSA** ideal of a barbershop performance: to sell the song using every means at the disposal of a quartet or chorus. A barbershop performance mobilizes a lyric text, a harmonic arrangement, vocal blend, facial expression, dress, choreography, gesture, and sometimes props to make a song persuasive, coherent, and moving. This chapter delves into the elements of barbershop singing and into the significance of song lyrics, sound, performance and social organization in barbershop harmony, starting with the element central to selling a song: the song itself.

The "Old Songs"

Barbershoppers exude an obvious reverence for "the old songs." Phil Embury, a former SPEBSQSA president, said: "They [the "old songs"] share in common, to a large degree, simple, sweet, easily remembered melodies, tunes that suggest harmony for which you can feel the parts, a tempo that enables your foursome to improvise original chord sequences and swipes, and lyrics that tell of sweetheart love, of mother, love of country, old Ireland, the dear old South, we can agree . . . that there is nostalgia in these songs."[1]

Of what direct relevance are these songs from a distant era to understanding the musical lives of barbershop singers, their beliefs, ideologies, or worldviews? I do not argue that barbershoppers mechanically adhere to a worldview encapsulated in the songs they sing. However, after looking closely at barbershop discourse on the "old songs," examining barbershop policies regarding competition song selection, and interviewing and polling barbershoppers, I have come to believe that lyric content is of real importance in motivating contemporary participation in barbershop harmony.

To begin my exploration of song texts, I performed a "content analysis" on all titles of approved SPEBSQSA arrangements from around 1990, and also on all song texts in the SPEBSQSA fiftieth anniversary commemorative "Heritage Medley." Both selections represent canons (canonized song titles on the one hand, canonized song texts on the other) as selected by the Society. The first analysis I performed was a simple frequency tabulation of the number of occurrences of each word. This produced the following two lists of the twenty most frequent key terms:[2]

20 most frequent key terms in titles of arrangements		20 most frequent key terms in SPEBSQSA "Heritage Medley" song texts	
No.	Term	No.	Term
49	old/en	35	old/en
41	song/s, sing/s/ing	35	song/s, sing/s/ing
27	love/s, loving	25	love/s, loving
22	little	25	girl/s, gal
21	home	21	all
20	girl/s, gal	15	then
20	day/s	14	like
18	sweet/est/ness	13	more
16	mother/mammy	12	day/s
13	baby, babe	12	baby, babe
13	down	12	time
13	all	12	up
13	world	12	there
13	rose/s	11	say, said, saying
12	back	10	now
12	there	10	one
11	barbershop	10	dear/ie
11	come	9	good
11	long/er	9	some
10	heart	9	never

I then carried out relational content analyses (looking for co-occurrence) on many of the above terms, starting with the one that leads the frequency list: "old." The terms that most frequently clustered with "old" or "olden" were:

1. songs
2. "gals" (various terms for women)
3. "pals" (various terms for male friends)
4. various states and regions
5. days, times
6. landscape features
7. town, neighborhood

This list of seven common relational pairs can be joined into four higher-level categories: old songs, old "faces" ("pals" and "gals"), old places, and old times.

Many of the old songs most favored by barbershoppers were already nostalgic at the time of their composition. They looked back to youth, hometowns, early courtship, family, friends and sometimes even to the "old quartet" as objects of nostalgic fascination.

> Last night I passed the corner where we used to harmonize
> I didn't see a soul I used to know
> The neighborhood looked different, I began to realize
> How things can change in just a year or so
> I'm all that's left of that old quartet
> That sang around the old hometown
> ("I'm All That's Left of That Old Quartet")

This song sketches the mythic geography of the corner, neighborhood, and hometown. Changes perceived to have occurred in the geography of this realm mirror the disappearance of the social group (the quartet). In songs like this, the barbershop is posited as a male space for socializing, away from the distractions of female company. Even more private and hidden away, the woodshed becomes a location of maximal authenticity, where songs can be extemporized freely—worked, chopped, and honed, with no thought of audience. The chorus to "I'm All That's Left of the Old Quartet," however, begins not in the woodshed nor in the barbershop, but in perhaps the most "authentic" of the quartet loci: the street corner. In *The Death of Rhythm and Blues*, Nelson George discussed the romance of "a corner under the streetlight" for fans of doo-wop harmony.[3] The doo-wop romance of the street corner echoes that of the earlier barbershop revival. Indeed, the number of early barbershoppers who spoke of hearing African American "blades" harmonizing on the streets, or the promoters who discovered black harmony groups on corners or in bars, would support speculation that the rhetoric of authenticity that surrounds the street corner may have had black ambulatory harmony quartets as its original reference.

The hometown so fondly recalled in many of these songs is a collective and social memory, an "American hometown." It is the hometown remembered fondly by Walt Disney and Meredith Willson and the hometown sung about by urban immigrant Tin Pan Alley songwriters. It is, finally, the hometown that continually calls to those rootless urbanites who have left it behind:

> Homesick, heartsick, nothing seems real
> That's how I feel today (today)
> Home town, my town, I hear you call
> Calling me far away (far away)
> *Chorus:*
> It's just a little street where old friends meet
> I'd love to wander back someday
> To you it may seem old and sort of tumble-down
> But it seems a lot to folks in my hometown
> Although I'm rich or poor, I still feel sure
> I'm welcome as the flowers in May
> It's just a little street where old friends meet
> And greet you in the same old way
> ("A Little Street Where Old Friends Meet")

On the hometown street, remembered through the lens of nostalgia, relationships are continuous, one is always welcome, and the concerns of the outside world with status and wealth are nonexistent. The phrase "far away" in this song refers no only to a distance of geography but also to a distance of time.

> Oh "Heart of My Heart," I love that melody
> "Heart of My Heart," brings back sweet memories
> When we were kids on the corner of that square
> We were rough and ready guys,
> But oh, how we could harmonize, to
> "Heart of my Heart," those friends were dearer then
> Too bad that we had to part
> I know a tear would glisten
> If once more I could listen
> To the gang that sang "Heart of My Heart"
> ("The Gang That Sang 'Heart of My Heart'")[4]

In many of these songs of the "pal" subspecies, the quartet functions as the condensation symbol of male fraternity. In the more self-consciously nostalgic songs, titles are sometimes interpolated, as they are here (the lyrics also mention the song "Sweet Roses of Morn"). Many of the pal songs construct a particular model of masculinity that allows for sentimental male bonding through the intimacy of singing together. In "That Old Quartet of Mine," the old singing buddies are held "dear," and that what is missed is the intimate "touch" of four-part harmony.

> Sitting by the fireside watching embers softly glow
> I put my daily cares aside and think of friends I used to know
> As I reach back in memory, I recall an old-time melody
> I can hear it yet, by my old quartet, in the days that used to be
> *Chorus:*
> I wonder what has happened to that old quartet of mine
> I hope and pray we'll meet again somewhere, some day, some time
> If only to remind them how dear they are to me
> And just how much I miss the touch of four-part harmony
> ("That Old Quartet of Mine")

As we see in the sampling of "pal" songs above, men are referred to in the plural—as "guys," "fellas," "gang," "bunch," "band," "boys," or "crowd." In the songs of the period dealing with courtship, love, romance, attraction, love lost, and mother, women are almost always referred to in the singular. In this Victorian model, male-male interactions are based in group activity outside of the home, while male-female relations are one-on-one and centered on the home. As I have stressed, a cornerstone of Victorian ideology was a belief that male companionship has ameliorative effects on the male psyche and that too much time spent with women feminizes and softens the male character.

Gender is usually immediately identifiable in golden-era songs: written by and large by men and providing men with the active voice, song texts assign to women a position as love interests and objects of male attention. Men describe women, idealize them, long for them, remember them, and sometimes scorn them.[5] The ideal of male-female relationships presented in many of the songs that are canonized in barbershop reproduces the marriage bond exemplified by the protagonist's parents in the barbershop "chestnut" "I Want a Girl (Just like the Girl That Married Dear Old Dad):"

> I want a girl just like the girl that married dear old dad
> She was a pearl and the only girl that daddy ever had
> A good old-fashioned girl with heart so true
> One who loves nobody else but you
> ("I Want a Girl" (Just like the Girl That Married Dear Old Dad)")[6]

Among the songs of scorn is "You're Nobody's Sweetheart Now," which castigates a former sweetheart. The lyrics contrast the girl she used to be— a girl in a gingham dress who brought a flower to the protagonist under an old oak tree—with the modernist, face-painted floozy she has become.

Few of the period songs deal with young married life or child rearing. The idealization of male-female relations takes place, rather, at the margins of the married life, during courtship and again during old age when the couple looks back fondly on a time, when (to quote a favorite of barbershoppers) "You and I Were Young, Maggie." Quite a few songs fall into this category, including some of the most often performed songs in barbershop style ("Put On Your Old Gray Bonnet," "Mandy Lee"):

> The old mill wheel is silent and has fallen down
> The old oak tree has withered and lays there on the ground
> While you and I are sweethearts, the same as days of yore
> Although we've been together forty years and more
> ("Down By the Old Mill Stream")[7]

A number of these songs place the nostalgic memory of courtship just after the passing of the loved one ("You Tell Me Your Dream," "In the Shade of the Old Apple Tree," "Dear Old Girl").

Marriage brings out the contradiction inherent in barbershop idealization of both "old pals" and "old gals," because marriage introduces a rift or disruption in the primacy of male fraternal relations. This rift is addressed in numerous texts such as this:

> Not a soul down on the corner, that's a pretty certain sign
> Those wedding bells are breaking up "That Old Gang of Mine"
> All the boys are singing love songs, they forgot "Sweet Adeline"
> ("Wedding Bells Are Breaking Up That Old Gang of Mine")[8]

Two songs are interpolated into this stanza: "That Old Gang of Mine," here representing the "old pals," and "Sweet Adeline," representing the "old gal(s)." The married men, apparently, have forgotten how to sing both songs, and have therefore lost the youthful innocence of first courtship and male camaraderie.

The types of songs beloved by barbershoppers tend to affirm the inevitability and importance of marriage but construct a frame of reference within which men interpret their conflicting desires, mourn the loss of freedom that they believe results from marriage, and (through singing barbershop harmony) reappropriate a certain amount of freedom in the form of all-male autonomous social activity. This schema (innocence, alienation, and redemption), which I have elsewhere linked to a widespread literary trope of paradise lost and found, can also be seen as a parable of American society as a whole and of the mythic history of barbershop singing. Singing the "old songs"—motivated by an ideology of "old-fashioned values"—is both commentary and cure, ideology and practice, restoring the fraternity whose loss it mourns. Nostalgia is encoded not only in song lyrics but in style, and in the entire set of vocal and harmonic practices and conventions that characterize barbershop singing.

Tags, Swipes, and Embellishments

In a 1943 *Harmonizer*, Sigmund Spaeth wrote to SPEBSQSA members:

> I still feel that barber shop harmony should be unaccompanied, re-
> stricted to male voices, with the tenor always singing above the lead.
> I believe there are certain chords which have a definite barber shop at-
> mosphere, particularly the diminished sevenths, augmented fifths,
> dominant sevenths, and the various inversions. I am in favor of mov-
> ing three parts around one sustained note, even the simultaneous mo-
> tion of all four parts, and I recommend that such effects be more fre-
> quently used for the traditional "barber shop endings." I find that the
> word "minor" is habitually misused, applying to almost any chord be-
> yond the obvious tonic, dominant, and sub-dominant, but seldom
> concerning itself with an actual minor chord.[9]

Barbershop revivalists decisively sided with the particular style of voicing that places the lead (tenor) voice on the melody, harmonizes it with a
tenor above and bass below, and fills in the harmony with the baritone line.
As we have seen, this voicing was common from the 1840s onward, although it was far from the only voicing used by minstrel, vaudeville, and
recording-era quartets. Another characteristic of the style the revivalists
sought to preserve was the "closeness" or "tightness" of harmony, in contrast to spread, open position, or "divorced" harmony. Close harmony
emphasizes close intervallic relationships, usually adjacent notes of the
chord, and the resultant chords seldom occupy a range of more than an octave and a half. One singer slides one note against the others to carve out
a new chord, a new experience, from the tissue of the former. As barbershop arrangers are the first to admit, barbershop harmony ignores many
of the rules of resolution and voice leading in order to keep the emphasis on the sonorous and sensuous quality of the chords. The baritone voice,
especially, often makes ungainly leaps, and may cross the lead voice in
order to maintain close voicing and complete consonant chords. The
chords thus generate a special energy and intensity: imagine for a moment
the feeling generated by standing in a close proximity to three other
singers, blending voices and creating compact clusters of locked-in, ringing, harmonized chords.

The ability of an arranger to keep the harmony close depends in part on
the nature of the melody of the song. Barbershop revivalists prefer songs
with a melodic range or ambitus of an octave or less, preferably lying
within the octave whose parameters are the notes *sol* to *sol* of the tonic
key. When the melody ranges too low into the bass register, barbershop
arrangers will generally spread the harmony a little wider, perhaps over
two octaves, and even exchange harmonic functions between the first
tenor and baritone, in order to preserve the sense of voicing.

Barbershop revivalists shunned the solo verses that were a staple of
golden-era quartet performance in favor of continuous four-part harmony,

and they also looked with disfavor on harmonizing a melody part with humming or untexted syllables, an approach that was in widespread use among African American jubilee quartets. Revivalists also strictly avoided instrumental accompaniment in favor of a cappella singing, harmonizing every note with consonant chords, and avoiding, if possible, suspensions and other non-chord tones. This imbued barbershop singing with a distinctive protean harmony.

Every quartet has its own sound, created by the individual vocal timbres and blend. Highly prized are first tenors with a crystalline-pure tone, and they have to be especially sensitive to dynamics so as to not overpower or drown out the lead. First tenors sometimes employ falsetto. In traditional barbershop arranging, one does not find the emphasis on a soaring high-lead voice that is found in many doo-wop and R&B groups, but one does often hear the tenor "cut loose" in a tag, hitting high, loud, sustained tones, while the other voices swipe below. Barbershop vocal parts can engage in responsorial and echo effects, but the general ideal remains homophonic textures throughout a song, with an abiding focus on a melody. This is, after all, about the songs.

Barbershoppers use the term "embellishment" for any arranging effect, technique, or device that enlivens the texture of the harmony. The best-known and most often used embellishments in barbershop harmony are swipes and tags.

A swipe refers to a movement from one chord to another on a single syllable, usually while the lead holds the melody note. Swipes often occur in measures where the melody has a held note (sections that might be filled with instrumental accompaniment if there were instruments accompanying), but the rhythmic flexibility of barbershop arranging allows for swipes nearly anywhere the arranger chooses to place them. The swipe is such a popular device in barbershop singing that it is often seen as the most diagnostic aspect of barbershop sound and aesthetic.

A tag is a special ending or coda to a song. Tags typically incorporate the final line of the song's chorus for the text and make great use of swipes and other arranging devices. Especially in the more exuberant tunes, known as "gut busters," tags will be sung open voiced with lots of dynamic intensity. Tags are extremely popular platforms for arranging skills, and medleys of tags from different songs are often sung at informal gatherings. A tag developed for one song will often migrate to others, with only a change in the lyrics. Tags are printed in barbershop newsletters and books and are available on the Web.

In 1925 Sigmund Spaeth recognized the appeal of tags of barbershop singers: "Barbershop harmony really begins at the end and works backwards. If a quartet is well equipped with 'wicked' endings, the body of the song may be fairly conventional. It is the close that leaves the final fragrance of the barbershop, and if this be beautifully flavored with a nostalgic aroma, it matters little what has gone before. . . . The first and most practical advice, therefore, to actual and potential singers of the barber-

Figure 5.1. A barbershop swipe

shop ballad is: get up plenty of good endings. Know them by heart and by number, so that they can be introduced at a moment's notice, to the amazement of every listener."[10] On the last note of the tag, basses commonly descend an octave (called simply "the drop").

Echo effects have been employed by quartet arrangers since the early nineteenth century, and along with swipes, they may be barbershop's quintessential sound (think of "Sweet Adeline"). Another early song associated with echoes is "By the Light of the Silvery Moon," in which early quartets almost always followed up the first line of the choral text, "By the light," with the other voices in echo mode ("by the light, by the light"). Echo effects were common in eighteenth-century English vocal music, but their centrality to the barbershop style may also be due to their similarity to African American responsorial or call-and-response singing.

Many other arranging devices are variations on the staggered-entry chord. If the four voices enter in succession from silence, it is generically called a "bell chord." Often, however, the voices begin together on a unison pitch and break off to create the chord. If these build up from bottom to top, starting on a low unison note, it is called a "pyramid." If they start on a middle note and go higher, then lower, then higher still, it is a called a "blossom." A "cascade" is the opposite of a pyramid, starting from a high unison note and cascading downward, with the bass breaking off last. Occasionally, while three voices hold their notes, a fourth voice will be assigned a melodic run in stepwise fashion, a device called a "Christmas tree." Another visual metaphor, "scissors," characterizes the crossing of two voices in opposite directions.

Barbershoppers are not bothered by the conventional nature of these effects, because the revivalists seek to preserve a style imbued with this type of melodic and harmonic gesture. However, skillful barbershop arrangers will refrain from overusing any single device or from loading a song down with so many of them that one loses the sense of the melody.

Whereas most of the popular music of the nineteenth century used the folklike tonic-subdominant-dominant chord progression popular in music of the British Isles, nineteenth-century experiments with circle-of-fifths progressions made their way into popular song (especially ragtime). As I have already mentioned, the practice of using the dominant of the dominant as a lead-in to a dominant-tonic cadence was at first a simple cadential extension of V^7–I. Composers began to structure entire sections of music around this type of pattern, even starting a melodic theme harmonized to one of these distant dominants. Charles Hamm notes: "Carried one step further, to yet another dominant, this mannerism results in a string of chromatic chords leading up to the final cadence. Such patterns are the basis for the characteristic harmonic style of 'barbershop harmony,' so linked in the popular mind with music of this period."[11] As noted by van der Merwe, Liszt's *Liebestraum* no. 3 outlines one such chord progression in the opening theme (I–III^7–VI^7–II^7–V^7–I). Van der Merwe dubs this the "ragtime progression" precisely because it was so heavily used by Tin Pan Alley composers of ragtime songs.[12] I argued in chapter 1 that the potential these progressions afforded for African American–style portamento within chromatic pitch areas contributed to establishing this progression in ragtime and coon songs.

In barbershop lingo, the major tonic triad is "home" or "home base." The progress of barbershop songs is referred to as the "harmonic highway," with important chords being called "signposts," or "road maps," and with harmonic digressions being called "side trips."[13] Barbershoppers are certainly not the only musical practitioners who use home and travel imagery in discussing harmonic progressions, but they are perhaps among the most self-conscious in employing this metaphor. With barbershop harmony conceived as a trip away from—and back to—home, a certain redundancy emerges between syntactics and semantics, or between the sound structure and its extramusical associations.

Singers "jump out" to a barbershop seventh chord a certain number of fifths away on the circle and return home through the series of secondary dominants. The jump-out chord can be referred to by the name of the best-known song that uses it, or—in an old system no longer in use—by fingers signaling how may steps away on the circle of fifths the chord is placed. This system was developed and popularized by Maurice A. "Molly" Reagan in the early 1940s and was transmitted to the revival movement in a series of articles in the *Harmonizer* called "The Mechanics of Barbershop Harmony." The so-called Reagan Clock System provided a singer-friendly discourse and pedagogy for singers who did not read music. It was an "ethnotheory" designed to elucidate the behavior of four-part close harmony within circle-of-fifths progressions. A song featuring a jump-out to a chord 4 fifths away from the tonic, starting and ending on the tonic triad (such as on the phrase "girl of my dreams" in the chorus of "The Sweetheart of Sigma Chi"), would be said to constitute a "12–4–3–2–1–12" sequence in the Reagan system. Reagan calls the chord based on the eighth position (i.e., an A-flat major triad in the key of C) the "barbershop chord," from its use in the vaudeville hit "(Mr. Jefferson Lord), Play That Barbershop

Chord." In golden-era songs, there may be an initial tonic chord, as in "Five Foot Two (Eyes of Blue)," or the progression can begin with the jump-out chord (the most distant secondary-dominant seventh-type chord used), as in "Sweet Georgia Brown." This type of harmony can be classified as centripetal, starting at a distant secondary dominant and moving (spiraling) closer to the tonic.

Obviously, this approach diminishes the traditional role of the subdominant as an approach to the dominant. The subdominant chord (IV, or the related chord in jazz progressions, the II^{m7}) is a diatonic chord—that is, all of its notes are found within the tonic scale. The new approach chord, the dominant of the dominant (II^7), introduces a chromatic note (a sharped fourth scale degree). Each subsequent dominant increases the number of nonscalar chromatic tones present in the harmonic progression. Such chromaticism might have been shocking for early audiences up until the 1870s or so, but the increasing ubiquity of this device in popular music naturalized the sound. In this way, popular music furthered the process by which chromaticism was made normative and integral, rather than decoratively expressive, in Western musical expectations. The singable melodies of the golden era, with their chromatic passages, evolved along with these explorations in centripetal harmony.

Centripetal progressions offered four-part harmony singers a number of distinct advantages. The four notes of the dominant seventh–style chord gave each voice a distinct note, with no doubling of voices, and thus maximized the expressive potential of a quartet, without requiring that the quartet omit chord tones (as would be the case with more extended chords). The chromaticism of the ragtime progressions allowed barbershoppers to snake or swipe chords with attention-grabbing chromatic slides. And, as an unintended consequence, the close-harmony voicing of dominant seventh chords in just tuning allowed for an especially vibrant "expanded" sound full of audible overtones, the acoustic principle that lends barbershopping its characteristic ringing timbre.

Barbershoppers do not sing only centripetal harmonies, of course; but these types of progressions lend themselves especially well to barbershop four-part close harmony. The dominant seventh–type chord (a major triad with a minor seventh scale degree) is so important to barbershop harmony that it is called the "barbershop seventh" or the "meat 'n' taters" chord. Society arrangers believe that a song should contain anywhere from 35 to 60 percent dominant seventh chords to sound "barbershop"—and when they do, barbershoppers speak of being in "seventh heaven."

Ringing Chords: Overtones and Metaphors

The more experienced singers of the barbershop revival (at least after the 1940s) have self-consciously tuned their dominant seventh and tonic chords in just intonation to maximize the overlap of common overtones, resulting in a ringing sound rich in harmonics. This sound is variously called "extended sound," "expanded sound," "fortified sound," or even (informally) "the voice of the angels."

I have not found early accounts describing this phenomenon; perhaps early close-harmony singers would occasionally ring chords but lacked a vocabulary with which to name this effect. Early revivalists, noting the shivers produced by some chords and the faint ethereal voices, debated whether this phenomenon was real. If it were real, they wondered, how was it produced? Singers noticed that certain predictable but subtle pitch adjustments produced better results. In a question-and-answer column from the *Harmonizer* in 1943, a singer asked, "In quartet arguments on how to sing some particular chord, I've heard it said for example the baritone is supposed to raise 'just a hair.' How can we tell how much is 'just a hair,' up or down?" The barbershop specialist Joe Stern responded, "This is a fallacy. I too have heard barber shop singers talk about 1/4 tones—1/8 tones, etc." Stern stated flatly that barbershop singers needed only to sing the "notes of the equal-tempered scales, recognizing no finer gradations than the half-tone."[14]

The first appearance of a theory of overtone production in Society contexts seems to have been in "Molly" Reagan's 1944 *Harmonizer* column, "Mechanics of Barber Shop Harmony." He noted that the timbral differences among instruments were related to the number and strength of the partials or harmonics (however, he misidentified partials simply as "octaves"). Although he did not reveal the problems of equal temperament, he did admit that barbershop singers need to sharpen or flatten notes "just a hair!" "One of the joys of barbershopping, unaccompanied, is the fact that true harmony can be attained, closer than notes on a piano or any other fixed-note instrument."[15]

Reagan gave the example of a dominant seventh chord based on a root whose fundamental was 100 hertz (Hz). The chord described would have notes with fundamentals at approximately 100, 125, 150, and 175 Hz. The most important issue in such a series is the fact that a dominant seventh chord with a root at 100 Hz is equivalent to the fourth, fifth, sixth, and seventh notes of an overtone series produced by a "missing root" of 25 Hz. In 1951 the mysteries of the ringing chords were described by the Society's international treasurer, Art Merrill: "There's a chord in barbershop that makes the nerve ends tingle. . . . We might call our chord a Super-Seventh! . . . The notes of our chord have the exact frequency ratios 4–5–6–7. With these ratios, overtones reinforce overtones. There's a minimum of dissonance and a distinctive ringing sound. How can you detect this chord? It's easy. You can't mistake it, for the signs are clear; the overtones will ring in your ears; you'll experience a spinal shiver; bumps will stand out on your arms; you'll rise a trifle in your seat."[16]

Merrill specified that barbershop had to be unaccompanied in order to free the singer from the tyranny of equal temperament (he referred to equal temperament improperly as the "chromatic scale"). He stressed that singers had to vary their pitches up to a "quarter tone" to achieve the properly tuned chords, and that they had to listen closely to each other to blend the chords. One other requirement for ringing chords was the avoidance of vibrato (which would of course vary the pitch and derail any effort to lock in the chord). An article on barbershop style once called vibrato "poison."

Some of the oral history interviews of early Society members include testimonies to the power of ringing chords, as in the following two accounts. The first is from Tom Massengale:

> We're singing down there one night and all of a sudden this violin starts playing up there, you know, obbligato, way up above our singing, and we sang a little while and we stopped with our mouths hanging open. And he [the director] said: "Well, you were in perfect harmony, perfect balance 'cause you created this overtone, created that other tone up there," and it's an eerie feeling.[17]

The second is from Gary Ives:

> Seeing other people react to a chord is just as much fun as singing it yourself. Seeing their faces . . . sometimes . . . it would just be a tear coming out of [my brother's] eye; it's happened may times to me. When you hit the right chord, it was just overwhelming. Our commentary was, "Did you hear the angels?" Today it's called "expanded sound" but we always referred to it as "the angels" . . . that overtone, that sound which is not sung.[18]

Barbershoppers have become partisans of this acoustic phenomenon, and they have made the physical experience of ringing chords a topic of lively discourse. Here is how that experience was described by the barbershop theorist Jim Ewin:

> We memorize just how these chords can sound if *struck* just right, and as we reach them in the song we tune our voices to *hit* the proper frequency. Of course, the more skilled the singers, the more Barbershop ringing chords they hit, and this is the area in which contests are won or lost. What happens when a *ringing* chord is struck? . . . If we could get a picture of this perfect chord on an oscilloscope [*sic*], we could see what it looks like. What it looks like isn't important *but what it does to us through our auditory nerves* is. The result is *a tingling of the spine, the raising of the hairs on the back of the neck, the spontaneous arrival of "goose flesh" on the forearm.* When all of this is happening, the human ear can hear only one sound through four voices combined to produce it. These four frequencies merged into a pattern which in effect produced a new sound, a fifth note of almost *mysterious propensities.* . . . It's the *consummation* devoutly wished by those of us who love Barbershop harmony. If you ask us to explain precisely and scientifically why we love it so, we are hard put to answer; *that's where our faith takes over.*[19]

Generations of barbershoppers have used this kind of rapturous language with hints of passion ("consummation") and quasi-religious belief ("devoutly," "mysterious properties," "faith takes over"). At the heart of the contemporary barbershop experience is this quest to produce and hear the harmonic phenomenon of ringing chords, making barbershop singers perhaps the most ardent proponents of harmonic singing this side of Tibet. Note that barbershoppers almost never speak of "singing" a chord, but almost always draw on a discourse of physical work and exertion; thus they "hit," "chop," "ring," "crack," and "swipe" (or in the old days, "snake") chords. This underlines that vocal harmony, which requires palpable physical exertion, is interpreted as an embodied musicking. Barbershoppers never lose sight (or sound) of its physicality.

In an article called "How We Train for Chorus Competitions," the East York Barbershoppers made clear the competitive edge that extended sound provides to a quartet or chorus: "Hit those special chords *hard* and *long*. After all, Society Judges are there to be 'moved,' so make that tingling sensation run up and down their spines and you will find their pencils being used to your advantage."[20] Compare two descriptions of the experience as described to me by barbershoppers:

> We create overtones by the voices being in a vowel formation the same, a blend the same. Voices of similar characteristics will create a tone above the four voices and that's the major thing we're looking for and that's the pleasure that we hear from it, and it's called the overtone [*sic*] . . . when the chord rings and it requires the chord to be perfectly tuned and balanced and so forth, but that's where the real pleasure comes from. And to ring one chord after another is a very difficult thing to do. Your fine competition quartet will hone their singing skills just like a golfer hones his golfing skills and they're capable of producing chord after chord of overtones.[21]

And:

> Then they hit the first chord and all of a sudden, "ring!" There are all these other notes, the overtones. If you hear a great quartet, they come to their last chord and it's just "whap!" There's a great big huge chord and that gets people hooked. A lot of people say, "Wow, I want to be a part of that." And it's fun to hear that chord around you.[22]

Note that this last comment also raises the discourse of addiction ("hooked"), which one finds often in barbershopping, beginning with the appearance of Deac Martin's book, *A Handbook for Adeline Addicts*.

So, how does this sound get produced? Barbershop revival singers rejected equal-tempered tuning early on because it sounded wrong for the chords. Equal temperament, the system used to tune Western fixed-pitch instruments such as a piano, constituted a historical compromise to an acoustic dilemma. Put simply, there is no fully adequate way of tuning notes on fixed-note instrument that will make all chords in a given key perfectly consonant and that will not produce strikingly dissonant chords when modulating to distant keys. Although the mathematics are complicated, tuning systems that produce well-tuned fifths produce awkward thirds, and vice versa. As I implied earlier in this section, a truly consonant triad or dominant seventh is produced when the frequencies of the various notes in a chord are simple multiples of a theoretical root note two octaves beneath the fundamental of the chord. Surprisingly, this consonance is especially noticeable when the timbres are complex, as is the case with voices.

Barbershoppers adjust each chord to the lead voice (melody) in a form of performance practice called just intonation. Just intonation is an ideal not often achieved except by well-trained quartets. In addition to producing consonant chords, this also creates audible overlaps in a few overtones of the chord tones, which, as I have mentioned, is perceived as a ringing acoustical phenomenon. Although the chords are tuned vertically (to the lead) in just intonation, the type of scale used by the lead voice to sing the melody is not specified, and this is especially important because the secondary-dominant progressions take the melody well outside the initial tonic scale. A just-tempered scale in the melody would accentuate the differences in these departures from the tonic key and make the adjustments made by the other voices more apparent. In practice, it seems that most leads rely on an approximation of an equal-tempered scale for the melody, to which the other voices adjust vertically in just intonation.

The nuanced adjustments necessary on the part of all four singers to achieve this intonation would represent an almost insurmountable barrier to producing ringing chords if there were no system of feedback to guide singers. Expanded sound functions as this feedback, letting singers know when their chord is properly tuned and when their individual pitches are perfectly aligned. Years of experience and close listening allow barbershoppers to know how to anticipate the adjustment needed to tune their parts when a given chord is called for in relation to a lead or melody note. Acoustic experiments by Ternström and Sundberg have shown that the common partials in a chord can be used by singers to tune chords in just intonation.[23]

Singing barbershop harmony requires a heightened perception of—and attention to—three other voices—their pitches, intensities, articulations, timbres, and tempi—and to the overtones of all ensemble voices together. This sophisticated sense of hearing and close listening have to be coupled to the singer's vocal production to blend the individual voice with the collective. Good overtone fortification is understood to reflect unified articulation, a balance of vocal intensities, and the presence of strong, resonant voices. It is produced only when all factors cohere. Because of this, the production of expanded sound and precise blend have become paramount aesthetic considerations in barbershop singing. In barbershop discourse, the ringing tone serves as a metaphor for group unity and camaraderie and a sublime experiential ideal. It has taken on a quasi-mystical significance for many barbershoppers, signaling that a kind of perfection in group harmony has been reached, a perfection that serves as a metaphor for the social unity and male fraternity (or female sorority, in the case of the women's barbershop groups) that inspire the practice of barbershop singing.[24]

Ringing chords would seem to be a rare aesthetic ideal amongst the world's many musical styles and forms, and yet there are a few oddly similar accounts from elsewhere in the world. The French ethnomusicologist Bernard Lorat-Jacob has written extensively on music of the Mediterranean island of Sardinia, home to a men's four-part singing style called *a tenore*. In Lorat-Jacob's words, "The exercise then consists of 'forming a block' with the other singers and, by following a soloist, of blending one's voice into those of the others. *A tenore* singing rests on principles of massed sound." After describing the basic practice, Lorat-Jacob expounds on the experience of producing "massed" sound:

> That cohesion—as I learned incidentally—has an objective feature; that is, it has the strange ability to manifest its existence acoustically. But for it to do so the four voices of the choir must be in perfect harmony. At that point a fifth voice, sung by no one in particular, makes its appearance in the upper register. It is called the *quintina* (literally the "little fifth") and is born of the harmonic fusion of the four real voices. Produced by the tight overlapping of the four consonant parts, the *quintina* testifies to the harmony of the singers and, as soon as they have made it "come out"—this is the goal the singers set themselves— it is present to the point of becoming overwhelming. . . . It is the acoustical proof of perfect harmony, and it is for that reason that the choir is called "concord" (*concordu* in Sardinian). Because it testifies to and at the same time reveals the perfection of the singing, the *quintina* is of a spiritual essence . . . the acoustic attribute of the ineffable.[25]

When I first read this account by Lorat-Jacob, I was stunned by the similarities in the way the sound was perceived and discussed in the two cultures, which have no obvious or direct historical connection. Parenthetically, like barbershop singing, the *a tenore* style often puts the melody in the second-highest voice.

The Music Men: Performance and Musical Lives

Early in my research, I used questionnaires to explore individual's motivations for singing barbershop harmony. The most common answers to my question about what attracted singers to barbershop (out of a list of ten possible choices) were "a love of music" and "fellowship."[26] Committed barbershop singers tend to be passionate about both. When asked about his most thrilling barbershop experience, Steve Ferrick replied:

I'm a great fan of Riptide's ability to Lock and Ring. . . . This brings me to my most thrilling singing experience, and I wasn't singing!! After Sat. eve at KC [the Kansas City barbershop convention], I went to the great VM [Vocal Majority, a chorus] afterglow. . . . It was over the top exceptional, kinda like a Spiritual experience. . . . After that I took a taxi up town to the main Hotel seeking Riptide [a quartet]. I spied them over in a corner singing to a group, so kinda just snuck up on 'em. They saw my name tag . . . and attacked me. . . . it was a hoot, got four great hugs, then they got right in my face and sang three songs at my nose . . . really not more than one foot away. . . . I WAS IN HEAVEN. I stood there with my eyes closed, which I like to do, and just let that awesome ring of theirs wash right over me. Some folks who were around took some pics—I look like I'm about to leave the body. To me, these guys have the best ring I've heard in more than 30 years. . . . In all those years, nothing has ever nailed me like hearing Riptide from one foot away . . . the sound is sooooooo pure, clean, balanced, blended, it's scary.[27]

These kinds of experiences, attested to by legions of barbershoppers, are both musical and social. They remind us that barbershop singing is enacted, lived, and experienced, and that it is a source of pleasure and joy as well as frustration and hard work. The major Societies (SPEBSQSA, Sweet Adelines International, and Harmony Incorporated, as well as non–North American societies) structure much of the organized barbershop activity of their members. Rehearsals, parades of quartets, chorus shows, sing outs, afterglows, competitions and conventions, volunteering, chapter meetings, and fundraisers make, for many barbershoppers, a lifestyle out of their singing hobby. The truly devoted may go to summer workshops and training sessions and participate as chapter or international officers. For many, especially those who hope to compete and who follow the competitions, the annual international conventions and the contests that build up to them are high points of the year. In the section that follows, I record some impressions, experiences, and testimony from an international SPEB-SQSA convention to better consider barbershop harmony as performance and practice.

The 2000 SPEBSQSA international convention was a "return to the womb" trip for barbershoppers—back to Kansas City, Missouri, and to the very hotel, the Muehlebach (now the Marriott-Muehlebach), where O. C. Cash and Rupert Hall convened a quartet in 1938 and had their fateful epiphany. The convention also celebrated two other cultural icons in barbershopping: *The Music Man* (which in 2000 was back for a run on Broadway) and the fiftieth anniversary of the championship of the Buffalo Bills, original stars of the *Music Man*'s Broadway and movie versions. The 2000 convention was also dedicated to recognizing the contributions of Walter Latzko, the band leader and arranger with the Arthur Godfrey shows, who arranged for both the Chordettes and the Buffalo Bills.

References to *The Music Man* were ubiquitous. The emcees for the quartet quarter-finals came onstage in the personae of Music Man characters, the daily bulletin that announced contest results was called the "River City Rag," and the banners and promotional material sported the logo for the year's convention, a graphic of a drum major right out of the musical's visual imagery.

Of course, when barbershoppers get together, they sing. I walked into the elevator of the fabled Muehlebach Hotel, and the first thing someone said was, "Hey, five people, we've got a quartet." His math was off, but the sentiment was there. Despite some nervous elevator laughter, no singing emerged by the second floor, but as we stepped out, the stranger behind me said to me, "I'm hungry to bust some tags. What part do you sing?" I looked around and realized he was talking to me.

"Baritone, but not a very good one," I answered, by no means modestly.

"Hey, no problem." And with that my new buddy, Doug, pulled me over just at the end of a glass walkway over the street between the two hotels.[28]

I hedged. "I don't have any tags *memorized*—I'm not active in a chorus."

"Let's try this," he said, pulling out some tags from his back pocket. "We'll use one that's got a nice bari part, if that's not too much of an oxymoron!" I had a feeling he had used that joke before. He paged through the dog-eared book and flipped to "Meet Me in Dreamland" (which I took to be a tag to "Meet Me Tonight in Dreamland," a song I'd been hearing a lot of lately in a television commercial for a mattress company),[29] and placed the book in my hands. "Sing [he sang] 'Meet me in dream - land' and hold 'land.' Start about here. [He hit a starting note for 'meet']."

I started up, and he joined me on lead below the baritone part. "Oh yeah, it's very crossed! Cool, huh. . . . . Now try, 'Sweet dream - y dream - land' and hold that there on the seventh chord . . . well, it *would* be a seventh chord" (meaning—I hoped—*if* we had four people, not *if* I could sing). I strained to reach the high D and sounded reedy, but I was trying desperately not to cop out and use falsetto. "Isn't that a stretch for a baritone!" he said, wincing. But we tried it again and he joined in and swiped "drea - eam – land," landing on a minor third.

"Hey, Jacko!" Doug called out. He introduced me to a member of his chorus who had just stepped off the escalator. "We're ripping some tags, and we need a tenor on 'Dreamland.'" We started off again as a trio and continued through to the end of the tag, sight-reading as necessary. I had to admit it was a nice bari part, chromatic and snaky, almost always above the lead until the last couple of bars.

Finally I excused myself: "Well, I've got to register and head outside to videotape the mass sing." We exchanged pleasantries, and Doug and Jackie headed off in the opposite direction to "Sing with the Champs," a chance for individual singers to get up on stage with championship quartets in front of the crowd at the Harmony Marketplace.

As I entered the registration area, I saw that scores of long-term and brand-new quartets had scattered themselves around the corners of the lobby, in doorways, behind exhibits, and in the middle of the room. I sidled

Figure 5.2. A tag to "Meet Me in Dreamland," arranged by Burt Szabo, 1981. Used by permission, Society for the Preservation and Encouragement of Barber Shop Quartet Singing in America, Inc.

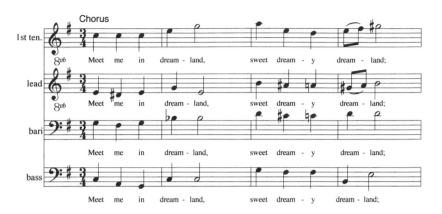

up behind a few to listen (but not to "fifth-wheel"!) and caught snippets of "Aura Lee," "MacNamara's Band," and "The Pal That I Loved Stole the Gal That I Loved" before picking up my tickets and badge. After baking in the sun with a couple of thousand barbershoppers for the "mass sing," I bought a bratwurst and wandered through the Harmony Marketplace, where merchants were selling everything from quartet videotapes to SPEB-SQSA monogrammed underwear and CD-ROM barbershop multimedia packages.

For the Quartet Semi-Final Competition, the central sections of Kemper Arena were nearly full. It was generally estimated that there were about ten thousand barbershoppers in town, most of whom, it seemed, were in attendance for the semifinals. Dennis, who was sitting next to me, sings in a newly organized urban Ohio chorus, although he himself lives some distance away from the city. He comes from a singing family, with sisters, brothers, and cousins all in one barbershop society or another. Dennis's new chorus is determined to qualify for the internationals, so it maintains a rigorous rehearsal schedule and has recruited a top director. The group only numbers about thirty-five to forty presently, but it intends to grow in the next year. Dennis frequently reached around to shake the hands of any number of people he knew who walked by. "This is the best place to sit," he confided, "because we're right above where all the former champions sit," and with that he started to list the names of people from right to left two rows in front of us, identified, as far as I can tell, by the backs of their heads. Clearly, he possesses a deep connoisseur's knowledge of barbershopping, knows the faces of hundreds of past international champions, remembers the renditions they performed for contests, and spots arranging infractions and style errors easily. After one excellent performance, he shouted "Awesome!" and pumped his fists.

Dennis is also intensely involved in "shadow judging," my term for the game played by so many who attend the convention. They mark score sheets of their own and compare their results to those of the panel of judges. As in so many competitive contexts for expressive culture, deep dissatisfaction with the judging is often expressed publicly. The pleasures experienced in this kind of audience reception (shadow judging) have not been well theorized. In contemporary adjudication, five judges are assigned to each of three separate categories: "music" (aspects of arrangement in the performance, such as melody, range, harmony, adherence to barbershop norms, embellishment, and so forth); "presentation" (how well a song is brought to life both visually and vocally); and "singing" (individual vocal skill as well as group blend, unity, precision, and ease of delivery). Each group presents two songs, and each judge awards up to 100 points per song. This means that, with a total of fifteen judges, a group can earn up to 3,000 points in a night's performance. For example, after performing "Basin Street Blues" and "Tin Roof Blues" in the quartet quarterfinals, Saturday Evening Post was in ninth place with 2,535 points; and they moved into the semifinals (top twenty groups) with a strong possibility of getting into the finals (the top ten point scorers advance). However, their semifinal contest performance of "I Thought about You" and "It Don't Mean a Thing" netted them only 2,490 points, dropping them in to a cumulative eleventh place and just out of the finals.

The most controversial performance of the evening was by Rumors, which performed a parody of "Please, Mr. Columbus," whose lyrics went: "Please style committee, turn this ship around." Their parody was aimed at the admission and too-lenient judging of what they considered to be non-barbershop material. The song had references to well-known performances of fringe material by other quartets and choruses. However, Rumors ended up in fourteenth place. The top three spots in each of the three nights of contest judging went to Platinum, Michigan Jake, and BSQ, in that order, all perennial finalists in recent years.

On the bus to the hotel after the quarters, semis, and finals, riders, myself included, shared the results of their shadow judging and compared their disgruntlement with others. A man with a white handlebar moustache shook his head:

> Four Voices in *thirteenth* place? What *were* they thinking? That was *good clean barbershop!* I counted other groups ending songs on major sevenths! That song by Rumors about the judges and style committee is dead on, you know?! Blues and swing are nice for enjoyment—I mean my chorus sings "As Time Goes By" and it's not based on a circle of fifths (the bridge maybe, but we don't sing it that way)—anyway . . . we sing it in parades but not for competition! Barbershop has got to have that circle of fifths. It's got to ring chords . . . or else it's just not barbershop. I just don't think "It Don't Mean a Thing" is barbershop. You know what I think? I think "It Don't Mean Barbershop"!

A woman across the aisle nodded. "I just kept hearing *modern* harmony. I don't even *know* what it was. Some of it was just *ugly.*" And so it went for the entire week of the convention, with spirited debates on tradition, judging criteria, appropriateness, quality and aesthetics emerging out of every contest and debated into the wee hours. (Months after the convention, some of this debate was still taking place on the Harmonet, a barbershop listserv). The gentleman quoted above was driving at a central distinction made in barbershopping between contest tunes and show or parade tunes. Songs for parades of quartets or chorus shows need not adhere to strict barbershop criteria and seldom do. Choruses and quartets have operated on the principle that their audiences need a more varied musical diet than that provided by the contest-worthy (often golden-era) songs. And so jazz standards, patriotic and religious songs, Broadway musical selections, and pop songs are liberally sprinkled into the non-contest performances. But when a group has polished a "show" tune to critical audience acclaim, there is always a tendency to want to bring the song into a contest and to perform one's best material regardless of the number of seventh chords or the singability of its melody.

In part because barbershoppers are so concerned about the graying of the tradition, younger quartets at Society conventions are often applauded regardless of ability. Emcees will typically say something like, "This is the future of our Society," followed by, "and the future of our Society appears to be in very good hands!" or "and our future seems to be very secure indeed!" SPEBSQSA has responded to the concerns over graying by forming the "Young Men in Harmony Committee," which designs youth programs and administers the MBNA America Collegiate Barbershop Quartet Contest. Sponsored by a credit card company, the collegiate competition is the barbershop Society's best hope for generating new audiences for barbershop among younger singers.[30]

At the collegiate competition, I happened to be sitting in the middle of a large family of singers. To my right was a teenager, Jason; his father, Dale, was in front of me. Dale, a father of five boys and one girl, hails from Montana. Dale's father came back from World War II embittered against the government, dropped out, took over a family farm, and discovered a growing network of barbershop singers. He passed on his love of barbershop to his son, as Dale did with the next generation. The males in the family all sing in a small local chapter ("It's not much of a chapter—sometimes ten people show up altogether"), but they also have a family quartet. Dale thinks his sons have an instinctual feel for barbershop, having been raised with the sound of ringing chords and hearing more than just "piano scales," while other quartets have to "learn to hear it, and undo all that other stuff." When the oldest joined the navy to pay for college, Dale recruited his youngest two boys to sing together on the tenor part, making his quartet a quintet. However, his two next oldest boys both plan to join the navy within two years, so the quartet will probably dissolve. In the meantime, however, the whole family came and participated in the fathers and sons chorus. "This is just what we like to do as a family. My boys have a lot of fun." Dale's son Jason enjoyed the anti-Montana jokes from the emcee the night previously, finding too much truth in jokes about the dearth of people and interesting things to do in Big Sky Country.

I was rooting for a group from Indiana that had accompanied one of my talks on barbershop, a group called Segway, and they performed an impressive rendition of the sentimental song "The Boy I Used to Be." Unfortunately for them, the same song was covered by the group that took first place, Millennium, in a clearly superior performance. Millennium followed that song with the biggest point-winning performance of the concert, a jazzy rendition of "I'm Beginning to See the Light." As the winning collegiate quartet, Millennium was scheduled to open ("mic test") the Quartet Semi-Final Competition. When their video feed appeared on the big screens at either side of the stage a few nights later, small groups of young women began screaming as though at a rock concert, especially for the members of the quartet deemed most "cute."

Back in Kemper Arena, our host and emcee for the chorus finals was the former Buffalo Bills baritone Dick Grapes, who mixed heartfelt stories about the Bills' singing career with jokes and asides. In an area beneath him and in front of the stage sat the fifteen judges, who activated a light to tell Grapes to halt whenever they were ready for the next chorus to begin.

Much of the drama of a competition takes place outside of the arena and before the convention, and a sense of suspense or tension can literally build over many years as some groups fail to win, feel slighted, and/or reposition themselves for success. Will the Alexandria Harmonizers continue their reign? Will Northbrook place in their perennial number-two position? Will Bank Street fall further from their once-heralded prospects? The drama of the convention plays out against the memory of all that has gone before in competitions.

No chorus has been pushing the envelope on integrating show tunes into barbershop in recent years more than the perennial second-place finishers, the New Tradition Chorus of Northbrook, Illinois. In 2000, the 112 members of the Northbrook chorus again staged their impressive and musically polished medley from the Broadway musical *Les Miserables*. With French Revolutionary–era costumes, elaborate staging, and extraordinary power and blend, the chorus is the darling of the arranging "progressives," who see their performance as simply one of the best choral presentations in North America. Traditionalists wonder why the chorus finishes so high even though they perform non-barbershop material! To no one's surprise, they placed—what else but?—second for an unprecedented ninth time.

Because a group's rank is the result of a cumulative total of the points awarded by all fifteen judges in three separate categories, it is almost impossible to conspire against or for a group. Nonetheless, conspiracy theories still take hold. Northbrook's ongoing also-ran ranking is partly a result of the presence of three dominant, professional, and exquisitely rehearsed groups with more mainstream approaches to barbershop harmony—Dallas's Vocal Majority, the Alexandria [Virginia] Harmonizers, and Masters of Harmony —which have rotated the championship on an almost routine three-year cycle for the last fifteen years. Championship choruses are barred from competition for two years after their championship, and as a result, the best choruses appear at the convention every three years to win first place. This compares with the quartet champions, who, owing to an early precedent, forever retire from international competition once they become Society champions (there are also limits on the number of singers from a championship quartet who can compete together in a new quartet).

There is indeed a heavy emphasis placed on becoming SPEBSQSA champions; a perennial second-place finish for a group like Northbrook may establish them as one of the greatest choruses in Society history, but they will never appear in the all-important lists of Society champions. To all but cognoscenti they will be relatively invisible in the historical accounts, which feature lists of former champions.

The first groups to perform for the chorus competition were two rather small choruses from Europe (one from the United Kingdom and one the Netherlands). During the performance by the Dutch chorus, a person in a chicken costume, serving as the mascot for the Big Chicken Chorus (Marietta, Georgia), solicited both attention and boos by clowning around in the front aisles of the auditorium. "That's just plain rude," said a barbershopper sitting next to me and pointing at the audience. "You would have never seen that a few years ago. Look at that—you've got supporters of Vocal Majority throwing Mardi Gras beads, fans of Excalibur [a quartet] waving laser sabers, train whistles a moment ago by fans of the Virginians, and a giant chicken doing . . . I don't know . . . the lambada . . . jeez. At least don't do it while the other group's on stage!"

Neil, my neighbor who spoke up, is an ardent barbershop traditionalist. He lives in an old mill town in upstate New York and started singing with a small chorus there last year. During the summer the chorus has close to forty members, but because many are elderly members who overwinter in Florida ("snowbirds"), the group is reduced to about ten of the younger members in the off season. This is fine with Neil, because the core membership selects tunes, mails them to the snowbirds, and rehearses them during the winter. The snowbirds learn their parts while in Florida and rehearse them about four to five times with the core group before performing in the major early-summer concert. Neil notes that the group's director is not first rate but that he is perfectly in keeping with the abilities and ambitions of the group, which are modest. The chorus enjoys a partnership with the local Harmony Incorporated chorus, with whom they share the billing at the annual summer concert. The local Harmony Incorporated chorus and its three competing quartets are, he added, much more professional than the SPEBSQSA group, and they regularly do very well at Harmony Incorporated conventions. Neil explained the connection: "Harmony Inc. sings the same kind of material as us. Sweet Adelines does more of the show tunes, and the '50s songs, and other kinds of harmony—it's nice, but it's not 'After Dark' and 'Coney Island Baby' like you hear from the men. We once did a concert with a Sweet Adelines group and they had a long argument before the show about what color stockings they were going to wear. Harmony Incorporated is a little more laid back than that. I mean, we [the men's group] don't care what color stockings you wear."

The Big Chicken Chorus ended their set with a humorous plea to the judges called "Someday We'd Like to Win International," which made lots of in-group references to the performances of recent champions and competitors. They marched in formation while imitating the Vocal Majority's rendition of "Jericho" and ran through a credible sample of Northbrook's "Les Miz" medley! They poked fun at last year's quartet champions, Fred, by singing "If Fred can win, anyone can," and ridiculed Northbrook's second-place reputation with the line "Say Jay [Northbrook's musical director], got a second?" The group donned the robes associated with a winning performance of the Alexandria Harmonizers, another dominant chorus, and played with the conventional wisdom that the Vocal Majority would win in 2000 ("And you know who's here!"). In any case, the judges were not impressed and dropped the Big Chicken Chorus to sixth place overall.

The surprise performance was by the Toronto Northern Lights, which managed to produce a big, extended sound and capture fifth place, despite being a relatively small chorus (34 members, compared to the Vocal Majority's 158). The Vocal Majority, however, lived up to its reputation with its powerful rendition of "The Sweetheart of Sigma Chi" and the "Mardi Gras March/South Rampart Street Medley," earning 2,866 points out of a possible 3,000. However, when I was spoke later with members of the Vocal Majority, they expressed disgruntlement with a point spread discrepancy on the part of one judge. His margin of difference was chalked up disapprovingly to a lack of training and experience, and his performance was compared to that of a former judge who often disagreed with his peers. The system of judging is expected to be so thoroughly scientific and so well managed through selection, training, and certification that few major discrepancies should emerge in individual point tallies.

The 2000 quartet finals were proceeded by a mass sing of "O Canada!" and "The Star-Spangled Banner" (led by Greg Lyne, the director of music education and services for SPEBSQSA), followed by another mass sing of "Lida Rose" from *The Music Man* with the women in attendance singing the counterpoint.

As if to remind us, unintentionally, that race is never far from the surface in barbershop, Excalibur began the contest with "Ain't Misbehavin'" and "Bill Bailey, Won't You Please Come Home?" both of which featured echoes of minstrelsy. A highlight of the competition was the rendition by the winning quartet, Platinum, of "Smilin' Through" and "Cuddle Up a Little Closer, Lovey Mine," for which the quartet earned a standing ovation. The levity was supplied by Fred's "halftime" performance. Fred, a comic quartet, was the previous year's champion group, and in 2000 it performed a contrafacta version of "It Was a Very Good Year" that described the ten years of competitions they endured (and lost, sometimes miserably) before winning first prize in 1999.

At a break in the competition, I turned to Hal, an older gentleman from western Kentucky with a big white handlebar moustache, and asked what he was likely to do when the convention was over. "I'm going to head up to Indiana for a weekend to catch an Acoustix [SPEBSQSA former international championship quartet] concert. We'll take the Winnebago up and make a weekend out of it—the wife and I do that every once in a while when a great group like Acoustix is singing. My daughter—she sings with a Sweet Adelines group down in Birmingham—she's going to come with us. She's a schoolteacher with twenty years seniority. . . . She's going to retire soon with a very good package. Anyway, this way we'll get some family time, 'cause we don't get to see too much of her these days, with her own family and all." I looked at him in amazement. A full week into nothing but barbershop and he was already plotting his next weekend's barbershop outing.

In looking back on my notes of conversations with barbershoppers at the convention—folks like Hal, Dale, Neil, and the others quoted here—I cannot help but worry that I have written my own ethnographic version of Norman Rockwell's "The Barbershop Quartet," peopled with friendly, down-home folk who spend weekends in Winnebagos and bust tags in American Legion halls. This is, of course, one face of the barbershop movement.

Tag: "Meet Me Tonight in Dreamland"

What separates this convention from any other hobbyist gathering, such as, for example, a Star Trek convention? At barbershop international conventions as at Trekker (or Trekkie) events, fans dress up, trade memorabilia, indulge their personal identification with the products of the popular culture industries, speak in rarified languages, and find meaning and fellowship in their shared passions. Conventions, especially conventions that focus on competition, partake of a generalized culture of conventions. From the registration booth, to the souvenir sales area, to the gatherings in arenas, to the parties that follow in restaurants and hotel rooms, conventioneering is a transposable experience. And yet there is something different in coming together to play music or to sing.

We perceive sound and music not as external but as part of ourselves, as incorporated. Steven Feld has noted that "sound both emanates from and penetrates bodies."[31] Indeed, we internalize the sounds of others through hearing even as we externalize the vibrations of our own vocal folds by speaking or singing. The act of hearing—in the presence of others—links participants in relationships of internalization and externalization of sound, enveloping listeners in auditory co-presence. The relationship of the internalizing and externalizing of the self and of others in collective musical encounters encourages the production of a powerful, transformative experience of the self as a participant in community, resulting in a greater sense of unity and solidarity. Collective audition—hearing together—is a persuasive, physical confirmation of connectedness.

Barbershop performances deploy texts ("the old songs") with nostalgic content; these texts originated in earlier times, and they serve as condensed articulations of late-Victorian ideology, betraying a longing for innocence, simplicity, and the assuredness that characterized—at least in the imagination—a previous historical epoch (although many texts also chronicle the heady optimism and brash cultural change at the turn of the century). Barbershop revivalists and their societies have selected a sample of the period's music as an appropriate canon for barbershop close harmony treatment. But it is not just the lyrics that speak of an earlier time. The preservation and codification of a set of sonic and stylistic practices or techniques nurture what are thought to be the auditory soundscapes of an earlier generation. There is a certain ecology manifest in these practices: "meat 'n taters" chords, four vocal parts, circle-of-fifths harmonic progressions, close harmony, *sol*-to-*sol* melodies, just intonation, swipes and embellishments, and ringing chords all fit together and cohere, in part because they emanate from a period of popular cultural production, and in part because barbershoppers have consolidated those practices seen as coherent and rejected those considered contradictory. In this fashion, the messy topography of history is smoothed out into a nostalgic cultural landscape.

Barbershop harmony saves its most serious payoffs for live performance. When discussing ringing chords, singers draw on metaphors of religious rapture, sexual pleasure, and drug addiction, among others, to describe the powerful experience of audible overtones in song. Quartets and choruses "sell" these packets of sounded ideology through persuasive choreography, expression, and gesture. The ringing chords that sometimes result are roundly interpreted as a metaphor for the unity, harmony, and fellowship sought in close harmony singing—sound structure as social structure.

Conclusion
Afterglow

With mournful voices, they howled that fine
Heart-rending song: "Sweet Adeline."
Their voices wailed from quavering throats
And clung fondly to the long, sad notes.
They swayed,
Leaned backward,
Closed their eyes
In sour attempts to harmonize.
　　　　　　　　　—Joseph Moncure March,
　　　　　　　　　　"The Wild Party" (1928)

The gin-soaked image of a barbershop quartet that Joseph March en-shrined in his ribald, Prohibition-era epic jazz poem "The Wild Party" is a far cry from the sanitized barbershop quartets of Norman Rockwell and Walt Disney. If we also consider Louis Armstrong's childhood quartet entertaining pimps and prostitutes for handouts in the streets of the Story-ville District of New Orleans, or blackface quartets performing travesties of African American music in turn-of-the-century minstrel productions, or the straightlaced recording quartets in Thomas Edison's early studios, we can begin to discern how malleable and protean an institution the barber-shop quartet has been.

W. E. B. Du Bois spoke of the centrality of the question of race in the twentieth century—in music as in all aspects of American life. I have worked the issue of race in this study from two angles: from the strikingly hybrid-ized cultural contributions that blacks and whites have made to barber-shop harmony and from the representations and the discourse about race that have emerged in and around barbershop quartet singing. I have at-tempted to show that barbershop harmony was neither a continuous Anglo-American singing style cultivated in quaint Victorian-era barber-shops, nor a product of an "authentic" black experience crudely appropri-ated by whites. Barbershop harmony, from my perspective, is a creolized and miscegenated product of American race relations, and it betrays the

179

traces left by Austrian and German harmonized folk song movements and their American imitators, by blackface minstrelsy and Stephen Foster's chorus songs, by black recreational harmonists, by ragtime composers, by pioneer recording quartets, and by the many and varied currents of the American musicscape that have spilled over into barbershop singing. This version of barbershop harmony is not set aside as an exceptional trinket of Americana but is woven into a tapestry of American vernacular harmony that connects doo-wop, the "high lonesome" sound of bluegrass, vaudeville comedy fours, black sacred quartet traditions, the Mills Brothers, and even (at some distance) the Beach Boys.

Barbershop harmony was embraced as an audio icon of the early century and as such was incorporated into later nostalgic evocations of the boisterous optimism of this period. The barbershop revivalists and the many pop cultural entrepreneurs enamored of barbershop harmony (Walt Disney, Arthur Godfrey, Robert Moses, Roy Rogers, Lawrence Welk, and Meredith Willson, and others) carefully honed these sounds and images to serve a peculiar form of American neo-Victorianism.

Our fascination with Victorian-era sociability and character may have passed its prime, but it is far from having disappeared from the American scene. It takes only a cursory look at the blueprints for new towns and developments (as well as old town center restoration projects) to note that many urban planners have fully embraced the vision of a livable small town of front porches and friendly storefronts, the kind of town we nostalgically imagine to be filled with sounds of brass bands and barbershop quartets. These neo-Victorian projects are seen as antidotes to alienated suburban sprawl, and at the heart of this movement in urban planning is a notion that somewhere along the line (with the advent of the automobile, the highway, and low-cost home loans) American cultural geography took a wrong turn. Like barbershop singing, this tendency in urban planning could be described as a fellowship restoration project.

Coincidentally, on the very day that I find myself writing this conclusion and finishing a first draft of this book, a national task force has released a report decrying the decline in civic participation, community ties, and citizenship. Called "Better Together: A Blueprint for Civil Renewal," the report faults the failure of the interwar generation to pass on a culture of active community involvement to the postwar baby boomers, which has resulted in a graying of civic connections. Not coincidentally, "graying" is the same term barbershoppers use to characterize the increase in the mean age of barbershop harmonists. The vitality of a barbershop movement is clearly challenged not only by a decline in associational activity and a continuing expansion of passive modes of cultural consumption, but also by the complicity of barbershop revivalists in whitewashing a rich and complex history of American vernacular four-part harmony.

The roots of barbershop singing enjoyed widespread commercial success in the first two decades of the century. The distinctive sound of barbershop harmony indexes that era and will continue to be nostalgically evoked, recycled, "preserved," and revived in the present. Barbershop harmony may indeed have a bright future as one of the many musics that generate subcultures and movements of affinity, the kinds of musical formations that dot the postmodernist soundscape.

The culture of amateur, participatory singing and the sound of well-rung barbershop chords in close harmony are among the assets that the barbershop revival movement brings to contemporary expressive culture. The aesthetic of barbershop singing, as it has developed over the course of the revival movement, is complex, fascinating, and esoteric, and it has made a unique contribution to the panorama of American (and world) music. It is my hope that as practioners of barbershop harmony explore their relationship to other a cappella (and accompanied) vernacular harmony styles, this book will offer them a better understanding of the historic links among these styles and genres. I also hope that it will facilitate a more frank confrontation with the legacy of black*voice* minstrelsy and thus empower the barbershop movement to preserve the "old songs" without the taint of the old racism.

The movement to "preserve and encourage" barbershop harmony has evolved in relation to a contest over alternative modernities. It has attempted to advocate for the values, real or imagined, of nineteenth-century small-town America–a system of beliefs that can be dubbed neo-Victorianism. This ideology incorporates an appreciation for gender segregation in recreational or hobby pursuits, an emphasis on fellowship and character, nostalgia for the turn of the century, and, obviously, a love of participatory, amateur harmony. Barbershop quartetting and harmony singing deserve to be much better understood as a musical and social practice, and it is hoped that this book will open the debate on the role of barbershop singing as a sonic icon of an American national mythology.

Notes

Preface

1. I adopt the common practice of dispensing with periods after each letter of SPEBSQSA, as I do with ASCAP, passim.

2. Gage Averill, "Four Parts, No Waiting: The Ideal of Male Camaraderie in Barbershop Harmony Singing," paper delivered at the Society for Ethnomusicology Annual Meeting, Oakland, California, November 5, 1990.

Introduction

1. On gospel quartets, see especially Kip Lornell, *"Happy in the Service of the Lord": African-American Sacred Vocal Harmony Quartets in Memphis,* 2d ed. (Knoxville: University of Tennessee Press, 1995), and Raymond Allen, *"Singing in the Spirit": African-American Sacred Quartets in New York City* (Philadelphia: University of Pennsylvania Press, 1992). On rhythm and blues harmony groups, see Philip Groia, *They All Sang on the Corner: New York City's Rhythm and Blues Vocal Groups of the 1950's* (Setauket, N.Y.: Edmond, 1974); Anthony Gribin and Matthew Schiff, *Doo-Wop: The Forgotten Third of Rock 'n' Roll* (Iola, Wisc.: Krause, 1992); and Jay Warner, *The Da Capo Book of American Singing Groups: A History, 1940–1990* (New York: Da Capo Press, 1992).

2. Charles Hamm's sole reference to close harmony singing and barbershop quartets in *Yesterdays* is: "Such patterns are the basis for the characteristic harmonic style of 'Barbershop harmony,' so linked in the popular mind today with music of this period" (New York: W. W. Norton, 1983), 296.

3. The sociologist of the arts Max Kaplan is the scholar most closely associated with barbershopping. His forty-year association with SPEBSQSA resulted in numerous commissioned studies and policy papers, along with an edited book called *Barbershopping: Musical and Social Harmony* (Cranbury, N.J.: Associated University Presses, 1993). Kaplan and Robert A. Stebbins, author of *The Barbershop Singer: Inside the Social World of a Musical Hobby* (Toronto: University of Toronto Press, 1996), have both emphasized empirical social science approaches to the study of leisure and hobbies. Their studies have counseled SPEBSQSA on improving recruitment and retention and stemming the "graying" of the barbershop movement. One of the chief drawbacks of both books has been their uncritical reliance on the conventional histories emanating from the barbershop revival societies.

4. "Vernacular" comes from the Latin word *vernâculus* (pertaining to domestic slaves, that is, slaves raised in the home of their masters). Such slaves were the masters of cultural in-betweenness and translation. In linguistics, "vernacular" refers to a nonstandard dialect or idiom used as a

language of common discourse, one that carries the tint of its lower-class origins or of its "popular" quality. The musicologist Christopher Small has used this sense of "vernacular" to title his book on African American music, *Music of the Common Tongue: Survival and Celebration in Afro-American Music* (New York: Riverrun Press, 1987). Vernacular musics are defined principally by what they are not: elite musics with pretensions to high art. Vernacular musics embody forms that might be classed as folk and/or popular-commercial, without worrying excessively about the boundaries of "folk"-ness. This is especially appropriate for barbershop, which passes so often back and forth from home and community-based music making to the commercial music industry and media.

5. Christopher Finch, *Fifty Norman Rockwell Favorites* (New York: Crown, 1977), 98–99.

6. Strangely enough, Foster's group looks as though it could be the same group that Rockwell featured, and it is standing in roughly the same formation, although the characters are a good twelve years younger. I believe that this similarity was probably unintentional (Rockwell employed his own live models from New Rochelle, New York, where he had his studio—one of those models was a New Rochelle barber), although it is conceivable that Rockwell had in mind an updating of the earlier cover art.

7. Warren Susman, ed., *Culture and Commitment, 1929–1950* (New York: George Braziller, 1973), 10.

8. Both accounts appeared in Joe Stern, "History of Barber Shop Harmony," *Harmonizer* 3, no. 4, 1944 (Advance Bulletin): 14, and in C. T. "Deac" Martin, *Keep America Singing* (1948; reprint, Kenosha, Wisc.: SPEBSQSA, 1970), 21–22.

9. Ibid.

10. Ibid. (Stern, reported by Van Vechten in *The Music of Spain*). Barbering in Europe and the early United States was a low-status occupation, typically occupied by members of intergenerationally low-status ethnic groups or castes. In Spain members of Rom (gypsy) groups often served as butchers and barbers; hence the connection to Spaniards (really Spanish gypsies) and to guitars. References to the use of guitars, citterns, and especially cymbals in the early accounts above suggest a Mediterranean association for various types of music being made in barbershops in England and even in the early urban United States. By the nineteenth century, throughout much of the United States and especially in the South, African Americans had taken over these low-status occupations, including barbering.

11. "Tampa Chapter's Oldest Charter Member," *Harmonizer* 5, no. 3 (February 1946): 41.

12. James Weldon Johnson, "The Origin of the 'Barber Chord,'" *Mentor* 17 (February 1929): 53.

13. Ed Lieberman, "Close Harmony or Barbershop, What Do You Think?" *Harmonizer* 8, no. 2 (December 1948): 8.

14. Stern, "History of Barber Shop Harmony," 14, and Martin, *Keep America Singing*, 22.

15. Lynn Abbott, "'Play That Barber Shop Chord': A Case for the African American Origin of Barbershop Harmony," *American Music* 10 (1992): 289–325.

16. James Earl Henry, "The Origins of Barbershop Harmony: A Study of Barbershop's Musical Links to Other African American Musics as Evidenced through Recordings and Arrangements of Early Black and White Quartets" (Ph.D. diss., Washington University, 2000). Henry's comparisons are, I suggest, unable to make a clear case for unilinear influence from Af-

rican American to white performance because, as he admits, he was unable to arrange these transcriptions of recordings into chronological order, an effort that would fail in any case owing to the lack of recording opportunities for most black quartets. He is left, therefore, to show examples of stylistic features in black examples and white examples and to assert that the former influenced the latter. His case is weakened by the fact that many of the stylistic influences he cites were not passed directly from black to white quartets but were a result of a pervasive African American influence in the popular music and songwriting industries of the late nineteenth and early twentieth centuries. For example, blues scales and dominant seventh chords need to be understood as part of the new pop music vernacular; they were not necessarily evidence of quartet-to-quartet transmission. In general, I find Henry's case overstated, but his many patient transcriptions should be helpful to scholars who continue this research.

17. Jeffrey Melnick, "'Story Untold': The Black Men and White Sounds of Doo-Wop," in *Whiteness: A Critical Reader*, ed. Mike Hill (New York: New York University Press, 1997), 147.

18. Russell A. Potter, "Race," in *Key Terms in Popular Music and Culture*, ed. Bruce Horner and Thomas Swiss (London: Blackwell, 1999), 71. As a result of its history, barbershop harmony becomes a sign in the continuing debate over authenticity, essentialism, and racial identity in music. As critical as black aesthetics have been to the evolution of barbershop harmony, barbershop quartet singing was always an unlikely candidate on which to posit a "coherent and stable racial culture" (this last phrase from Paul Gilroy, *The Black Atlantic: Modernity and Double Consciousness* [Cambridge: Harvard University Press, 1993], 97). My focus on cultural interaction runs afoul of interpretations of black and white cultural history that emphasize cultural separation. Even Eric Lott, in his brilliant *Love and Theft: Blackface Minstrelsy and the American Working Class* (New York: Oxford University Press, 1993), emphasizes bounded cultures in arguing that minstrelsy served as an exception to the rule: "the minstrel show worked for over a hundred years to facilitate safely an exchange of energies *between two otherwise rigidly bounded and policed cultures*"(6, emphasis added). This remark is belied by his later observation of minstrel men visiting "racially integrated theaters, taverns, neighborhoods, and waterfronts" (41). Indeed, this latter observation speaks to the incompleteness and failures of the segregationist project (Jim Crow laws, the one-drop rule, and so on). Minstrelsy reveals the anxieties of contact, the sexual tensions percolating in a nation with a history of visible miscegenation, clumsy readings of cultural difference, and fears of lower-class black physicality and resentment. Cultural representations of the minstrel show (and its descendants) were made in what Christopher A. Waterman calls "a system of interracial musical calculation that originated in the paternalistic social relations of slavery and survived thoroughgoing institutionalization of the one-drop ideology in the decades following Reconstruction" (Waterman, "Race Music: Bo Chatmon, 'Corrine, Corrina,' and the Excluded Middle," in *Music and the Racial Imagination*, ed. Ronald Radano and Philip V. Bohlman [Chicago: University of Chicago Press, 2000]).

19. See Eric Hobsbawm and Terence Ranger, *The Invention of Tradition* (New York: Cambridge University Press, 1983). Also see Edward Said, *Orientalism* (New York: Vintage Books, 1979).

20. I refer the reader to the wealth of detail in David Lowenthal, *The Past Is a Foreign Country* (Cambridge: Cambridge University Press, 1985).

21. Martin, "Three Eras of Barbershop Harmony," *Harmonizer* 15, no. 2

(June 1955): 20. Martin's version of the decline of barbershopping likewise excludes commercial concerns and the media. He claims that Prohibition made drinking more popular, even among former teetotalers, and that attempts at drunken harmony caused barbershop to fall into disrepute.

22. Hamm, *Yesterdays*, 182.

23. Maurice Halbwachs, *On Collective Memory*, ed. and trans. Lewis A. Coser (Chicago: University of Chicago Press, 1992; first published in 1941 under the title *La mémoire collective*), helped to shift attention in the social sciences and humanities toward the social construction of memory (and away from its neuropsychological basis).

24. Mieke Bal, introduction, *Acts of Memory: Cultural Recall in the Present*, ed. Mieke Bal, Jonathan Crewe, and Leo Spitzer (Hanover: Dartmouth University Press, 1999), xi.

25. Lowenthal, *The Past Is a Foreign Country*, 4–13.

26. Renato Rosaldo, *Culture and Truth: The Remaking of Social Analysis* (Boston: Beacon Press, 1989), 69–73.

27. Jean-Jacques Rousseau, *The New Eloise*, cited in Marshall Berman, *All That Is Solid Melts into Air: The Experience of Modernity* (New York: Simon and Schuster, 1982), 18.

28. Fredric Jameson, *The Cultural Turn: Selected Writings on the Postmodern, 1983–1998* (London: Verso), 10. Jameson calls contemporary fads for realism—especially in political movements that seek the solidity of the past as a balm for current ills—a "replay of the empty stereotypes of all those things, and a vague memory of their fullness on the tip of the tongue"(189). He coins the term "hauntology" to refer to the studying the spectral apparition of the past in the present. Jean Baudrillard devoted his influential volume *Simulations* (New York: Semiotext(e), 1983) to the notion that what passes for real in the contemporary world is a play of images and symbols that no longer stand for anything outside of other symbols and therefore constitute mere simulacra. "When the real is no longer what it used to be, nostalgia assumes its full meaning. There is a proliferation of myths of origin and signs of reality; of second-hand truth, objectivity and authenticity" (12).

29. See Richard V. Francaviglia, *Main Street Revisited* (Iowa City: University of Iowa Press, 1966), for a look at the legacy of small-town main streets in American life.

30. Imaginative geographies have not figured prominently in recent major works of cultural geography. Henri Lefebvre's 1974 *Production de l'espace*, translated into English as *The Production of Space* (Oxford: Blackwell, 1991), attempted to wrest notions of space away from Cartesian absolutism and Kantian mentalism and to produce a historical materialist philosophy of space in which space is understood as being socially produced by spatial practices. Indeed, the increasing attention to space may be generated by contemporary transformations of the planet's demographics through human population movements, problematizing the relationship of space and place to identity. Some of the ethnographic accounts of place and space found in Steven Feld and Keith H. Basso, *Senses of Place* (Santa Fe: School of American Research Press, 1996), especially those that correlate mythic and real spaces, reach in the direction of imaginative spaces, or as I call them, "unreal estate," dealing with how real spaces coexist with sacred, ancestral, and spiritual spaces. For a poetics of space and identity, see Lucy Lippard, *The Lure of the Local: Senses of Place in a Multicentered Society* (New York: New Press, 1997).

31. Barbara Kirshenblatt-Gimblett, *Destination Culture: Tourism, Museums, and Heritage* (Berkeley: University of California Press, 1998), 7.

32. Mark Slobin, *Fiddler on the Move: Exploring the Klezmer World* (New York: Oxford University Press, 2000), 32.

33. See especially Raymond Williams, *Marxism and Literature* (Oxford: Oxford University Press, 1977).

34. I have not attempted a full history of the barbershop organizations, in part because this kind of book has been written by barbershop enthusiasts and published by SPEBSQSA, Sweet Adelines International, and Harmony, Inc. See Martin, *Keep America Singing;* Will Cook, *Melodies for Millions* (Kenosha, Wisc.: SPEBSQSA, 1962); Val Hicks, *Heritage of Harmony* (Kenosha, Wisc.: SPEBSQSA, 1988); Holly Weberling Romine, compiler, *Sweet Adelines International 50th Anniversary Commerative Album (Fifty and Forward: 1945–1995)* (Tulsa: Sweet Adelines International, 1995); and G. Ruth Geils, *Harmony from Our Hearts: Harmony, Inc., 1959–1984* (Kenosha, Wisc.: Harmony, Inc., 1985).

Chapter 1

"A Little Close Harmony" is the title of a medley of close harmony songs composed/compiled by songwriter and barbershop singer Geoffrey O'Hara in 1921. Including segments from popular "old songs" favored by quartets (mostly African American, minstrel, and coon songs), O'Hara's medley was intended to evoke the quartetting songscape of the nineteenth century, and for this reason it seemed a fitting title for this chapter that itself samples the century's history of close harmony.

1. A classic account of song forms in this period can be found in Irving Lowens's *Music and Musicians in Early America* (New York: W. W. Norton, 1964). Also see general treatments of American musical history, such as Gilbert Chase, *America's Music: From the Pilgrims to the Present* (Urbana: University of Illinois Press, 1987); Richard Crawford, *The American Musical Landscape* (Berkeley and Los Angeles: University of California Press, 1993); and H. Wiley Hitchcock, *Music in the United States: A Historical Introduction* (Englewood Cliffs, N.J.: Prentice Hall, 1988).

2. George Pullen Jackson, *The Story of the Sacred Harp, 1844–1944* (Nashville: Vanderbilt University Press, 1944), xvii; cited in John Bealle, *Public Worship, Private Faith: Sacred Harp and American Folksong* (Athens: University of Georgia Press, 1997). 168. Emphasis added.

3. Kip Lornell hints that black close-harmony quartets may have been influenced by shape-note singing on the basis of shape note's "four-part harmony," "prescribed training system," and "formal performance contexts." See Lornell, *"Happy in the Service of the Lord": African-American Sacred Vocal Harmony Quartets in Memphis,* 2d ed. (Knoxville: University of Tennessee Press, 1995), 10. In contrast, I suspect that recreational black harmony evolved largely outside systems of formal training and performance contexts (and I view the impact of the singing university groups as more inspirational than pedagogical).

4. However, glee clubs become ardent popularizers of barbershop-style harmony in the 1910s and 1920s, and many visual evocations of (white) barbershop singing are sprinkled with university banners and other signs of a lively campus barbershop scene.

5. See Dale Cockrell's *Demons of Disorder: Early Blackface Minstrels and Their World* (Cambridge: Cambridge University Press, 1997), 151. Also see

Cockrell's edition of the Hutchinson Family's journals, *Excelsior: Journals of the Hutchinson Family Singers, 1842–1846* (Stuyvesant: Pendragon Press, 1989), xxi–xxiv.

6. A history of "Stille Nacht" and the role of the Strasser and Rainer Families in disseminating the song can be found on the "Silent Night" "cyber-museum" created by Bill Egan, which can be found at <www.fortunecity.com/victorian/museum/59/index.html>.

7. This quote came from a Web site called "The Hutchinson Family Singers Home Page," curated by Alan Lewis (2000), <www.geocities.com/unclesamsfarm/hutchinsons.htm>.

8. John Wallace Hutchinson, *Story of the Hutchinsons (Tribe of Jesse)*, 2 vols. (Boston: Lee and Shepard, 1896), 2:304–5; cited in Charles Hamm, *Yesterdays: Popular Song in America* (New York: W. W. Norton, 1983), 144. Emphasis added.

9. "The Old Granite State," composed, arranged and sung by the Hutchinson Family, words by Jesse Hutchinson Jr. (New York: C. Holt, Jr., 1843).

10. For a short history of the Luca Family, see Ronald Henry High, "Black Male Concert Singers of the Nineteenth Century: A Bibliographic Study," in *Feel the Spirit: Studies in Nineteenth-Century Afro-American Music*, ed. George R. Keck and Sherrill V. Martin (New York: Greenwood Press, 1988), 117–34; and James M. Trotter, *Music and Some Highly Musical People: Remarkable Musicians of the Colored Race* (1881; New York: Johnson Reprint, 1968), chap. 6, 88–105.

11. *Cincinnati Enquirer*, January 19, 1859; cited in Bealle, *Public Worship, Private Faith*, 72.

12. "Johnny Schmoker," composer, B. F. Rix (Chicago: Root and Cady, 1863). In the Rare Book, Manuscript, and Special Collections Library, Duke University.

13. "The Sword and the Staff: A National Anthem," words by George P. Morris, music by W. Vincent Wallace (New York: J. L. Hewitt, 1843). In the Lester S. Levy Collection of Sheet Music, Johns Hopkins University. My use of the letters TTBB refers to arrangements originally designated either for tenor 1– tenor 2–baritone–bass or for those in which the baritone was called a first bass. Where it is known, I will underline the part that sings an identifiable lead or melody line (e.g., TTBB). In some early examples, the highest male part is called the alto.

14. Gerhard Kubik, *Africa and the Blues* (Jackson: University Press of Mississippi, 1999), 106. Kubik gives credit to Percival R. Kirby for first identifying this process. The term "functional harmony" is not a value judgment (as in functional versus dysfunctional) but a reference to the logic of Western harmony in which the hierarchy of pitches in a scale helps to determine the sequence of chords. Each chord has a functional role in a composition, rather than being simply a coincidence of tones or a decorative feature.

15. Ibid., 114–17.

16. William Francis Allen, Charles Pickard Ware, and Lucy McKim Garrison, compilers, *Slave Songs of the United States* (New York: A. Simpson, 1867), v; emphasis added.

17. This appeared in Frederika Bremer's *The Homes of the New World: Impressions of America* (New York: Harper and Bros., 1853) and was included in Dena Epstein's *Sinful Tunes and Spirituals* (Urbana: University of Illinois Press, 1977), 164.

18. Kubik, *Africa and the Blues*, 113; emphasis added.

19. Ibid., 142. This is a part of a much larger argument by Kubik about the origins of common Sudanic African scalar types.

20. Portia K. Maultsby, "Africanisms in African-American Music," in James E. Holloway, ed., *Africanisms in American Culture* (Bloomington: Indiana University Press, 1990), 194.

21. The development of African American rhythmic, melodic, and harmonic approaches has been the subject of sustained interest and argument throughout the twentieth century (generating theories and nomenclatures of African retention, syncretism, creolization, transculturation, hybridization, and much more), and it is not my goal to reinvent the wheel here or detail the evolution of African American musical style. Rather, I have attempted a plausible framework for the interaction of European and African American approaches to part-singing that could account for some of the distinctive characteristics of barbershop-style close harmony as described in various nineteenth- and early-twentieth-century accounts. Similar in spirit to my attempts at retroactive theorizing is the remarkable work of Samuel A. Floyd Jr. in *The Power of Black Music: Interpreting Its History from Africa to the United States* (New York: Oxford University Press, 1995), in which he theorizes the interaction of black folk materials, especially those of the ring shout, with European musics to produce a variety of creolized genres from rags to gospel.

22. See Henry Louis Gates Jr., *The Signifying Monkey: A Theory of African-American Literary Criticism* (New York: Oxford University Press, 1988), and Floyd, *The Power of Black Music*, 1995. Floyd offers an alternative derivation for the term "rag," citing nineteenth-century reports of African Americans "flaunting rags [handkerchiefs]" as a way of calling people to a dance as well as various dance steps know as "ragging" (70).

23. For a history of the minstrel show, see Robert C. Toll, *Blacking Up: The Minstrel Show in Nineteenth-Century America* (New York: Oxford University Press, 1974); Eric Lott, *Love and Theft: Blackface Minstrelsy and the American Working Class* (New York: Oxford University Press, 1993); William J. Mahar, *Behind the Burnt Cork Mask: Early Blackface Minstrelsy and Antebellum American Popular Culture* (Urbana: University of Illinois Press, 1999), and Cockrell, *Demons of Disorder*.

24. This connection was argued first, I believe, by Hans Nathan in *Dan Emmett and the Rise of Early Negro Minstrelsy* (Norman: University of Oklahoma Press, 1962).

25. From a Baltimore 1844 playbill quoted from Cockrell, *Demons of Disorder*, 153.

26. See Hamm, *Yesterdays*, 137–39.

27. Jon W. Finson, *The Voices That Are Gone: Themes in Nineteenth-Century American Popular Song* (New York: Oxford University Press, 1994), 198. For a detailed history of Foster and an analysis of his place in American music, see Ken Emerson, *Doo-Dah! Stephen Foster and the Rise of American Popular Culture* (New York: Da Capo Press, 1998).

28. Finson, *Voices That Are Gone*, 198–99.

29. Lott, *Love and Theft*, 8.

30. For an extended discussion of the possible origins of this song, see the fascinating study of "Dixie" by Howard L. Sacks and Judith Rose Sacks, *Way Up North in Dixie: A Black Family's Claim to the Confederate Anthem* (Washington: Smithsonian Institution Press, 1993). The Sackses substantiate the claim made by the family and supporters of Emmett's con-

temporaries, the African American performers Ben and Lew Snowdon, that the Snowdons taught the song to Dan Emmett.

31. Many references in this section to black minstrel troupes, their personnel, names, and dates are unless otherwise noted from Bernard L. Peterson Jr., *The African American Theater Directory, 1816–1960: A Comprehensive Guide to Early Black Theater Organizations, Companies, Theaters, and Performing Groups* (Westport, Conn.: Greenwood Press, 1997). This is an alphabetical listing, so I will not include page numbers for each reference.

32. Henry T. Sampson, *The Ghost Walks: A Chronological History of Blacks in Show Business, 1865–1910* (Metuchen, N.J.: Scarecrow Press, 1988), 5. An early source of information on black quartets is the memoirs of Ike Simond, a minstrel performer, titled *Old Slack's Reminiscences and Pocket History of the Colored Profession from 1865–1891* (Chicago: By the author, 1891.

33. Don B. Wilmeth, *Variety Entertainment and Outdoor Amusements: A Reference Guide* (Westport, Conn.: Greenwood Press, 1982), 111. This book is my primary source on the medicine shows.

34. "Tom the Tattler," *Indianapolis Freeman*, December 8, 1900; cited in Lynn Abbott, "'Play That Barber Shop Chord': A Case for the African American Origin of Barbershop Harmony," *American Music* 10 (1992): 308; emphasis added.

35. Abbott, "'Play That Barber Shop Chord'," 290.

36. See, for example, Floyd, *The Power of Black Music*, 64.

37. Abbott, "'Play That Barber Shop Chord'," 299.

38. Ibid., 298–99; emphasis added.

39. Ibid., 204–5.

40. Trotter, *Music and Some Highly Musical People*, 295; emphasis added.

41. Edward A. Berlin, *King of Ragtime: Scott Joplin and His Era* (New York: Oxford University Press. 1994), 25. Joplin's quartet seems to have changed membership over time, and it is not made clear to which period this particular membership list applied.

42. Rudi Blesh and Harriet Janis, *They All Played Ragtime*, 4th ed. (New York: Oak Publications, 1971). My account here of Joplin's early vocal quartet activities is based in part on Berlin, *King of Ragtime*, 34–40.

43. W. C. Handy, *Father of the Blues: An Autobiography*, ed. Arna Bontemps (New York: Macmillan, 1941), 15. The discussion of Handy's quartet and minstrel activities is taken from his autobiography.

44. Willie "The Lion" Smith with George Hoefer, *Music on My Mind: The Memoirs of an American Pianist* (New York: Doubleday, 1964), 24.

45. Louis Armstrong, *Satchmo: My Life in New Orleans* (New York: Prentice-Hall, 1954), 36. Also, see Abbott, "'Play That Barber Shop Chord'," 318. Armstrong's early experiences in quartets are detailed in *Satchmo*, 86–87. Did his quartet imitations of instruments inform his innovative scat singing? Did his experience in ragging standard barbershop numbers predispose him to find improvisational models in Tin Pan Alley pop songs (another of his many contributions to jazz performance)? Finally, did his very vocal trumpet lines owe a debt to his years as a tenor?

46. MacKinley Helm, *Angel Mo' and Her Son, Roland Hayes* (New York: Greenwood Press, 1969), 72–73; cited in Abbot, "'Play That Barber Shop Chord'," 313–14.

47. Abbott, "'Play That Barber Shop Chord'," 289–325, 290.

48. Christopher Small, *Music of the Common Tongue: Survival and Cel-*

ebration in Afro-American Music (New York: Riverrun Press, 1987), 83. Small quotes Gilbert Chase, *America's Music* (New York: Norton, 1983), 27–28.

49. J. George O'Brien, "Do You Remember," *Harmonizer* 7, no. 4 (May 1948): 38. The practice of singing vocables in close harmony was already mentioned in relation to the song "Johnny Schmoker," by B. F. Dix, sung by Father Kemp's Old Folks' Shows. This tendency became very pronounced at the turn of the century with songs that imitated trains, birds, and instruments. Groups such as the Mills Brothers later became famous for such imitations.

50. "Old Folks at Home," by Stephen C. Foster, arr. Wilson G. Smith (Boston: Oliver Ditson, 1887). As some of the contemporaneous accounts I include have attested, black harmonizing was often cited for its vigorous use of portamento and for the chord progressions created by the sliding movement in one or more voices ("snaking"). Indeed, without recorded sound evidence, and owing to the notoriously ambiguous musical nomenclature used by observers in the period, my conclusions about the association of African Americans with swipes must remain a hypothesis. I also observe that tags seem to be used with increasing frequency for quartet harmony arrangements with an African American connection (and that they often contained swipes), and so I surmise that they provided the opportunity for groups and arrangers to hammer home a showy form of black close harmony at the close of a song. I do not argue that tags (codas) have any kind of essential or original relationship to African-derived music forms.

51. See Sandra Graham, "The Fisk Jubilee Singers and the Concert Spiritual: The Birth of an American Tradition" (Ph.D. diss., New York University, 2001).

Chapter 2

1. Bernard L. Peterson Jr., *The African American Theater Directory, 1816–1960: A Comprehensive Guide to Early Black Theater Organizations, Companies, Theaters, and Performing Groups* (Westport, Conn.: Greenwood Press, 1997), 193. Many of the groups and performances in this section can be found in this guide or in either of Henry T. Sampson's guides, *The Ghost Walks: A Chronological History of Blacks in Show Business, 1865–1910* (Metuchen, N.J.: Scarecrow Press, 1988) or *Blacks in Blackface: A Sourcebook of Early Black Musical Shows* (Metuchen, N.J.: Scarecrow Press, 1980). Also see Paul Oliver, Max Harrison and William Bolcom, eds., *The New Grove Gospel, Blues, and Jazz with Spirituals and Ragtime* (New York: Norton, 1986).

2. See Thomas L. Riis, *Just Before Jazz: Black Musical Theater in New York, 1890–1915* (Washington: Smithsonian Institution Press, 1989), 22–24.

3. For a history of music and comedy in Harlem, see the chapters devoted to expressive culture in Jervis Anderson, *This Was Harlem: A Cultural Portrait, 1900–1950* (New York: Farrar Straus Giroux, 1982).

4. Originally from a column called "The Stage" in the *Indianapolis Freeman*, May 11 and April 19, respectively. Cited in Abbott, "'Play That Barber Shop Chord'," 309.

5. The first quotes are from "Tom the Tattler," *Indianapolis Freeman*, December 8, 1900; quoted in Abbott, "'Play That Barber Shop Chord'," 308. The latter review comes from a San Diego paper quoted in the *Freeman;* reprinted in Abbott, 310.

6. My material on Tin Pan Alley is indebted especially to Nicholas Tawa, *The Way to Tin Pan Alley: American Popular Song, 1866–1910* (New York: Schirmer Books, 1990); Don B. Wilmeth, *Variety Entertainment and Outdoor Amusements: A Reference Guide* (Westport, Conn.: Greenwood Press, 1982); Wilmeth, *American and English Popular Entertainment* (Detroit: Gale Research, 1980); and Philip Furia, *The Poets of Tin Pan Alley: A History of America's Great Lyricists* (New York: Oxford University Press, 1990). Furia's book focuses on a later generation of Tin Pan Alley songwriters but makes a historical connection to earlier styles and composers. I have also relied on the few published insider accounts, such as Charles K. Harris, *After the Ball* (New York: Frank-Maurice, 1926); Edward B. Marks (as told to Abbott Liebling), *They All Sang: From Tony Pastor to Rudy Vallee* (New York: Viking, 1934); and Isidore Witmark and Isaac Goldberg, *The Story of the House of Witmark* (New York: Furman, 1939). The racial politics of Tin Pan Alley, especially the production of African American style by Jewish songwriters, is the focus of Jeffrey Melnick, *A Right to Sing the Blues: African Americans, Jews, and American Popular Song* (Cambridge: Harvard University Press, 1999). Two excellent general works on the entertainment industry are Robert C. Toll, *The Entertainment Machine: American Show Business in the Twentieth Century* (New York: Oxford University Press, 1982), and Russell and David Sanjek, *American Popular Music Business in the Twentieth Century* (New York: Oxford University Press, 1991).

7. Paul Théberge points out in *Any Sound You Can Imagine: Making Music, Consuming Technology* (Hanover, N.H.: Wesleyan University Press, 1997), 29–30, that the advertising relationship of hardware and software extends well back into the history of the publishing and musical instrument building industries in Europe. Early music reproduction technology was considered a stimulus to sales of instruments. In Théberge's analysis, the player piano represented a seminal moment in the transition from nineteenth-century "producer ethics" to consumerist (recreation, leisure, instant gratification).

8. Jon W. Finson, *The Voices That Are Gone: Themes in Nineteenth-Century American Popular Song* (New York: Oxford University Press, 1994), 440. For themes in nineteenth-century song, also see Nicholas Tawa, *Sweet Songs for Gentle Americans: The Parlor Song in America, 1790–1860* (Bowling Green, Ohio: Bowling Green University Popular Press, 1980), and Tawa, *A Sound of Strangers: Musical Cultures, Acculturation, and the post–Civil War Ethnic American* (Methuen, N.J.: Scarecrow Press, 1982).

9. See, for example, Edward A. Berlin, *King of Ragtime: Scott Joplin and His Era* (New York: Oxford University Press, 1994), 12; or, for more general background, Berlin, *Ragtime: A Musical and Cultural History* (Berkeley and Los Angeles: University of California Press, 1980); William J. Schafer and Hohannes Riedel, *The Art of Ragtime: Form and Meaning of an Original Black American Art* (Baton Rouge: Louisiana State University Press, 1974); Rudi Blesh and Harriet Janis, *They All Played Ragtime*, 4th ed. (New York: Oak Publications, 1971); and David A. Jasen and Trebor Hay Tichenor, *Rags and Ragtime: A Musical History* (New York: Seabury Press, 1978).

10. Vaudeville and the recording industry evolved in tandem (along with Tin Pan Alley); my decision to treat them sequentially in this chapter represents my interest in exploring the issues unique to each. In practice, some of the vaudeville quartets made recordings, and some of the recording quartets pursued careers on the stage.

11. Marks, *They All Sang*, 12. Other sources consulted for this section include John E. Dimeglio, *Vaudeville U.S.A.* (Bowling Green, Ohio: Bowling Green University Popular Press, 1972); Douglas Gilbert, *American Vaudeville: Its Life and Times* (New York: Dover, 1941); Anthony Slide, *The Vaudevillians: A Dictionary of Vaudeville Performers* (Westport, Conn.: Greenwood Press, 1981); Bill Smith, *The Vaudevillians* (New York: Macmillan, 1976); Charles W. Stein, *American Vaudeville as Seen by Its Contemporaries* (New York: Alfred A. Knopf, 1984); and Henry Jenkins, *What Made Pistachio Nuts? Early Sound Comedy and the Vaudeville Aesthetic* (New York: Columbia University Press, 1992).

12. Robert W. Snyder, *The Voice of the City: Vaudeville and Popular Culture in New York* (New York: Oxford University Press, 1989), 12.

13. Ibid., 12.

14. Ibid., 132.

15. Joe Stern, "History of Barber Shop Harmony," *Harmonizer* 3, no. 4 (1944): 14. A musical tabloid show was a loosely thematized touring variety show with an emphasis on music. Also see the *Harmonizer* 8, No. 2 (December 1948): 32, and the *Harmonizer 9, no. 2* (December 1949): 28.

16. Snyder, *The Voice of the City*, 43.

17. Nicholas Tawa, *The Way to Tin Pan Alley: American Popular Song, 1866–1910* (New York: Schirmer Books, 1990), 81. Not all comedy fours featured the same stock characters, of course.

18. "Fred Stein Recalls Days B. B. S. (Before Sound Systems)," *Harmonizer* 4, no. 4 (May 1945): 39. Stein was later a bass with the Four Harmonizers, a SPEBSQSA group from Chicago.

19. A letter from Rus Cole, excerpted in J. George O'Brien, "Do You Remember?" *Harmonizer* 10, no. 3 (March 1951): 30.

20. The best-known version of the Empire City Quartette included Harry Cooper, Irving Cooper, Harry Tally, and Harry Mayo.

21. Snyder, *The Voice of the City*, 37.

22. Much of the information on the Avon Comedy Four comes from two articles, "Birth of the Avon Comedy Four," *Harmonizer* 7, no. 3 (February 1948): 54, and G. H. "Curly" Crossett's "Pioneer Recording Quartets: The Avon Comedy Four," *Harmonizer* 7, no. 1 (May 1947): 46.

23. Harry P. Harrison and Karl William Detzer, *Culture under Canvas* (New York: Hastings House, 1958); cited in Dean Snyder, "Chautauqua and Male Quartets," *Harmonizer* 28, no. 1(January–February 1968): 21. An extensive collection of chautaqua playbills and brochures has been assembled in the Redpath Chautauqua Collection at the University of Iowa Libraries Special Collections Department. Much of this material is available in digital form on the World Wide Web at <http://memory.loc.gov /amen/award98/iauhtml/tccchome.html> as part of the Library of Congress American Memory Project. The Redpath Collection contains references to hundreds of male and female quartets appearing on the chautauqua circuit.

24. Thomas Alva Edison, *North American Review* (June 1878); cited in Daniel J. Boorstin, *The Americans: The Democratic Experience* (New York: Vintage Books, 1974), 307.

25. Boorstin, *The Americans*, 307.

26. Robert M. W. Dixon, John Godrich, and Howard Rye, *Blues and Gospel Records 1890–1943*, 4th ed. (New York: Clarendon Press, 1997), 964.

27. Ibid., 857.

28. John H. Bieling, "Reminiscences of Early Talking Machine Days,"

Talking Machine World (April 1914): 18, cited in William Howland Kenney, *Recorded Music in American Life: The Phonograph and Popular Memory, 1890–1945* (New York: Oxford University Press, 1999), 32.

29. Ibid.; p. 23 in the original.

30. Ulysses "Jim" Walsh, "The Coney Island Crowd," *Hobbies: The Magazine for Collectors* (July 1942): 16.

31. Ulysses "Jim" Walsh, "Favorite Pioneer Recording Artists," *Hobbies: The Magazine for Collectors* (November 1943): 32.

32. Ulysses "Jim" Walsh, "Favorite Pioneer Recording Artists," *Hobbies: The Magazine for Collectors* (January 1944): 22.

33. Ulysses "Jim" Walsh, "The Coney Island Crowd," *Hobbies: The Magazine for Collectors* (September 1942): 13. Women were deemed to be the target audience for home phonograph use because the recording companies presumed that women, holding sway in family parlors, would be more responsible than men for introducing the phonograph to the entire family and for choosing the recordings for home play.

34. Music by John Sylvester Fearis, words by Jessie Brown Pounds (Chicago: Forster Music Publisher, 1901); held by the Rare Book, Manuscript, and Special Collections Library, Duke University.

35. Walsh, "Favorite Pioneer Recording Artists," 12.

36. The notion of ranking hit recordings in the period before *Variety* and *Billboard* began to publish reliable charts (1929 and 1935 respectively) begs explanation. For this material, I rely on Joel Whitburn's extrapolation of data from a number of sources, including lists published in *Talking Machine World* (the record industry publication first called *Phonogram* and later *Phonoscope*), Jim Walsh's columns in *Hobbies* magazine, and record label publications. Individual record labels routinely exaggerated the popularity of their own artists, just as industry statistics most likely overstated aggregate trends. These rankings should therefore not be regarded as conclusive, only as productively suggestive. For a more in-depth description of this methodology, see either *Joel Whitburn's Pop Memories, 1890–1954: The History of American Popular Music* (Menominee Falls, Wisc.: Record Research, 1986) or *Joel Whitburn Presents a Century of Pop Music* (Menominee Falls, Wisc.: Record Research, 1999), ix–xi. The latter publication relies on the same research done for the former but covers a slightly different period and often extends the rankings. For the remainder of this chapter, references to the relative rankings of recordings are drawn from these two sources, unless otherwise noted.

37. Jay Warner, *The Da Capo Book of American Singing Groups: A History, 1940–1990* (New York: Da Capo Press, 1992), 2. Although the material in this book on groups before 1940 is sketchy and often inaccurate, its detailed coverage of the harmony groups from the 1940s on is impressive.

38. Dixon et al., *Blues and Gospel Records,* 259. Work led the group up until 1915, after which various versions of the group performed with James A. Myers and his wife.

39. The best concise source for information on this group is Jas Obrecht, "Polk Miller's Old South Quartette," *Victrola and 78 Journal* (Spring 1996): 8. I rely on Obrecht's work in this section and on the documentation of recordings in Dixon et al., *Blues and Gospel Records.*

40. Ibid. The original source was a *Richmond Journal* article from January 3, 1912.

41. Ibid.; italics added by the author.

42. Polk Miller's Old South Quartette (and the Old South Quartette

without Miller) can be heard on *The Earliest Negro Vocal Quartets, 1894–1928* (Document Records DOCD-5061, 1991).

43. Kenney, *Recorded Music in American Life,* 19.

44. Hooley had sung briefly in another quartet called the American Quartet that recorded for Gram-o-Phone at the turn of the century. Detailed information on personnel changes in the later version of this quartet can be found in Ulysses "Jim" Walsh, "The Coney Island Crowd," *Hobbies: The Magazine for Collectors,* June 1942, 21–23.

45. Additional information on the song can be found in "How 'Sweet Adeline' Came into Being," *Harmonizer* 6, no. 4 (May 1947): 33, and David C. Wright, "Harry Armstrong's 'Sweet Adeline' Tells Story of His Biggest Song Hit," *Harmonizer* 25, no. 5 (September–October 1965): 8.

46. From the text of a letter written by Armstrong to Joe Laurie Jr. in June 1945; reprinted in Holly Weberling Romine, comp., *Sweet Adelines International Fiftieth Anniversary Commemorative Album (Fifty and Forward: 1945–1995)* (Tulsa: Sweet Adelines International, 1995), 3.

47. Ibid.

48. Information on Billy Murray is drawn from Ulysses "Jim" Walsh's series "The Coney Island Crowd," in *Hobbies: The Magazine for Collectors,* April 1942, 15; May 1942, 15; and June 1942, 21.

49. Ulysses "Jim" Walsh, "The Coney Island Crowd," *Hobbies: The Magazine for Collectors,* May 1942, 15.

50. Whitburn, *Joel Whitburn's Pop Memories,* 327.

51. With lyrics by William Tracey and Ballard MacDonald, music by Lewis Muir.

52. Given the number of examples I have encountered of the use of the term "minor" for dominant seventh–type chords and diminished chords, it would appear to have been a relatively common expression in the late nineteenth century. The "minor" may refer to the additional minor interval added to the chord (between the fifth scale degree and the seventh), or it may refer only to the sensory impression made by the chords on listeners, and thus may have served as a shorthand for chord types other than major triads.

53. This anecdote was relayed in "Curly" Crossett, "The Edison Quartet," *Harmonizer* 8, no. 2 (December 1948): 18.

54. Whitburn, *Joel Whitburn's Pop Memories,* 90. For biographical information on Collins, see Ulysses "Jim" Walsh's column "Favorite Pioneer Recording Artists," *Hobbies: The Magazine for Collectors,* November 1942, 111–12.

55. Lyrics by Will Dillon, music by Albert Von Tilzer (New York: Broadway Music, 1915).

56. Words by Alfred Bryan, music by Al Piantadosi (New York: Leo Feist, 1915).

57. Music by Arthur Lange, lyrics by Andrew B. Sterling (New York: Joe Morris Music, 1917).

58. Albert Collins departed from the Peerless Quartet in 1918; as a result, Frank Croxton took over on bass, while John Meyer moved to baritone. Between 1918 and 1925, the personnel stabilized with Burr, Campbell, Meyer, and Croxton on most recordings. Also in 1918, William Hooley, the bass of the Haydn, American, and Orpheus Quartets, died and was replaced by Donald Chalmers of the Criterion Quartet. The American Quartet continued to record for Victor until 1925, but its personnel was essentially the same as that of the Peerless Quartet except for the lead singers

(Burr for Peerless and Murray for American). In 1925, Henry Burr fronted for an otherwise new Peerless Quartet, which continued recording until 1928.

59. The Four Harmony Kings were Ivan Harold Browning, William H. Berry, Charles E. Drayton, and William A. Hann. Together until 1929, the quartet endured only minor substitutions in the line-up.

60. Many of the African American quartets of the race-record era, including those in this section, are listed along with their recordings in Robert M. W Dixon, John Godrich, and Howard Rye, *Blues and Gospel Records, 1890–1943*, 4th ed. (New York: Clarendon Press, 1997). The classifications of "gospel," "spiritual," and jubilee" are tenuous. Gospel referred to a religious music with a strong New Testament influence. It featured a popular sound that mixed blues, jazz, ragtime, and spirituals and, of course, barbershop-style close harmony; and it expressed a lively, syncopated, and charismatic spirit. Jubilee quartets and gospel fours performed gospel as well as spirituals, older hymns, and occasional secular songs. The term "jubilee" increasingly identified groups that came out of the spiritual tradition but performed more secular material. However, the newly popular rubric "jazz" was sometimes used for this purpose as well (as in the Norfolk Jazz Quartet, which really sang little of what would today be called jazz). In any case, these terms ("gospel," "spiritual," "jubilee," and "jazz") were not applied consistently, and in fact the groups often changed their repertory, style, and sometimes names (e.g., the Monarch Jazz Quartet also performed as the Monarch Jubilee Quartet) to suit different contexts.

61. This appearance was noted in *Talking Machine World* (March 1927) and was discussed in a profile of Franklyn Baur by Tim Gracyk. Gracyk's book *Popular American Recording Pioneers, 1895–1925* (N.p., 2000) was published shortly before this book went to press; however, a few profiles from the book were posted on Gracyk's Web site at <http://www.garlic.com/~tgracyk/>.

62. Slide, *The Vaudevillians*, 529.

63. Mark Booth, "Jingle: Pepsi-Cola Hits the Spot," in *On Record: Rock, Pop, and the Written Word*, ed. Simon Frith (New York: Pantheon Books, 1990), 322.

64. This quote, and much of the information on the Maple City Four is from a profile on the SPEBSQSA Web page at <http://www.spebsqsa.com>.

65. The biographic material on the Capitol City Four is from Roy L. Fox, "The Capitol City Four of Springfield, Ill." *Barber Shop Re-Chordings* 2, no. 2 (1942): 15.

66. "The Four Harmonizers," *Harmonizer* 3, no. 2 (December 1943): 22.

67. Lawrence O'Connor, "Forty-Four Years of Harmony: The Globe Quartet," *Harmonizer* 9, no. 2 (December 1949): 28. This suggests a striking parallel to the rise of doo-wop close harmony in the 1950s, which also became popular on a neighborhood-by-neighborhood basis among black and white teenagers.

68. Joe Stern, "History of Barber Shop Harmony," *Harmonizer* 3, no. 4, 1944: 14.

Chapter 3

"The Lost Chord" was a popular nineteenth century song by Sir Arthur Sullivan based on a poem by Adelaide Anne Procter (1825–1864). Barbershop revivalists often referred to the song to suggest that there had been a period in the 1920s and 1930s in which the barbershop chords were "lost" before being rediscovered by the revival movement, although this has little to do with the sentiment of the original verses.

1. Sigmund Spaeth, ed., *Barber Shop Ballads: A Book of Close Harmony* (New York: Simon and Schuster, 1925); C. T. Martin, *A Handbook for Adeline Addicts: A Starter for Cold Voices and a Critical Survey of American Balladry* (Cleveland: Schonberg Press, 1932); George Shackley, *Close Harmony: Male Quartets, Ballads, and Funnies with Barber Shop Chord* (New York: Pioneer Music, 1925).

2. Spaeth, *Barbershop Ballads*, 26.

3. Sigmund Spaeth, *Harmonizer* 2, no. 4 (1943): 15.

4. Cited in Robert A. Stebbins, *The Barbershop Singer: Inside the Social World of a Musical Hobby* (Toronto: University of Toronto Press, 1996), 61 (no original citation provided); emphasis added. Note the ways in which potentially "feminine" concerns such as butterfly collecting or iris cultivation are masculinized and "hardened" by employing the equestrian metaphor (with its sexual overtones) of riding a horse hard.

5. Neil Harris, introduction, *The Land of Contrasts, 1880–1901*, ed. Neil Harris (New York: George Braziller, 1970), 17.

6. Music by Ray Henderson, words by Billy Rose and Mort Dixon, 1922.

7. Spaeth, *Barbershop Ballads*, 61.

8. Warren Susman, ed., *Culture and Commitment, 1929–1950* (New York: George Braziller, 1973), 9.

9. Henri Lefebvre, *The Production of Space*, translated by Donald Nicholson-Smith (Oxford and Cambridge, Mass.: Blackwell, 1991), 25.

10. George Lipsitz, *Time Passages: Collective Memory and American Popular Culture* (Minneapolis: University of Minnesota Press, 1990), 9.

11. Stanley Coben, *Rebellion against Victorianism: The Impetus for Cultural Change in 1920s America* (New York: Oxford University Press, 1991), 4.

12. Gail Bederman, *Manliness and Civilization: A Cultural History of Gender and Race in the United States, 1880–1917* (Chicago: University of Chicago Press, 1995), 137.

13. For a reinterpretation of the politics of the interwar era, see Ellis W. Hawley, *The Great War and the Search for a Modern Order: A History of the American People and Their Institutions, 1917–1933*, 2d ed. (Prospect Heights, Ill.: Waveland Press, 1992), especially his discussion of "ethnocultural tensions and issues" (57–60, 89–91).

14. Herbert Agar, "Culture versus Colonialism in America," in Susman, *Culture and Commitment*, 29–31 (originally published in *Southern Review* (July 1935): 1–19); emphasis added. The scope of antimodernist organizing is captured in T. J. Jackson Lears, *No Place of Grace: Antimodernism and the Transformation of American Culture, 1880–1920* (New York: Pantheon Books, 1981).

15. Henry Seidel Canby, *The Age of Confidence* (New York: Farrar and Reinhart, 1934), 79, 257–8; cited in Coben, *Rebellion against Victorianism*, 19.

16. Hawley, *The Great War and the Search for a Modern Order*, 103.

17. Michael Denning, *The Cultural Front: The Laboring of American Culture in the Twentieth Century* (New York: Verso, 1998). Denning charts the aesthetic and cultural politics of the 1930s and 1940s, linking the progressive politics of the folk balladeers and the black modernist spirit of swing to avant-garde trends in cinema and literature. In short, he weaves together the various progressive and modernist cultural tendencies of the period.

18. "Barber Shop Airs Will Rise in Parks," *New York Times*, July 17,

1935. As to the claim of "first," this is difficult to substantiate, although I wish to stress that it is the first I have found. It is possible that such contests were established in many municipalities in the United States in the same period.

19. As a trio of very influential politicians, Smith, Moses, and La Guardia have been the subjects of many biographies that have informed this section. Among them I would note Matthew and Hannah Josephson, *Al Smith: Hero of the Cities* (Boston: Houghton Mifflin, 1969); Robert Moses, *A Tribute to Governor Smith* (New York: Simon and Schuster, 1962); Robert A. Caro, *The Power Broker: Robert Moses and the Fall of New York* (New York: Alfred A. Knopf, 1974); Thomas Kessner, *Fiorello H. La Guardia and the Making of Modern New York* (New York: McGraw-Hill, 1989); August Heckscher, *When La Guardia Was Mayor: New York's Legendary Years* (New York: W.W. Norton, 1978); Lawrence Elliott, *Little Flower: The Life and Times of Fiorello La Guardia* (New York: Morrow, 1983); and Cleveland Rogers, "Robert Moses," *Atlantic Monthly*, February 1939, 225–34. Such biographies rarely mention the barbershop interests of their subjects.

20. Smith's Catholicism was the subject of remark in an article in *Time* magazine about the 1935 contest: "Al Smith may have felt a sympathy with the Blessed Sacrament Lyceum Quartet of Queens" ("Barber Shop Chords," *Time*, September 23, 1935, 26). Like many barbershop enthusiasts, Fiorello La Guardia was a Mason, initiated in 1913 into the Italian immigrant Garibaldi Lodge. Later in this chapter I discuss the importance of Freemasonry to the barbershop revival.

21. Words by James W. Blake, music by Charles B. Lawlor (1894).

22. Moses, *A Tribute to Governor Smith*, 46.

23. "Bronx Teams Lead Barber Shop Glee," *New York Times*, August 29, 1935.

24. Ibid.

25. "Eight Thousand Shaving Mugs Found in 5-hour Hunt for Prizes for Barber Shop Quartets," *New York Times*, August 2, 1935.

26. "Going Back to the Good Old Days!" *Recreation*, November 1936, 407, 420–21.

27. Some aspects of this latter account were not backed up by former Society president Carroll P. Adams and may be apocryphal. This account appeared in a letter in the *Harmonizer* 4, no. 1 (1944): 25.

28. The most complete biography of Owen Clifton Cash was the obituary written by Deac Martin for the *Harmonizer* 13, no. 1(1953): 4–5, from which some of this material was gleaned.

29. Although this letter is frequently cited in brief, it appeared in its entirety in "And How They Grew," *Harmonizer* 4, no. 1 (September 1944): 26.

30. Will Cook, "Melodies for Millions," *Harmonizer* 24, no. 1 (January–February 1964): 9.

31. Cash's most detailed recounting of the early meetings was in "The Founder's Column," *Harmonizer* 12, no. 4 (June 1953): 2.

32. The Tulsa riots occurred after a rumor spread that a white woman had been harassed by a black man. Up to ten thousand whites ransacked and burned the Greenwood neighborhood, deputized lynch mobs rounded up blacks thought to be "uppity," local planes with machine guns strafed the streets, and members of the Ku Klux Klan shot blacks who were running from the mobs. Despite the death of perhaps three hundred residents and the devastation of an entire neighborhood, the memory of the riot was suppressed within the space of a single generation. For an update on this

tragedy, see Brent Staples, "Unearthing a Riot," *New York Times Magazine*, December 19, 1999, 64–69.

33. The source of this quote from O. C. Cash has been lost. The inspiration for some of Cash's humor and rural western folksiness was Will Rogers, whom Cash occasionally quoted in his "Founder's Column" in *The Harmonizer*.

34. O. C. Cash, "Founder's Message," *SPEBSQSA Barber Shop Re-Chordings* 1, no. 1 (November 1941), 3.

35. "Apostle of Harmony," *Harmonizer* 3, no. 2 (December 1943): 3; emphasis added.

36. Interview with Betty Anne Cash by Grady Kerr, April 4, 1988. SPEBSQSA Oral Histories.

37. "Musical Revival," *Detroit Plain Dealer and Daily Leader*, June 30, 1943.

38. "Flat Feet v. Barflies," *Time*, August 5, 1940, 46.

39. Mark C. Carnes, "Scottish Rite and the Visual Semeiotics of Gender," in *Theatre of the Fraternity: Staging the Ritual Space of the Scottish Rite of Freemasonry, 1896–1929, curated by C. Lance Brockman* (Jackson: University of Mississippi, 1996), 74.

40. Both symbols, with their obvious phallicism, signified the masculine social worlds of their respective organizations.

41. Kenneth L. Ames, "The Lure of the Spectacular," in Brockman, *Theatre of the Fraternity*, 23.

42. Caroll P. Adams, *Harmonizer* (1941): 3.

43. "Tulsa's Initiation Ceremony," *Harmonizer* 3, no. 2 (1943): 20. The title of Grand Keeper of the Minor Keys, which Rupert Hall claimed in the initial organizing letter, is a play on the keys to the temple alluded to in Masonic rituals.

44. "Flat Feet v. Barflies," *Time*, August 5, 1940, 46.

45. Caro, *The Power Broker*, 1084. A good general introduction to the fair is Helen Harrison, ed., *The Dawn of a New Day: The New York World's Fair, 1939–40* (New York: Queens Museum, 1980). This is the exhibit catalog.

46. "Barber Shop Warblers to Trill at Fair; Mayor, as Chief Patron, Issues Cordial Bid," *New York Times*, March 10, 1940.

47. "Smith Warms Up Barber-Shop Baritone; Vigorous, if Not Very Pretty, He Admits," *New York Times*, March 11, 1940.

48. "Barber Shop Foursomes," *New York Times*, March 12, 1940.

49. The Flat Foot Four consisted of Britt Stegall, Johnny Whalen, "Red" Elliott, and Sam Barnes, all policemen on the Oklahoma City police force.

50. "Flat-Foot Four 4 Wins Barber-Shop Mug," *New York Times*, July 27, 1940.

51. "Vibrations at N.Y. Fair: Barber Shop Quartets Compete for National Championship," *Newsweek*, August 5, 1940, 43–44.

52. "Redcap Singers Win," *New York Times*, June 27, 1941.

53. See Raymond Allen, *"Singing in the Spirit": African-American Sacred Quartets in New York City* (Philadelphia: University of Pennsylvania Press, 1992), 30.

54. "Negro Singers Out, Smith, Moses Quit," *New York Times*, July 3, 1941.

55. Ibid.

56. An extensive account of Smith's travails in Oklahoma during the campaign can be found in Josephson, *Al Smith*, 380–85.

57. Cited by barbershopper Joe Wodicka, SPEBSQSA Oral History Interview, p. 15.

58. James Earl Henry, "The Origins of Barbershop Harmony: A Study of

Barbershop's Musical Links to Other African American Musics as Evidenced through Recordings and Arrangements of Early Black and White Quartets" (Ph.D. diss., Washington University, 2000), provides an excellent annotation of the materials on this subject in the SPEBSQSA files.

59. This article, by Alvin Goldstein, was quoted originally in Kerill Rubman, "From 'Jubilee' to Gospel in Black Male Quartet Singing" (master's thesis, University of North Carolina, 1980), 40, and cited in Allen, *Singing in the Spirit*, 27.

60. Henry, *The Origins of Barbershop Harmony*, 44–45. The author also includes a fascinating exchange on race and barbershop singing involving three early SPEBSQSA leaders, Joe Stern, "Deac" Martin, and Bro Adams (47–50).

61. "Smith and Moses Carol in Quartet," *New York Times*, June 19, 1942.

62. The Golden Gate Quartet was made up of Henry Owens, William Langford, Willie "Bill" Johnson, and Orlandus "Dad" Wilson.

Chapter 4

1. Edwin S. Smith, "President's Column," *Harmonizer* 12, no. 4 (1953): 5; emphasis added.

2. George W. Stark, "Talk of the Town," *Detroit News*, June 21; quoted in the *S.P.E.B.S.Q.S.A. Barber Shop Re-Chordings* 2, no. 1 (September 1942): 4; emphasis added.

3. Hal Staab, "A Message from President Hal Staab," *S.P.E.B.S.Q.S.A. Barber Shop Re-chordings* 2, no. 1 (September 1942): 5.

4. "The Will to Win," *S.P.E.B.S.Q.S.A. Barber Shop Re-Chordings* 2, no. 1 (September 1942): 9, and "No Rationing of Barber Shop Harmony," *S.P.E.B.S.Q.S.A. Barber Shop Re-Chordings* 2, no. 2 (December 1942): 11.

5. "Society Has Chance to Christen Two B-29's, Let's Go!!," *Harmonizer* 4, no. 4 (May 1945): 3.

6. Crosby's story originally appeared in his "Call Me Lucky" series in the *Saturday Evening Post* and was excerpted in "Keeping Posted," *Harmonizer* 12, no. 4 (June 1953): 46.

7. "Deac" Martin, "The Way I See It," *Harmonizer* 9, no. 4 (June 1950): 54.

8. Will C. Cook, "Melodies for Millions," *Harmonizer* 25, no. 2 (March–April 1965): 11. This series was initiated by Will C. Cook but was finished by others after Cook's death in 1964.

9. In order of appearance in the text, Decca 261, nos. 3422, 3448, 3583, 3651, and 3744; Columbia C-35, nos. 35795–35798; and Victor P 26, nos. 26630–26632.

10. "Swipes," *Harmonizer* 5, no. 3 (February 1946): 34.

11. Hal Staab, "Vision of the Future," *Harmonizer* 2, no. 4 (May 1943): 2, emphasis added.

12. Cook, "Melodies for Millions," *Harmonizer* 25, no. 2 (May–June 1965): 17–18.

13. For an analysis of the ubiquity of contestation in human society, see Walter J. Ong, *Fighting for Life: Contest, Sexuality, and Consciousness* (Ithaca: Cornell University Press, 1981). Ritualized conflict as an element in forms of play is the theme of Johan Huizinga's *Homo Ludens: A Study of the Play Element in Culture* (Boston: Beacon Press, 1955), which offers stimulating arguments despite its dated rhetoric. There are enough examples of musical competition around the world to suggest that we further theorize the relationship between expressive culture and ritualized

conflict. Obvious questions include: How do music contests respond to specific constructs of masculinity or femininity? Do music contests draw on (or influence) other agonistic cultural forms such as sports and warfare? And, of course, what does competition do for—and to—musical sound, style, and performance practice?

14. "Deac" Martin and Frank H. Thorne, "What About Our National Contests?" *Harmonizer* 2, no. 4, 1943: 18–19.

15. Stafford R. Taylor, "The Way I See It," *Harmonizer* 16, no. 1 (March 1958): 48.

16. Cook, "Melodies for Millions," *Harmonizer* 24, no. 2 (March–April 1964): 9.

17. Deac Martin, "The Way I See It," *Harmonizer* 8, no. 3 (March 1949): 42.

18. Max H. Brandt, "The Respectable Art of Woodshedding in World Music," in *Barbershopping: Musical and Social Harmony,* ed. Max Kaplan (Rutherford, N.J.: Farleigh Dickinson University Press, 1993), 25.

19. Deac Martin, "The Way I See It," *Harmonizer* 3, no. 2 (December 1943): 8.

20. Charles M. Merrill, "President's Column," *Harmonizer* 7, no. 2 (May 1947): 6.

21. Each of these women's barbershop groups was profiled in the *Harmonizer* 2, no. 4 (May 1943): 16–17, from which some of this material was culled.

22. O. C. Cash, "Founder's Column," *Harmonizer* 5, no. 1 (August 1945): 18, 35; emphasis added.

23. The original British version of the musical opened in 1899 at the Lyric Theatre on London's West End. With various changes in the songs, an American version opened on Broadway in 1900. The book was by Owen Hall (whose real name was Jimmy Davis), with lyrics by E. Boyd-Jones and Paul Reubens and music by Leslie Stuart. Two recordings survive of the song, one from Gramophone's original British cast recording (the first-ever cast recording) featuring the Lyric Theatre Chorus and the other a recording of American members, here called the "Floradora Girls," made in 1902 by Columbia records. Both recordings are available on a historic rerelease, *Florodora: A Musical Comedy* (Opal CD 9835).

24. "I See the Papers," *Harmonizer* 8, no. 3 (March 1949): 41.

25. *Barber Shop Re-Chordings* 2, no. 2: 14.

26. "Swipes," *Harmonizer* 5, no. 3 (February 1946): 44.

27. This split is discussed in G. Ruth Geils, *Harmony from Our Hearts: Harmony, Inc., 1959–1984* (Kenosha, Wisc.: Harmony, 1985), 5–7.

28. Deac Martin, "The Way I See It," *Harmonizer* 8, no. 3 (March 1949): 42.

29. Bill C. Malone, *Country Music U.S.A.,* rev. ed. (Austin: University of Texas Press, 1985), 21.

30. Ibid., 145–49.

31. Maurice "Molly" Reagan, "What Is Happening to 'Preservation'?" *Harmonizer* 21, no. 5: 12.

32. Jay Warner, *The Da Capo Book of American Singing Groups: A History, 1940–1990* (New York: Da Capo Press, 1992), 205–9.

33. "Keep Posted," *Harmonizer* 7, no. 3 (February 1948): 11.

34. Additional information on the Flying L Ranch Quartet is posted on a SPEBSQSA web page at <http://www.spebsqsa.org>.

35. *Wait Till the Sun Shines, Nellie* was directed by Henry King and based on a book by Ferdinand Reyher called *I Heard Them Sing.* The prolific film score composer Alfred Newman wrote the music.

36. Bosley Crowther, "Wait Till the Sun Shines, Nellie,"*New York Times*, June 28, 1952.

37. Some of the material on the Chordettes in this section is drawn from Dennis Garvey's "The Chordettes: From Barbershop to 'Lollipop'," *Goldmine* (July 10, 1992): 13–18.

38. Ibid., 13.

39. From a broadcast of *Arthur Godfrey's Talent Scouts*, transcribed in Arthur J Singer, *Arthur Godfrey: The Adventures of an American Broadcaster* (Jefferson, N.C.: McFarland, 2000), 91. Arthur Godfrey was yet another popularizer of barbershop who was himself a Freemason. Others in this category included Fiorello La Guardia, Roy Rogers, Red Skelton, and Irving Berlin.

40. Warner, *The Da Capo Book of American Singing Groups*, 42.

41. A series of articles in entertainment journals and newspapers chronicled Godfrey's troubles. Bleyer's dismissal was ascribed by one commentator to a recording made by Cadence Records of an ABC radio personality whom Godfrey saw as a competitor with Godfrey's own radio program. For example, see "Ouster of Bleyer Laid to Recording," *New York Times*, October 21, 1953.

42. There is a certain irony in a steam locomotive serving as Disney's inspiration for his foray into a pastoral Americana. As Leo Marx makes clear in *The Machine in the Garden: Technology and the Pastoral Ideal in America* (New York: Oxford University Press, 1964), the locomotive generally served in American literature as a metaphor for the noisy, intrusive impact of modernity. Living in southern California at the onset of the automobile age, however, Disney could not help but notice the contrast in transportation and nurture a fondness for the vehicles that tied together the Midwest of his youth. Indeed, the locomotive seems an apt symbol for the new turn-of-the-century "pastoralism" associated not with the rural village but with the American town.

43. Randy Bright, *Disneyland: Inside Story* (New York: Harry N. Abrams, 1987), 41.

44. Bob Thomas, *Walt Disney: An American Original* (New York: Simon and Schuster, 1976), 17; italics in original.

45. Ibid., 246.

46. Richard Schickel, *The Disney Version: The Life, Times, Art, and Commerce of Walt Disney* (New York: Simon and Schuster, 1968), 361.

47. Related by Dick Grapes in his public address (while emceeing the chorus finals) at the 2000 SPEBSQSA International Convention.

48. "The Music Man," *Variety*, April 11, 1962, 6; "Too Many Trombones," *Time*, July 20, 1962, 79; "The Music Man," *Sight and Sound* 31 (Summer 1962): 147; "Sweet Corn," *New Yorker*, September 8, 1962, 80.

49. Bob Williams, "Evolution of a Great Quartet: 'The Buffalo Bills'," *Buffalo Evening News*, May 20, 1979; reprinted in the *Harmonizer* 28, no. 5 (September–October 1967): 2–3.

Chapter 5

1. Phil Embury, "1956 International Convention Keynote Speech," *Harmonizer* 16, no. 3 (September 1956): 33.

2. The frequency, relational, and contextual analyses that informed this section were produced with "Tex" software. To focus on significant terms, I filtered out articles, conjunctions, pronouns, helping verbs, and prepositions—in other words, terms that had largely a syntactical function—in

favor of those terms with more semantic importance (verbs, nouns, adjectives, etc.).

3. Nelson George, *The Death of Rhythm and Blues* (New York: Pantheon, 1988).

4. Words and music by Ben Ryan, 1926.

5. There were clear exceptions to this trend among golden-era songs, such as the songs written for the female vaudevillians Belle Baker, Nora Bayes, or Fanny Brice ("Second Hand Rose," "Has Anybody Here Seen My Kelly," "My Man"). These songs could be ribald, assertive, self-deprecatory, or humorous. However, these songs were seldom performed by quartets at the time and had little impact on the barbershop revival.

6. Words by William Dillon, music by Harry von Tilzer, 1911.

7. Words and music by Tell Taylor, 1910.

8. Words by Irving Kahal and Willie Raskin; music by Sammy Fain.

9. Sigmund Spaeth, "A Message from Sigmund Spaeth," *Harmonizer* 3, no. 4 (May 1943): 6. Some of the material in this section first appeared in Gage Averill, "Bell Tones and Ringing Chords: Sense and Sensation in Barbershop Harmony," *World of Music* 41, no. 1 (1999): 37–51.

10. Sigmund Spaeth, *Barbershop Ballads: A Book of Close Harmony* (New York: Simon and Schuster, 1925).

11. Charles Hamm, *Yesterdays: Popular Song in America* (New York: W. W. Norton, 1983), 294–96.

12. Peter Van der Merwe, *Origins of the Popular Style: The Antecedents of Twentieth-Century Popular Music* (Oxford: Clarendon Press, 1989), 250–51.

13. See *Barbershop Arranging Manual* (Kenosha, Wisc.: SPEBSQSA, 1980).

14. Joe Stern, "Questions and Answers," *Harmonizer* 3, no. 1 (September 1943): 6.

15. Maurice E. "Molly" Reagan, "Mechanics of Barber Shop Harmony," *Harmonizer* 3, no. 3: 10.

16. Art Merrill, "You Can Call Off the Search—For We've Found the Lost Chord," *Harmonizer* 10, no. 3: 27.

17. Interview with Tom Massengale, 1988, from the SPEBSQSA Oral History Archives.

18. Interview with Gary Ives, 1991, from the SPEBSQSA Oral History Archives.

19. Jim Ewin, "Barbershop Harmony: A Natural Science," *Harmonizer* 21, no. 2 (1943): 19, 30; emphasis added.

20. Al Shields [director of the East York (Toronto) Ontario Chorus], "How We Train for Chorus Competitions," *Harmonizer* 15, no. 1 (March 1955): 47.

21. Interview with Bob Summers; Fort Myers, Florida, 1987.

22. Interview with Rob Mitchell, Redmond, Washington, 1990.

23. Johan Sunderberg, *The Science of the Singing Voice* (Dekalb, Ill.: Northern Illinois University Press, 1987), 136–37. Sunderberg points to the importance of formants in amplifying certain partials and recommends that choral directors assign selected formants to each chord while teaching choral arrangements so as to aid singers in locking in the best tuning possible. "Again, the results showed that the singers agreed more closely in phonation frequency when the common partial was enhanced by a formant"(137).

24. The ideological construction of barbershop singing as an exercise in social and musical harmony (or fellowship or camaraderie) and its connection to nostalgic evocations of a "lost" structure of feeling (along with

its political, gender, and racial underpinnings) was the subject of my first barbershop paper at the 1990 meeting of the Society for Ethnomusicology ("Four Parts, No Waiting: The Ideal of Male Camaraderie in Barbershop Harmony Singing"). Liz Garnett, "Ethics and Aesthetics: The Social Theory of Barbershop Harmony," *Popular Music* 18, no. 1 (1999): 41–61, also identified the relationship between musical and social harmony (and its expression in egalitarianism and participation) as an expression of ideology in barbershop singing. However, Garnett's interests were not historical, and she treats barbershop as "a largely self-enclosed musical culture" (41) Thus, she does not connect the ideology of fellowship and harmony with ideological currents beyond the barbershop movement, nor directly with gender relations.

25. Bernard Lorat-Jacob, *Sardinian Chronicles*, trans. Teresa Lavender Fagan (Chicago: University of Chicago Press, 1995), 75, 94.

26. I administered these questionnaires to three choruses and received about fifty-five responses out of perhaps ninety-five distributed. Because of this thin sample, I used the questionnaires to direct my attention to issues of motivation rather than drawing strong conclusions from them.

27. Steve Ferrick, addressing a question posed over the "Harmonet" barbershop listserv on November 12, 2000. Used with permission.

28. The conversations recorded in this section were transcribed by me from memory, for the most part shortly after they occurred. I have tried to be true to the syntax and flow of the conversations, but I do not claim that they are perfect word-for-word transcriptions. I was able to explain my role to most of those to whom I was speaking, but as I did not procure explicit permission to print these interactions, I have changed the names of my contacts, and, when necessary, excised explicit identifying comments or remarks. The conversations recorded were chosen from those I transcribed not because they represent an adequate and representative sampling, but because I thought that they elegantly expressed the kinds of conversations and interactions—the "texture" of conventions—as I experienced them. I hoped that they would also provide a window into the commitment to singing, aesthetic discourse and contest, and camaraderie that I found to be present in these events.

29. Words by Beth Slater Whitson, music by Leo Friedman, 1909. The tag book that Doug carried was, I found, *A Pocketful of Tags, no. 2* (Kenosha, Wisc.: SPEBSQSA 1992); the tag in question had been arranged in 1981 by Burt Szabo.

30. There is some concern in men's and women's barbershop societies that the a cappella movement on campuses largely bypasses barbershop singing entirely in favor of an eclectic mix of pop, hip-hop, and jazz arrangements. To begin to address this gulf, SPEBSQSA's 2001 international convention was scheduled in Nashville, Tennessee, immediately following a three-day a cappella workshop called "Sing! An A Cappella Celebration." The 2001 international SPEBSQSA convention was called "2001: A Barbershop Odyssey," in reference to the science fiction film by Stanley Kubrik. The poster featured a circular pitch pipe represented as an orbiting space station.

31. Steven Feld, "Sound Worlds," in *Sound*, ed. Patricia Kruth and Henry Stobart (Cambridge: Cambridge University Press, 2000), 184.

Glossary

afterglow The informal party that follows a barbershop performance. Quartet singing dominates the afterglow.

ambitus A term used to describe the range of scale degrees used in a melody.

anchor man An occasional term for the bass voice in a barbershop quartet, especially when a quartet woodsheds.

augmented chord A triad consisting of two major thirds.

balance The relative volume or intensity of the four voices.

barbershop seventh chord A chord consisting of the root, third, fifth, and flatted seventh degrees of the scale. It is characteristic of barbershop arrangements. When used to lead to a chord whose root is a fifth below the root of the barbershop seventh chord, it is called a dominant seventh chord. Barbershoppers sometimes refer to this as the "meat 'n' taters chord." In the nineteenth and early twentieth centuries, these chords were sometimes called "minors."

barbershop style A stylization and codification of close-harmony singing practices. Its main features include absence of vibrato, close-harmony voicing, a lead (melody) voice under the tenor harmony, just intonation, consonant four-part singing, a preponderance of dominant seventh–type chords, and the use of arranging conventions such as swipes, tags, and bell chords.

barrel tone A barbershop term for a full-voiced vocal production.

barroom tenor See *whiskey tenor.*

bell chord An arranging technique. Four voices enter in succession to create a chord, each voice ringing in like a bell. Not to confused with "bell tone," which is occasionally used to describe the effect of harmonics (i.e., "extended sound").

blend Unlike "balance" this 'refers not to volume but to pitch. A proper blend maximizes the coincidence of overtones such that the chord "rings."

blossom An arranging technique by which four voices begin in unison and expand to a four-part chord in contrary motion (i.e., one goes lower, the next higher, the next lower, and the last higher).

brassy tone A metallic vocal timbre employed in loud passages.

bust a chord Colloquial barbershop usage for "sing a song" (also "split a chord" or "crack a chord").

cadence A cadence initiates a sense of rest or resolution in a harmonic progression. Cadences are often used to affirm a section of music's tonality and are usually found at the conclusion of a phrase or piece of music.

cascade An arranging technique. The four voices begin in unison, and, while the highest voice maintains the note, the lower voices move downward in succession to their chord tones.

centripetal harmony Harmonic progressions that spiral progressively toward the tonic triad. In the case of barbershop harmony, this is used to describe the resolutions of dominant-style seventh chords around the circle of fifths. This is not a term in use by barbershoppers.

chestnut Old favorite tune or standard.

Christmas tree A melodic run (as in up and down a sequence of notes) performed by any one of the voices as an embellishment.

chromaticism See *diatonicism*.

circle of fifths The name given to the arrangement of the twelve keys, situated such that each successive note is a fifth above (or below, if the movement is in the opposite direction) the one that precedes it. Hence, starting with C: G, D, A, and E (or, in the opposite direction, from E: A, D, G, and C).

clock system An approach to the secondary-dominant style of harmonic progression developed by barbershop revivalist Maurice E. "Molly" Reagan in the 1940s. Reagan taught singers to find their proper accompaniment notes in a chord progression in which the tonic triad is designated the twelve o'clock chord and in which the harmony "jumps out" to a sequence of secondary dominants starting somewhere between two and five o'clock on the clock face. This then would be designated the "jump-out" chord. The harmonic progression would then resolve counterclockwise on the clock face back to the twelve o'clock chord via a circle of fifths. As an ideational device, the clock system was supposed to make singing this type of harmony accessible for the untrained singer with a visual mnemonic and a system of finger signals. It worked poorly, if at all, for songs built on other types of chord progressions.

close-harmony singing or *close-position voicing* or *close-position harmony* A style of harmony singing in which the four voices remain relatively proximate to each other and generally do not exceed much more than and octave to an octave and a half from lowest to highest notes of the chord.

combination tone Another term used by barbershop singers to describe the production of audible harmonics from chord singing. See also *bell tone* and *difference tone*.

crow Someone attracted to barbershop singing by the fraternity and the activity, but who lacks vocal skills.

diatonicism The reliance, in musical composition, on the diatonic scale, based on the division of an octave into seven notes, five of which are a whole tone above the preceding tone and two of which are a semitone above the one below. Musical compositions that introduce scale tones not included in diatonic scales are said to be chromatic.

diminished chord This is a triad built up from minor thirds. A fully diminished seventh chord adds an additional fourth tone a minor third above the fifth.

divorced voicing A voicing of a chord that leaves the tenor or bass (i.e., the outer parts) far removed from the other voices. See *open-position harmony.*

dominant seventh chord or *dominant* See *barbershop seventh.*

drop A common arranging technique in which the bass drops an octave on the last note of the song.

echo An arranging effect whereby words or phrases are repeated by different voices.

embellishment A word barbershoppers use for any arranging effect, technique, or device that enlivens the texture of the harmony, e.g., swipe, modulation, cascade effect, echo.

expanded sound This is the most popular term among barbershop organizations for the vibrant group sound that results from the production and reinforcement of overlapping overtones. The effect is not unlike that of additional singers on higher notes. See *lock and ring.*

fifth wheel An unwelcome interloper singing along with a quartet.

folk-song style In barbershop jargon, this refers to a style of song with a limited chord progression (usually I–IV–V) and a largely diatonic melody. Many songs of this type have been incorporated into the barbershop repertory (especially "Irish" songs), but they are considered to be weak candidates for good barbershop arranging.

four-act A vaudeville term for a quartet (sometimes but not always a vocal quartet). These were typically comedy groups.

functional harmony A theory of tonal harmony that argues for a functional, developmental, and mathematical (i.e., not simply sensual or decorative) role for all harmonies, and in which harmonies are typically viewed as fulfilling one of three functions: tonic, dominant, or subdominant.

gang-sing In the early days of the barbershop revival when the style was practiced primarily by quartets, a gang-sing was what occurred when more than a quartet participated. Gang-sings became popular features of annual conventions and chapter meetings in the early barbershop movement. For some time, the harmonies sung by each section were not standardized and were largely woodshedded or, when standardized, were taught quickly by rote. Extemporized gang sings were gradually replaced by a growing emphasis on participating in chapter choruses, which increasingly used standardized arrangements.

glee-club style In barbershop jargon, glee-club style refers to arrangements that place the melody in the highest voice and lack the emphasis on golden-era songs, with their dominant seventh chords. The diatonic harmony of glee-club singing often requires doubling of parts.

gut-buster A song or tag suitable for loud, expressive singing.

heterophony A term used to describe polyphonic music in which a single melody is simultaneously varied in each voice.

homophony A term used to describe polyphonic music in which all voices move collectively at the same basic pace. The best-known type of homophony consists of melody with chordal accompaniment. Barbershop singing is typically homophonic.

intonation Intonation is the measure of accurate pitch in performance. Subtle variations in intonation can be valuable as an expressive tool and can be used to generate tension and excitement and to provide character to melody.

jazz style See *modern style.*

just intonation An interval tuned such that it is acoustically pure. Typically, intervals that are justly intoned are tuned to the lowest corresponding partial in the overtone series.

leaner A "follower," or someone not up to the task of singing their part alone.

lock-in Sound that emerges when group vocal production is properly executed (with matched vowel sounds, intensity, intonation, and vocal quality) and the group achieves a pure and piercing tone. See *expanded sound* and *unit sound.*

lock-and-ring sound Similar to lock-in, this term also denotes the resultant harmony, which has a ringing quality rich in overtones. See *expanded sound* and *unit sound.*

mass sing Practiced by both SPEBSQSA and Sweet Adelines, this is the successor to early gang-sings. Mass sings occur at annual conventions when everyone in attendance is invited to gather in a public place to sing barbershop harmony.

meat 'n' taters chord See *barbershop seventh chord.*

modern style In barbershop jargon, this refers to group harmony with a high lead voice, extended chords, and lots of dissonance.

open-position voicing or *open-position harmony* A chord in which the lead, tenor, and baritone are not on adjacent chord tones, as opposed to close-position voicing or close-position harmony. A chord produced in this style is called a "spread chord."

ostinato (pl. *ostinati*) The repetition of a short musical pattern (a melodic and rhythmic entity) throughout a piece or a section of a piece.

overtone In acoustics, an overtone is one of the frequencies that sound above a fundamental frequency. When an instrument produces a tone, the ear perceives a composite sound made up of a fundamental and many less apparent overtones. Overtones, while typically less audible than the fundamental, are an integral part of a note's character.

parade of quartets An old barbershop term for a quartet "show" with more than one quartet, not typically connected to competitions.

polecat A standard barbershop song. SPEBSQSA published collections of arrangements of these songs, and hence the common association of "polecat" with a readily available arrangement.

portamento In vocal music, portamento is a gesture that connects two pitches by moving continuously through all the pitch area in between.

precision A competition judging category referring to the accuracy of attack and release, and the synchrony of sung lyrics.

putting over a song This phrase came out of vaudeville and refers to the ability of a singer or quartet to "sell" a song to the audience, a skill highly valued by Tin Pan Alley, which relied on the performers to popularize their material.

pyramid An arranging technique that builds on a low pitch, adding higher voices until a four-part chord is achieved.

ragtime progression A chord progression that was popular in the early part of the twentieth century. It follows the following progression: I–III^7–VI^7–II^7–V^7–I (see *circle-of-fifths* and *centripetal harmony*).

reinforced sound See *ringing chord.*

ringing chord A chord in which the various partials or overtones present in the voices produce audible overtones and thus a peculiar ringing sensation. Over the years, this sensation has been described by barbershop singers and theorists as a combination tone, a bell tone, a difference tone, reinforced sound, expanded sound, or a summation tone. As noted in the text, some of these terms derive from antiquated theories of the mechanisms behind ringing chords.

scissors An arranging technique that features the crossing of two voices in opposite directions.

scoop A barbershop term for a slide upward onto a desired pitch.

secondary dominant chord or *secondary dominant progression* This term is seldom used by barbershoppers, but it refers to the types of harmonic progressions that form the backbone of the barbershop repertory. Many of these songs are characterized by the resolution of a dominant seventh–style chord not to its tonic triad but to another seventh chord built on the note a fifth below the root note of the chord. This seventh chord would resolve in similar fashion, and it was popular for progressions to include three, four, or five of these resolutions around the circle of fifths back to the tonic triad in the initial key of the song. Drawing on the spatial metaphor of a chord progression spiraling back into the tonic triad, I have also used the term "centripetal harmony" for this type of progression. See *barbershop seventh chord, meat 'n' taters chord,* and *ragtime progression.*

show A musical event hosted by a barbershop chapter and featuring quartet and chorus performances.

show tunes Songs that depart from rigid barbershop criteria but that are allowable for non-competition performances, either in shows or singouts.

singout Sometimes used to describe an engagement in which barbershop quartets are hired by outside groups to perform.

slide A smooth movement onto new chord tones from other pitches.

split a chord With a pun on the word "chord" (i.e., a cord of wood), this is another colloquial term for "busting a chord" or singing in close harmony.

stage presence A competition judging category that comprises costuming, gesture, comportment, poise, and showmanship. Preparing a group in stage presence is the province of the stage presence coach.

spark-plugs Barbershop singers who have a reputation as dynamic organizers and motivators.

spread chord See *open-position voicing* or *open-position harmony.*

summation tone See *ringing chord.*

swipe An extremely popular device in barbershop singing, consisting of the movement from one chord to another on a single word or syllable while one or another of the singers (often the lead tenor) holds a single note. A swipe is a harmonic technique used to embellish melodically stable moments or held notes where a fermata might otherwise govern, or where there are naturally occurring pauses in the melody.

tag A special ending or coda to a song. Tags usually use the final line of the song's chorus for the text, and they typically employ swipes and other arranging devices. Tags are extremely popular platforms for arranging skills, and medleys of tags from different songs may be sung at informal gatherings.

tear jerker A sad or sentimental song.

tiddlies A barbershop term for small embellishments added by arrangers or singers (in woodshedding) and which typically involve non-chord tones (suspensions, appoggiaturas, and so forth).

unit sound An ideal of quartet or choral sound production that results from balance, blend, intonation, controlled vowel production, and expression. Attention to all of these factors should produce a tightly unified sound with a strong overtone component.

whiskey tenor A singer of barbershop-like material, derived from the caricatures of inebriated quartets in vaudeville.

woodshed To sing a song in barbershop style without printed arrangements, extemporizing voice leading and harmonies in the course of performance. The ability to do this is considered the mark of an experienced and serious barbershopper. In the early days of amateur barbershop singing, woodshedding was the laborious process of working out an arrangement by trial-and-error such that it could be performed in public.

Bibliography

Articles in daily, weekly, monthly, or quarterly lay periodicals are not listed in the bibliography, only in the notes section. Examples include *Hobbies: The Magazine for Collectors*, the *New York Times*, *Time* magazine, and the *Harmonizer* (SPEBSQSA).

Abbott, Lynn. "'Play That Barber Shop Chord': A Case for the African American Origin of Barbershop Harmony." *American Music* 10 (1992): 289–325.

Ames, Kenneth L. "The Lure of the Spectacular." In *Theatre of the Fraternity: Staging the Ritual Space of the Scottish Rite of Freemasonry, 1896–1929*, curated by C. Lance Brockman. Jackson: University of Mississippi Press, 1996.

Allen, Raymond. *"Singing in the Spirit": African-American Sacred Quartets in New York City*. Philadelphia: University of Pennsylvania Press, 1992.

Allen, William Francis, Charles Pickard Ware, and Lucy McKim Garrison, compilers. *Slave Songs of the United States*. New York: A. Simpson, 1867.

Anderson, Jervis. *This Was Harlem: A Cultural Portrait, 1900–1950*. New York: Farrar Strauss Giroux, 1982.

Anonymous. *Barbershop Arranging Manual*. Kenosha, Wisc.: SPEBSQSA, 1980.

Armstrong, Louis. *Satchmo: My Life in New Orleans*. New York: Prentice-Hall, 1954.

Averill, Gage, "Four Parts, No Waiting: The Ideal of Male Camaraderie in Barbershop Harmony Singing." Paper delivered at the Society for Ethnomusicology Annual Meeting, Oakland, Calif., November 5, 1990.

Averill, Gage. "Bell Tones and Ringing Chords: Sense and Sensation in Barbershop Harmony," *World of Music* 41, no. 1 (1999): 37–51.

Bal, Mieke. Introduction to *Acts of Memory: Cultural Recall in the Present*, edited by Mieke Bal, Jonathan Crewe, and Leo Spitzer. Hanover: Dartmouth University Press, 1999.

Baudrillard, Jean. *Simulations*. New York: Semiotext(e), 1983.

Bealle, John. *Public Worship, Private Faith: Sacred Harp and American Folksong*. Athens: University of Georgia Press, 1997.

Bederman, Gail. *Manliness and Civilization: A Cultural History of Gender and Race in the United States, 1880–1917*. Chicago: University of Chicago Press, 1995.

Berlin, Edward A. *Ragtime: A Musical and Cultural History*. Berkeley: University of California Press, 1980.

Berlin, Edward A. *King of Ragtime: Scott Joplin and His Era.* New York: Oxford University Press, 1994.

Berman, Marshall. *All That Is Solid Melts into Air: The Experience of Modernity.* New York: Simon and Schuster, 1982.

Blesh, Rudi, and Harriet Janis. *They All Played Ragtime.* 4th ed. New York: Oak Publications, 1971.

Boorstin, Daniel J. *The Americans: The Democratic Experience.* New York: Vintage Books, 1974.

Booth, Mark. "Jingle: Pepsi-Cola Hits the Spot." In *On Record: Rock, Pop, and the Written Word,* edited by Simon Frith. New York: Pantheon Books, 1990.

Brandt, Max H. "The Respectable Art of Woodshedding in World Music." In *Barbershopping: Musical and Social Harmony,* edited by Max Kaplan. Rutherford, N.J.: Farleigh Dickinson University Press, 1993.

Bright, Randy. *Disneyland: Inside Story.* New York: Harry N. Abrams, 1987.

Carnes, Mark C. "Scottish Rite and the Visual Semiotics of Gender." In *Theatre of the Fraternity: Staging the Ritual Space of the Scottish Rite of Freemasonry, 1896–1929,* curated by C. Lance Brockman. Jackson: University of Mississippi Press, 1996.

Caro, Robert A. *The Power Broker: Robert Moses and the Fall of New York.* New York: Alfred A. Knopf, 1974.

Chase, Gilbert. *America's Music: From the Pilgrims to the Present.* Urbana: University of Illinois Press, 1987.

Coben, Stanley. *Rebellion against Victorianism: The Impetus for Cultural Change in 1920s America.* New York: Oxford University Press, 1991.

Cockrell, Dale, ed. and compiler. *Excelsior: Journals of the Hutchinson Family Singers, 1842–1846.* Sociology of Music Series 5. Stuyvesant, N.Y.: Pendragon Press, 1989.

Cockrell, Dale. *Demons of Disorder: Early Blackface Minstrels and Their World.* Cambridge: Cambridge University Press, 1997.

Cook, Will. *Melodies for Millions.* Kenosha, Wisc.: SPEBSQSA, 1962.

Crawford, Richard. *The American Musical Landscape.* Berkeley and Los Angeles: University of California Press, 1993.

Denning, Michael. *The Cultural Front: The Laboring of American Culture in the Twentieth Century.* New York: Verso, 1998.

Dimeglio, John E. *Vaudeville U.S.A.* Bowling Green, Ohio: Bowling Green University Popular Press, 1972.

Dixon, Robert M. W., John Godrich, and Howard Rye. *Blues and Gospel Records, 1890–1943.* 4th ed. New York: Clarendon Press, 1997.

Elliott, Lawrence. *Little Flower: The Life and Times of Fiorello La Guardia.* New York: Morrow, 1983.

Emerson, Ken. *Doo-Dah: Stephen Foster and the Rise of American Popular Culture.* New York: Da Capo Press, 1998.

Epstein, Dena. *Sinful Tunes and Spirituals.* Urbana: University of Illinois Press, 1977.

Feld, Steven. "Sound Worlds." in *Sound,* edited by Patricia Kruth and Henry Stobart. Cambridge: Cambridge University Press, 2000.

Feld, Steven, and Keith H. Basso. *Senses of Place.* Santa Fe, N.M.: School of American Research Press, 1996.

Finch, Christopher, ed. *Fifty Norman Rockwell Favorites.* New York: Crown, 1977.

Finson, Jon W. *The Voices That Are Gone: Themes in Nineteenth-Century American Popular Song.* New York: Oxford University Press, 1994.

Floyd, Samuel A. Jr. *The Power of Black Music: Interpreting Its History from Africa to the United States*. New York: Oxford University Press, 1995.

Francaviglia, Richard V. *Main Street Revisited*. Iowa City: University of Iowa Press, 1966.

Furia, Philip. *The Poets of Tin Pan Alley: A History of America's Great Lyricists*. New York: Oxford University Press, 1990.

Garnett, Liz. "Ethics and Aesthetics: The Social Theory of Barbershop Harmony." *Popular Music* 18, no. 1 (1999): 41–61.

Garvey, Dennis. "The Chordettes: From Barbershop to 'Lollipop'," *Goldmine*, July 10, 1992, 13–18.

Gates, Henry Louis Jr. *The Signifying Monkey: A Theory of African-American Literary Criticism*. New York: Oxford University Press, 1988.

Geils, G. Ruth. *Harmony from Our Hearts: Harmony, Inc., 1959–1984*. Kenosha, Wisc.: Harmony, Inc., 1985.

George, Nelson. *The Death of Rhythm and Blues*. New York: Pantheon, 1988.

Gilbert, Douglas. *American Vaudeville: Its Life and Times*. New York: Dover, 1941.

Gilroy, Paul. *The Black Atlantic: Modernity and Double Consciousness*. Cambridge: Harvard University Press, 1993.

Gracyk, Tim. *Popular American Recording Pioneers, 1895–1925*. N. p., 2000.

Graham, Sandra. "The Fisk Jubilee Singers and the Concert Spiritual: The Birth of an American Tradition." Ph.D. diss., New York University, 2001.

Gribin, Anthony and Matthew Schiff. *Doo-Wop: The Forgotten Third of Rock 'n' Roll*. Iola, Wisc.: Krause, 1992.

Groia, Philip. *They All Sang on the Corner: New York City's Rhythm and Blues Vocal Groups of the 1950's*. Setauket, N.Y.: Edmond, 1974.

Halbwachs, Maurice. *On Collective Memory*. Edited and translated by Lewis A. Coser. Chicago: University of Chicago Press, 1992.

Hamm, Charles. *Yesterdays: Popular Song in America*. New York: W. W. Norton, 1983.

Handy, W. C. *Father of the Blues: An Autobiography*. Edited by Arna Bontemps. New York: Macmillan, 1941.

Harris, Charles K. *After the Ball*. New York: Frank-Maurice, 1926.

Harris, Neil, ed. *The Land of Contrasts, 1880–1901*. New York: George Braziller, 1970.

Harrison, Helen, guest curator. *The Dawn of a New Day: The New York World's Fair, 1939–40* [exhibition catalogue]. New York: Queens Museum, 1980.

Hawley, Ellis W. *The Great War and the Search for a Modern Order: A History of the American People and their Institutions, 1917–1933*. 2d ed. Prospect Heights, Ill.: Waveland Press.

Heckscher, August. *When La Guardia Was Mayor: New York's Legendary Years*. New York: W. W. Norton, 1978.

Henry, James Earl. "The Origins of Barbershop Harmony: A Study of Barbershop's Musical Links to Other African American Musics as Evidenced through Recordings and Arrangements of Early Black and White Quartets." Ph.D. diss., Washington University, 2000.

Hitchcock, H. Wiley. *Music in the United States: A Historical Introduction*. Englewood Cliffs, N.J.: Prentice Hall, 1988.

Hicks, Val. *Heritage of Harmony*. Kenosha, Wisc.: SPEBSQSA, 1988.

High, Ronald Henry. "Black Male Concert Singers of the Nineteenth Century: A Bibliographic Study." In *Feel the Spirit: Studies in Nineteenth-*

Century Afro-American Music, edited by George R. Keck and Sherrill V. Martin. New York: Greenwood Press, 1988.

Hobsbawm, Eric, and Terence Ranger. *The Invention of Tradition.* New York: Cambridge University Press, 1983.

Huizinga, Johan. *Homo Ludens: A Study of the Play Element in Culture.* Boston: Beacon Press, 1955.

Jameson, Fredric. *The Cultural Turn: Selected Writings on the Postmodern, 1983–1998.* London: Verso, 1998.

Jasen, David A., and Trebor Hay Tichenor. *Rags and Ragtime: A Musical History.* New York: Seabury Press, 1978.

Jenkins, Henry. *What Made Pistachio Nuts? Early Sound Comedy and the Vaudeville Aesthetic.* New York: Columbia University Press, 1992.

Johnson, James Weldon. "The Origin of the 'Barber Chord'." *Mentor* 17, February 1929.

Josephson, Matthew, and Hannah Josephson. *Al Smith: Hero of the Cities.* Boston: Houghton Mifflin, 1969.

Kaplan, Max, ed. *Barbershopping: Musical and Social Harmony.* Cranbury, N.J.: Associated University Presses, 1993.

Keck, George R., and Sherrill V. Martin, eds. *Feel the Spirit: Studies in Nineteenth-Century Afro-American Music.* New York: Greenwood Press, 1988.

Kenney, William Howland. *Recorded Music in American Life: The Phonograph and Popular Memory, 1890–1945.* New York: Oxford University Press, 1999.

Kessner, Thomas. *Fiorello H. La Guardia and the Making of Modern New York.* New York: McGraw-Hill, 1989.

Kirshenblatt-Gimblett, Barbara. *Destination Culture: Tourism, Museums, and Heritage.* Berkeley and Los Angeles: University of California Press, 1998.

Kubik, Gerhard. *Africa and the Blues.* Jackson: University Press of Mississippi, 1999.

Lears, T. J. Jackson. *No Place of Grace: Antimodernism and the Transformation of American Culture, 1880–1920.* New York: Pantheon Books, 1981.

Lefebvre, Henri. *The Production of Space.* Translated by Donald Nicholson-Smith. Oxford and Cambridge, Mass.: Blackwell, 1991.

Lippard, Lucy. *The Lure of the Local: Senses of Place in a Multicentered Society.* New York: New Press, 1997.

Lipsitz, George. *Time Passages: Collective Memory and American Popular Culture.* Minneapolis: University of Minnesota Press, 1990.

Lorat-Jacob, Bernard. *Sardinian Chronicles.* Translated by Teresa Lavender Fagan. Chicago: University of Chicago Press, 1995.

Lornell, Kip. *"Happy in the Service of the Lord": African-American Sacred Vocal Harmony Quartets in Memphis.* 2d ed. Knoxville: University of Tennessee Press, 1995.

Lott, Eric. *Love and Theft: Blackface Minstrelsy and the American Working Class.* New York: Oxford University Press, 1993.

Lowens, Irving. *Music and Musicians in Early America.* New York: W. W. Norton, 1964.

Lowenthal, David. *The Past Is a Foreign Country.* Cambridge: Cambridge University Press, 1985.

Mahar, William J. *Behind the Burnt Cork Mask: Early Blackface Minstrelsy and Antebellum American Popular Culture.* Urbana: University of Illinois Press, 1999.

Malone, Bill C. *Country Music U.S.A.* Rev. ed. Austin: University of Texas Press, 1985.

Marks, Edward B., as told to Abbott Liebling. *They All Sang: From Tony Pastor to Rudy Vallee.* New York: Viking, 1934.

Martin, Claude Trimble "Deac." *A Handbook for Adeline Addicts: A Starter For Cold Voices and a Survey Of American Balladry.* Cleveland: Schonberg Press, 1932.

———. *Keep America Singing.* Kenosha, Wisc.: SPEBSQSA, 1948.

Marx, Leo. *The Machine in the Garden: Technology and the Pastoral Ideal in America.* New York: Oxford University Press, 1964.

Maultsby, Portia K. "Africanisms in African-American Music." In *Africanisms in American Culture,* edited by James E. Holloway. Bloomington: Indiana University Press, 1990.

Melnick, Jeffrey. "'Story Untold': The Black Men and White Sounds of Doo-Wop." In *Whiteness: A Critical Reader,* edited by Mike Hill. New York: New York University Press, 1997.

Melnick, Jeffrey. *A Right to Sing the Blues: African Americans, Jews, and American Popular Song.* Cambridge: Harvard University Press, 1999.

Moses, Robert. *A Tribute to Governor Smith.* New York: Simon and Schuster, 1962.

Nathan, Hans. *Dan Emmett and the Rise of Early Negro Minstrelsy.* Norman: University of Oklahoma Press, 1962.

Obrecht, Jas. "Polk Miller's Old South Quartette." *Victrola and 78 Journal* (Spring 1996).

Oliver, Paul, Max Harrison, and William Bolcom, eds. *The New Grove Gospel, Blues, and Jazz with Spirituals and Ragtime.* New York: Norton, 1986.

Ong, Walter. *Fighting for Life: Contest, Sexuality, and Consciousness.* Ithaca: Cornell University Press, 1981.

Peterson Bernard L. Jr. *The African American Theater Directory, 1816–1960: A Comprehensive Guide to Early Black Theater Organizations, Companies, Theaters, and Performing Groups.* Westport, Conn.: Greenwood Press, 1997.

Potter, Russell A. "Race." In *Key Terms in Popular Music and Culture,* edited by Bruce Horner and Thomas Swiss. London: Blackwell, 1999.

Riis, Thomas Lawrence. *Just before Jazz.* Washington, D.C.: Smithsonian Institution Press, 1989.

———. *More Than Just Minstrel Shows: The Rise of Black Musical Theatre at the Turn of the Century.* Brooklyn: Institute for Studies in American Music, 1992.

Rodgers, Cleveland. "Robert Moses." *Atlantic Monthly,* February 1939, 225–34.

Romine, Holly Weberling, comp. *Sweet Adelines International Fiftieth Anniversary Commerative Album (Fifty and Forward, 1945–1995).* Tulsa: Sweet Adelines International, 1995.

Rosaldo, Renato. *Culture and Truth: The Remaking of Social Analysis.* Boston: Beacon Press, 1989.

Sacks, Howard L., and Judith Rose Sacks. *Way up North in Dixie: A Black Family's Claim to the Confederate Anthem.* Washington, D.C.: Smithsonian Institution Press, 1993.

Said, Edward. *Orientalism.* New York: Vintage Books, 1979.

Sampson, Henry T. *Blacks in Blackface: A Sourcebook of Early Black Musical Shows.* Metuchen, N.J.: Scarecrow Press, 1980.

————. *The Ghost Walks: A Chronological History of Blacks in Show Business, 1865–1910*. Metuchen, N.J.: Scarecrow Press, 1988.

Sanjek, Russell, and David Sanjek. *American Popular Music Business in the Twentieth Century*. New York: Oxford University Press, 1991.

Schafer, William J., and Hohannes Riedel. *The Art of Ragtime: Form and Meaning of an Original Black American Art*. Baton Rouge: Louisiana State University Press, 1974.

Schickel, Richard. *The Disney Version: The Life, Times, Art and Commerce of Walt Disney*. New York: Simon and Schuster, 1968.

Shackley, George. *Close Harmony: Male Quartets, Ballads and Funnies with Barber Shop Chords*. New York: Pioneer Music, 1925.

Siebenmorgen, Klaus-Wilfred. "Barbershop Singing as a Special Phenomenon in American Musical Life." Written assignment presented in connection with the first state examination for the office of Secondary School Teacher, Level II. Universität Dortmund, 1983.

Simond, Ike. *Old Slack's Reminiscences and Pocket History of the Colored Profession from 1865–1891*. Chicago: By the author, 1891.

Singer, Arthur J. *Arthur Godfrey: The Adventures of an American Broadcaster*. Jefferson, N.C.: McFarland, 2000.

Slide, Anthony. *The Vaudevillians: A Dictionary of Vaudeville Performers*. Westport, Conn.: Greenwood Press, 1981.

Slobin, Mark. *Fiddler on the Move: Exploring the Klezmer World*. New York: Oxford University Press, 2000.

Small, Christopher. *Music of the Common Tongue: Survival and Celebration in Afro-American Music*. New York: Riverrun Press, 1987.

Smith, Bill. *The Vaudevillians*. New York: Macmillan, 1976.

Smith, Willie "The Lion," with George Hoefer. *Music on My Mind: The Memoirs of an American Pianist*. New York: Doubleday, 1964.

Snyder, Robert W. *The Voice of the City: Vaudeville and Popular Culture in New York*. New York: Oxford University Press, 1989

Spaeth, Sigmund, ed. *Barbershop Ballads: A Book of Close Harmony*. New York: Simon and Schuster, 1925.

————. *Barbershop Ballads and How to Sing Them*. New York: Prentice-Hall, 1940.

Stebbins, Robert A. *The Barbershop Singer: Inside the Social World of a Musical Hobby*. Toronto: University of Toronto Press, 1996.

Stein, Charles W. *American Vaudeville as Seen by Its Contemporaries*. New York: Alfred A. Knopf, 1984.

Sunderberg, Johan. *The Science of the Singing Voice*. Dekalb, Ill.: Northern Illinois University Press, 1987.

Susman, Warren, ed. *Culture and Commitment, 1929–1950*. New York: George Braziller, 1973.

Tawa, Nicholas. *Sweet Songs for Gentle Americans: The Parlor Song in America, 1790–1860*. Bowling Green, Ohio: Bowling Green University Popular Press, 1980.

Tawa, Nicholas. *A Sound of Strangers: Musical Culture, Acculturation, and the Post–Civil War Ethnic American*. Metuchen, N.J.: Scarecrow Press, 1982.

Tawa, Nicholas. *The Way to Tin Pan Alley: American Popular Song, 1866–1910*. New York: Schirmer Books, 1990.

Théberge, Paul. *Any Sound You Can Imagine: Making Music, Consuming Technology*. Hanover, N.H.: Wesleyan University Press, 1997.

Thomas, Bob. *Walt Disney: An American Original*. New York: Simon and Schuster, 1976.

Toll, Robert C. *Blacking Up: The Minstrel Show in Nineteenth-Century America.* New York: Oxford University Press, 1974.

———. *The Entertainment Machine: American Show Business in the Twentieth Century.* New York: Oxford University Press, 1982.

Trotter, James M. *Music and Some Highly Musical People: Remarkable Musicians of the Colored Race.* Boston: Lee and Shepard, 1881; reprint, New York: Johnson Reprint Corporation, 1968.

Van der Merwe, Peter. *Origins of the Popular Style: The Antecedents of Twentieth-Century Popular Music.* Oxford: Clarendon Press, 1989.

Warner, Jay. *The Da Capo Book of American Singing Groups: A History, 1940–1990.* New York: Da Capo Press, 1992.

Waterman, Christopher A. "Race Music: Bo Chatmon, 'Corrine, Corrina,' and the Excluded Middle." In *Music and the Racial Imagination,* edited by Ronald Radano and Philip V. Bohlman. Chicago: University of Chicago Press, 2000.

Whitburn, Joel. *Joel Whitburn Presents a Century of Pop Music.* Menominee Falls, Wisc.: Record Research, 1999.

———. *Joel Whitburn's Pop Memories, 1890–1954: The History of American Popular Music.* Menominee Falls, Wisc.: Record Research, 1986.

Williams, Raymond. *Marxism and Literature.* Oxford: Oxford University Press, 1977.

Wilmeth, Don B. *American and English Popular Entertainment.* Detroit: Gale Research, 1980.

———. *Variety Entertainment and Outdoor Amusements: A Reference Guide.* Westport, Conn.: Greenwood Press, 1982.

Witmark, Isidore, and Isaac Goldberg. *The Story of the House of Witmark.* New York: Furman, 1939.

Web Pages Cited and Additional Web Pages of Interest

Barbershop Quartet Arrangement Books and Folios, <http://www.ms.uky.edu/~sills/bsbooks.html> This is an excellent and comprehensive listing of books of barbershop arrangements, including cover art and contents.

Parlor Songs, 1880s–1920s: In Search of American Popular Song, <http://parlorsongs.com/> In addition to an extensive collection of cover art, this site features notated piano arrangements of popular songs of the era that can be played using a free browser. The site hosts a monthly newsletter with feature articles.

Society for the Preservation and Encouragement of Barber Shop Quartet Singing in America, Inc., <http://www.spebsqsa.org/>

Sweet Adelines International, <http://www.sweetadelineintl.org/>

Harmony Incorporated, <http://www.harmonyinc.org/index.html>

Ancient Harmonious Society of Woodshedders (AHSOW), <http://www.harmonize.com/ahsow/>

A Cappella Almanac (the online source from CASA: The Contemporary A Cappella Society), <http://www.casa.org>

Tim Gracyk's home page for *Popular American Recording Pioneers, 1895–1925,* <http:www.garlic.com/~tgracyk/>

Silent Night "cyber-museum," created by Bill Egan, <http://fortunecity.com/victorian/museum/59/index.html> "Silent Night" ("Stille Nacht") was the best-known song to come out of the German-speaking *Singverein* movement of the early nineteenth century, popularized by singers such as the Rainer Family Singers and the Strasser Family Singers, both of which are featured on this site.

"The Hutchinson Family Singers Home Page," curated by Alan Lewis (2000), <http://geocities.com/unclesams farm/Hutchinson.htm>

Sites Featuring Important Sheet Music and Musical Ephemera Collections

Keffer Collection of Sheet Music, ca. 1790–1895, Annenberg Rare Book and Manuscript Collection, University of Pennsylvania Library, <http://www.library.upenn.edu/special/keffer/index.html>

Lester S. Levy Collection of Sheet Music, Milton S. Eisenhower Library, Johns Hopkins University, <http://levysheetmusic.mse.jhu.edu/>

The Historic American Sheet Music Project, Rare Book, Manuscript, and Special Collections Library, Duke University, <http://scriptorium.lib.duke.edu/sheetmusic>

Redpath Chautauqua Collection, University of Iowa Libraries Special Collections Department, <http://memory.loc.gov/ammem/award98/iauhtml/tcchome.html>, hosted by the Library of Congress American Memory Project.

African American Sheet Music, 1850–1920, John Hay Library, Brown University, <http://memory.loc.gov/ammem/award97/rpbhtml/aasmhome.html>, hosted by the Library of Congress American Memory Project.

America Singing: Nineteenth-Century Song Sheets, Rare Book and Special Collections Division, Library of Congress, <http://memory.loc.gov/ammem/amsshtml/amsshome.html>

Historic American Sheet Music Collection, Rare Book, Manuscript, and Special Collections, Library, Duke University, <http://memory.loc.gov/ammem/award97/ncdhtml/hasmhome.html>, hosted by the Library of Congress American Memory Project.

Index

Abbott, Lynn, 10, 13, 39, 40, 44, 45, 52
Abt, Franz, 22
Acoustix, 177
Adams, Carroll P., 104
Aeolian Singers, 24
Africa, 30, 31
African Americans
  appreciation of Euro-American music, 11
  in armed forces quartets, 119
  and barbershop harmony, 9–10, 32–33, 39, 177, 179–80, 185n.18, 189n.21
  close harmony in second half of nineteenth century, 45
  in competitions, 97, 109–12
  dance crazes, 80
  dignified presentations, 40–43, 50–51
  early recordings, 62
  gray areas of black and white harmony, 46–48, 179
  influence in popular music, 185n.16
  instrumental music and quartet harmonizing, 43–44
  jubilee quartets, 40–42
  Luca family singers, 27–28, 40, 42, 46
  minstrel shows, 37, 46, 51
  polyphonic singing, 30–31
  quartets of 1890s, 50–52
  quartets with barbershop sound, 133–35
  racism against, 54, 90, 110–14, 131–33, 198n.32
  recording opportunities, 65–66, 79–80
  shape-note singing, 22, 187n.3

  slave singing, 30–31, 45
  southern white nostalgia about, 68
  street-corner singing, 155–56
  swipes and tags, 191n.50
  transformations of harmony singing, 45
  in vaudeville, 58
African pitch area concept, 32, 33
Agar, Herbert, 90–91
A. G. Fields's Minstrels, 73
Albee, Edward F., 56, 58, 82
Alexandria Harmonizers, 175, 176
Alleghanians, 26
Allen, William Francis, 30–31
amateurism. See recreational music
"America, Here's My Boy," 78
American Ballad Contest for Amateur Barber-Shop Quartets, 94–97, 112
American national imaginary, 8
American Quartet, 64, 72–74, 78–79, 195n.58
American Recording Company, 64
American Society of Composers, Authors, and Publishers. See ASCAP
Ames, Kenneth L., 103
Anderson, Edna Mae, 127, 128
Anderson, Ken, 144
Apollo Minstrels, 37
Arion Quartet, 42
armed forces quartets, 118–19
Armstrong, Harry, 70, 108, 148
Armstrong, Louis, 44, 179
Arthur Godfrey's Talent Scouts (radio/TV show), 140–41, 149
ASCAP (American Society of Composers, Authors, and Publishers), 105, 107

219

Johnson Sisters, 126, 127, 129
Jolson, Al, 58, 133
Jones, Ada, 73, 74
Jones, Will C. "Billy," 64
Joplin, Scott, 40–41, 43–44
Jordanaires, 135
Jubilaires, 140
jubilee quartets, 38, 40–42, 79–80,
     196n.60
"Jump Jim Crow," 34–35
jump-out chord, 162–63
just intonation, 167, 208

Kaiser, Herman, 105–6
Kaplan, Max, 183n.3
Kaufman, Irving, 59
"Keep America Singing," 119
Keith, Benjamin Franklin, 56, 58,
     82
Kemp, "Father" Robert, 14, 28
Kennedy, John F., 151
Kenton, Stan, 137
Kickapoo Indian Medicine Com-
     pany, 38
kickapoo shows, 38
Kilgallen, Dorothy, 151
Kirby, Percival, 188n.14
Kirshenblatt-Gimblett, Barbara, 15
Knickerbocker Quartet, 50, 51, 78
Kubik, Gerhard, 30, 32, 188n.14
Ku Klux Klan, 90, 112, 198n.32

Lacey, Franklin, 150
La Guardia, Fiorello, 18, 92–94, 97,
     107–8, 109, 114, 198n.20
LaRosa, Julius, 142
Latzko, Walter, 141–42, 144, 169
Lauretta Quartet, 43
Lawler, Charles, 70
Leavitt's High Rollers, 72
Lefebvre, Henri, 89, 186n.30
Lester, Will, 59
Lew Johnson's Baby Boy Min-
     strels, 38
Lew Johnson's Minstrels, 37
Lew Johnson's Plantation
     Minstrels, 37–38
Lew Johnson's Refined Min-
     strels, 51
Liederkranz Society, 23
Likins, Bill, 138–39
Lime Kiln Quartette, 51
"Little Close Harmony, A," 153
"Little Street Where Old Friends
     Meet, A," 156

locomotives, 202n.42
Lorat-Jacob, Bernard, 168
"Lost Chord, The," 196
Lott, Eric, 36, 185n.18
Love and Theft (Lott), 36
Lowe, Bill, 99
Lowenthal, David, 3
Luca, Alexander C., Sr., 27
Luca, Cleveland O., 27–28
Luca family, 27–28, 40, 42, 46
Lucy Show, The (TV show), 130
Lyne, Greg, 176

MacDonough, Harry, 63, 69, 72,
     74–75
Magnolia Quartet, 38, 51
Mahoney, Jere, 69
Mainstreeters, 138
Majors, Joe, 75
Male Quartet and Chorus Books
     (Giffe), 46
Male Quartet and Chorus Books
     (Herbert), 46
Manhansett Quartette, 62–64, 69
Manning, D., 134
Maple City Four, 82–83
Maple Leaf Club, 43
Marceline (Mo.), 145
March, Joseph Moncure, 179
Mariners, 142
Marks, Edward, 55, 64
marriage, 157–58
Martin, Deac, 10, 13, 40, 71, 87,
     89, 119, 120–22, 124–25, 135,
     166
Marx Brothers, 58
masking, 11–12
Massengale, Tom, 165
McAdoo, O. M., 52
McCaslin, George, 105–6, 138–39
McClain, Billy, 39, 51
McClelland, James, 40
McFerrin, Bob, 148
McGuire Sisters, 143
McKenna, William J., 134
Mediterranean Theater of Opera-
     tions United States Army
     (MTOUSA), 118
"Meet Me in Dreamland," 170–71
"Meet Me Tonight in Dreamland,"
     115
Melnick, Jeffrey, 11
melodic range, 159
Mendelssohn glee club, 23
Merrill, Art, 164

CD Contents

The selections on the companion CD are intended not to form a representative audio history of the barbershop close-harmony style but, instead, to illustrate a number of issues, performance groups, styles, and genres discussed in the book. The examples are weighted heavily to songs recorded between 1894 and the mid-1920s for which copyright has lapsed; later recordings on the disc contain a preponderance of songs in public domain. Beware: many of the historic recordings were recorded on cylinders and 78 rpm discs and are extremely low fidelity.

1. New Hutchinson Family Singers, Robert DeCormier, conductor. "Excelsior." From *Homespun America*, VoxBox (The American composers series). Englewood Cliffs, NJ: VoxBox CDX 5088. 1993 © 1976, used by permission.

   The sound of mid-nineteenth-century close harmony as performed by The Hutchinson Family was reconstructed by the New Hutchinson Family Singers, led by Robert DeCormier. "Excelsior," along with "The Old Granite State," was one of The Hutchinson Family's most popular songs, and it demonstrates the T1-T2-Bari-Bass voicing of barbershop-style close harmony. In this example, the female voice, originally Abby Hutchinson, carries the high tenor harmony. *Homespun America*, from which this recording was licensed, contains period music for brass band, social dance orchestra, and music of The Hutchinson Family Singers. The New Hutchinson Family Singers are accompanied by members of the Eastman Wind Ensemble and Chorale; Donald Hunsberger and Robert DeCormier, directors. See pp. 24–27.

2. Standard Quartette (1894). "Keep Movin'" (unnumbered wax cylinder). From *The Earliest Negro Vocal Quartets (1894–1928)*. Document 5061, © 2000 (Johnny Parth, producer; original notes by Ray Funk). Used by permission.

   The Standard Quartet, an African American group, may have been the second quartet to record for a phonograph company following the sessions featuring the Unique Quartet in 1891. The Standard Quartet's early Columbia cylinders have been lost, but some of their 1894–97 session material survives. This excerpt from their song "Keep Movin'," although marred by terrible surface noise, allows the listener to imagine the effect of the exciting close-harmony choruses. With its reference to "darkies singing," this song seems to have one foot in the blackface minstrel tradition, despite its surface similarity to late-nineteenth-century spirituals. See p. 62.

3. Haydn Quartet (1901). "Farmyard Medley." Composer unknown. Improved Berliner Gram-O-Phone, Issue no. 496. Reproduced from the National Library of Canada's Web site (www.nlc-bnc.ca).

This song starts out as a standard nostalgic evocation of pastoral homeland, only to descend into sung imitations of barnyard animals, ending in a full comic romp of spoken dialogue, imitations of musical instruments (banjo), and a song that would have been quite at home on the minstrel stage. The banjo-strumming imitation on the syllables "Rang a dinga ding," etc., is often heard in period performances of "The Levee Song" (also known as "I've Been Working on the Railroad"). See pp. 69–70.

4. Haydn Quartet (1903). "The Sidewalks of New York." By James W. Blake and Charles B. Lawlor, 1894. Berliner Gram-O-Phone Co. of Canada / Victor / Grand Prize. Issue no. 48. Reproduced from the National Library of Canada's Web site (www.nlc-bnc.ca).

Far from a straightforward treatment of Blake and Lawlor's song, this recording presents an ethnic vaudeville "shtick" about street vendors in New York's tenement districts, complete with dialogue, sound effects, evocations of children's playground songs ("London Bridge"), and ethnic slurs. See pp. 55–56, 91–95.

5. Billy Murray and Hayden Quartet (1909). "By the Light of the Silvery Moon." By Gus Edwards and Edward Madden, 1909. Victor 16460-A. *The Heritage Hall Museum of Barbershop Harmony Presents Close-Harmony Pioneers*, HHM 1000, © 1994 Society for the Preservation and Encouragement of Barber Shop Quartet Singing in America, Inc. Used by permission.

One of the great "spooning" songs of the turn of the century, its lyrics play with contemporaneous courtship slang and a theatrical view of romance. Many songs of the period had long pauses (as here after "light") that quartets could fill with devices such as echo effects and swipes. The instrumental accompaniment was very common in the era. This was the recording that made the song a hit. See p. 70.

6. Polk Miller and His Old South Quartette (1909). "Watermelon Party." 2178-Edison Amberole 392 cylinder. From *The Earliest Negro Vocal Quartets (1894–1928)*. Document 5061, © 2000. Johnny Parth, producer.

This was the black quartet fronted by a white "darky dialectician," discussed on pp. 67–69. With its guitar accompaniment and the alternation of Polk Miller's verses and the quartet's choruses, this represents a slice of minstrel-style repertory, but note the very interesting proto-talking-blues style or heightened speech delivery that Miller uses for the verses.

7. Columbia Quartette (1911). "I Want a Girl." By William Dillon and Harry Von Tilzer, 1911. Columbia A1034. *The Heritage Hall Museum of Barbershop Harmony Presents Close-Harmony Pioneers*, HHM 1000, © 1994 Society for the Preservation and Encouragement of Barber Shop Quartet Singing in America, Inc. Used by permission.

    Essentially a "mother" song and nostalgic tribute to long-lasting love, this song was set to a lively march beat and became a top hit of 1911, later surfacing as a chestnut of the barbershop tradition. See pp. 75–76.

8. American Quartet (1911). "Oh, You Beautiful Doll." By Nat D. Ayer and A. Seymour Brown. Victor 16979-A. *The Heritage Hall Museum of Barbershop Harmony Presents Close-Harmony Pioneers*, HHM 1000, © 1994 Society for the Preservation and Encouragement of Barber Shop Quartet Singing in America, Inc. Used by permission.

    This was another favorite recording from the peak years of the barbershop tradition. The "ping" of lead singer Billy Murray's voice can clearly be heard on this recording, as on the recordings earlier on this disc in which he fronts for the Haydn Quartet. See pp. 73–75.

9. Henry Burr and the Peerless Quartet (1920). "Cornfield Medley" [or "Way Down Yonder in the Corn Field"]. Composer unknown. Reproduced from the National Library of Canada's Web site (www.nlc-bnc.ca).

    Although this recording was made quite late (1920), this was perhaps the most-often-performed quartet song of the 1890s. The shockingly racist minstrel dialogue may appear to be its most prominent feature now, but in its day, singers delighted in the chord changes of its chorus, in its various sound and instrument imitations, and in the interpellated songs (e.g., "Massa's in de Cold, Cold Ground," "Way Down upon the Swanee River," "The Levee Song").

10. Columbia Stellar Quartette (1918). "You're the Flower of My Heart, Sweet Adeline." Harry Armstrong and Richard Gerard, 1896. *The Heritage Hall Museum of Barbershop Harmony Presents Close-Harmony Pioneers*, HHM 1000, © 1994 Society for the Preserva-tion and Encouragement of Barber Shop Quartet Singing in America, Inc. Used by permission.

    "Sweet Adeline" (as it is most often known) is sometimes called the "anthem" of barbershop singers, and this rendition demonstrates why it was so enduringly popular among close-harmony enthusiasts: dramatic pauses in the melody to accommodate barbershop-style arranging effects, chromatic possibilities in the chord progression, and a straightforward sentimentality. See pp. 70–73.

11. Henry Burr and the Peerless Quartet (1920). "Beautiful Isle of Some-where." By Jessie Brown Pounds and John Sylvester Fearis, 1901. Berliner Gram-O-Phone / His Master's Voice. Issue no. 216108 B. Reproduced from the National Library of Canada's Web site (www.nlc-bnc.ca).

    Although written at the turn of the century, "Beautiful Isle of Some-where" was reprised by the Peerless Quartet in a lovely rendition in 1920. This is a classic "hearth and home" song of the close-harmony tradition. See pp. 65–66.

12. The Peerless Quartet (1921). "My Mammy." By Walter Donaldson, 1921. Victor 18730-A. Collection of Val Hicks, used by permission.

    In 1921, The Paul Whiteman Orchestra had a hit with this nos-talgic minstrel-style song, originally from the Broadway musical *Sinbad*. The Peerless Quartet followed with their own popular version a few months later. Six years later, a blackface Al Jolson revived the song for the movie *The Jazz Singer*. This rendition has a distinctive echo in the bass voice in the chorus ("little Mammy").

13. The Shannon Quartet (1926). "Let Me Call You Sweetheart." By Leo Friedman and Beth S. Whitson, 1911. Recorded (Victor 19941-B). *The Heritage Hall Museum of Barbershop Harmony Presents Close-Harmony Pioneers*, HHM 1000, © 1994 Society for the Preservation and Encouragement of Barber Shop Quartet Singing in America, Inc. Used by permission.

    A classic "waltz song" from 1911, "Let Me Call You Sweetheart" was first popularized by the Peerless Quartet. The Shannon Quartet recorded material in the Irish and traditional barbershop quartet repertory under their original name but, after the advent of elec-tronic recording, recorded a jazzier and more modern repertory under the name The Revelers. Note the nice tag that starts at 2'45".

14. The Southern Negro Quartet (1921). "Sweet Mama." Columbia A-3450. From *Earliest Negro Vocal Groups Vol. 3, 1921–1924*. Collection of Val Hicks, used by permission.

    Vocal impressions of instruments, sobbing-like vocal effects, and effective falsetto singing characterize this animated performance from the early 1920s. Its harmonic progression and lyric content and the vocal freedom evident in its bridge section suggest some of the solo vocal recordings of the classic jazz period, a touch of the collective improvisatory playing of early New Orleans jazz. This is representative of the directions in which black quartets were taking the close-harmony style in the 1920s.

15. Pullman Porters Quartet (1927). "Pullman Passenger Train." From *Black Secular Vocal Groups Vol. 1, 1923–1929*, Document Records, DOCD-5546.

Again, innovations in harmony singing are front-and-center in an African American quartet's performance from the 1920s. The group features a powerful bass voice in a semi-oratorical style.

16. The Avon Comedy Four (1915). "Yaaka Hula Hickey Dula." Victor 18081. Collection of Val Hicks, used by permission.

This excerpt of a popular vaudeville novelty song comes from perhaps the best-loved vaudeville comedy four (and Bing Crosby's favorite group), the Avon Comedy Four. In 1916, Al Jolson achieved a hit recording with this song.

17. Bartlesville Barflies, 1939 SPEBSQSA Quartet Champions. Medley: "Wait 'Til the Sun Shines, Nellie" (Andrew B. Sterling and Harry Von Tilzer, 1905); "By the Watermelon Vine (Lindy Lou)" (Thos S. Allen, 1904); "By the Light of the Silvery Moon" (Edward Madden and Gus Edwards, 1909). *Best of Barbershop Quartets: 38 Years of Winners*, BH 60177. © 1977, Society for the Preservation and Encouragement of Barber Shop Quartet Singing in America, Inc. Used by permission.

Here is a great representation of the first generation of barbershop revivalists from the heartland, recorded at the first SPEBSQSA competition. See pp. 105–6.

18. Flatfoot Four, 1940 SPEBSQSA Quartet Champions. "Annie Laurie," traditional. *Best of Barbershop Quartets: 38 Years of Winners*, BH 60177. © 1977, Society for the Preservation and Encouragement of Barber Shop Quartet Singing in America, Inc. Used by permission.

The Flatfoot Four won the quartet competition at the New York World's Fair with this rendition of a traditional Scottish song (chock full of swipes) that had already become a barbershop standard. The group's use of echo effects at 2'04" hearkens to African American quartets of the previous decades. See pp. 109–12.

19. Buffalo Bills, 1950 SPEBSQSA Quartet Champions. "Goodbye, Old Dixie, Goodbye" (Medley). Arranged by Phil Embury. *Best of Barbershop Quartets: 38 Years of Winners*, BH 60177. © 1977, Society for the Preservation and Encouragement of Barber Shop Quartet Singing in America, Inc. Used by permission.

This was one of the Dixie-oriented medleys that the Bills used to win the 1950 International Quartet Competition. Even a casual listener should be able to discern the increasing precision, blend, dynamic control, and virtuosic swipes (listen to the swipes on "die" at 2'17" to 2'23") that The Buffalo Bills were helping to establish in the barbershop competitions. Arrangements, too, had become more demanding in the aftermath of Frank Thorne's work. See pp. 147–50.

20. Second Edition, 1989 SPEBSQSA Inc. International Quartet Champions. "Hello! My Baby." Ida Emerson and Joe Howard, 1899. Arranged by Ed Waesche. *SPEBSQSA Presents Barbershop Harmony Favorites, Volume 1.* © 1991 Society for the Preservation and Encouragement of Barber Shop Quartet Singing in America, Inc. Used by permission.

Although now well over a decade old, this recording by the 1989 SPEBSQSA International Champion Quartet, Second Edition, represents a high contemporary standard for men's barbershop vocal production, with clear ringing chords, a superb vocal blend, and a subtle use of timing, dynamic variations, staggered entry effects, and even modulations (1'37") to sell the song. The tag that begins at 1'44" provides an excellent example of the current emphasis on ending on a powerful note.

21. Rich-Tone Chorus (Sweet Adelines International Region 25; Dale K. Syverson, director). "Pal of My Cradle Days." Al Piantadosi, 1925. Arranged Brian Beck. *Portland Perfection: International Chorus Finalists.* © 2001 Sweet Adelines International. Used by permission.

One legitimate criticism of this companion CD could be that it doesn't include enough chorus recordings. Ever since the 1950s, choruses have become principal organizing units of the barbershop revival movement and the ensemble of choice for the majority of barbershoppers. This lovely rendition of a sentimental favorite of the 1920s is by a champion Sweet Adelines International chorus. Many Sweet Adelines International arrangements feature songs composed after the so-called golden era of barbershop harmony, but this tune was written in the latter decade of that era. See pp. 126–30 for the early history of Sweet Adelines International.

22. Fanatix (Sweet Adelines International Region 21). "I Love to Hear That Old Barbershop Style." Words and music by Einar Pedersen, © 1973; arr. Hicks, Lund. *Portland Perfection: International Quartet Finalists.* © 2001 Sweet Adelines International. Used by permission.

All the hallmarks of barbershop style are in evidence in this song written to capture the style and sentiment of the barbershop era by SPEBSQSA member Einar N. Pedersen. The song has become something of a contemporary barbershop anthem. Fanatix won the 2001 Sweet Adelines International Quartet Championship with a set of performances that included this rendition.